QUINN

Trevor Birney is an Emmy-nominated film producer, director and journalist who began his career at *The Impartial Reporter* newspaper on the border in Fermanagh. In 2017 he produced the ground-breaking documentary *No Stone Unturned*, about the 1994 murder by UVF gunmen of six Catholics in Loughinisland, County Down. Following the film's premiere, the PSNI launched an investigation into the alleged leaking of secret documents and arrested Birney and his colleague, Barry McCaffrey. Police later apologised and paid both journalists significant damages. He lives in Belfast.

QUINN

TREVOR BIRNEY

MERRION
PRESS

First published in 2022 by
Merrion Press
10 George's Street
Newbridge
Co. Kildare
Ireland
www.merrionpress.ie

© Trevor Birney Publishing Ltd, 2022

978 1 78537 399 2 (Paper)
978 1 78537 400 5 (Ebook)

Typeset in Calluna 11.5/16

Front and back cover images courtesy of Jan McCullough

Internal images courtesy of Lorraine Teevan, excluding Teemore Shamrocks (courtesy of Quinn family archive); Sean Quinn outside his quarry at Derrylin (courtesy of Independent News and Media/Getty Images); Kevin Lagan and the Slieve Russell Hotel (courtesy of Fine Point); Quinn's quarry on Doon Mountain and Sean Quinn looks out over his former empire (courtesy of Jan McCullough); Cyril McGuinness (courtesy of Collins Photo Agency); Police cordon close to the home of Kevin Lunney (courtesy of Pacemaker).

Cover design: edit+ www.stuartcoughlan.com

Merrion Press is a member of Publishing Ireland.

To my dearest, Sheila, Ella, Mia and Freya.

And to border people.

Contents

Prologue   1

1   The Dig   7

2   Trouble at a Border Bank   28

3   Stone and Shite   40

4   Monopoly   59

5   Cavan's Versailles   75

6   Border State of Mind   95

7   Failing to Compute   114

8   'Fuck It, Let's Get a Jet'   134

9   215,619,414   152

10   'More than a Billion, Yes'   178

11   The Molly Maguires   201

12   Is This What You Want?   228

13   Mission Accomplished   259

14   Border People   279

Epilogue   301

Bibliography   307

Acknowledgements   309

Index   313

Prologue

17 September 2019
Derrylin, Co. Fermanagh

As he pulled out onto the main road from the Quinn Industrial Holdings car park, with Slieve Rushen Mountain in his rear-view mirror, Kevin Lunney's mind was on the evening ahead: dinner with the family, possibly cutting the lawn afterwards, definitely looking through papers ahead of an important board meeting the following morning. Distracted by these thoughts, he failed to notice the black Audi tailing him.

He sped along in his Toyota Land Cruiser, unhindered. Traffic congestion in Derrylin was never a concern. That's the way he liked it. His evening commute was less than ten minutes, door to door. A much different scenario to what he'd faced during his time away from this place, his home. He'd left many years earlier to study electrical engineering at Queen's University in Belfast and, after university, got a job with Andersen Consulting in Dublin, a role that took him across the Atlantic for a while to work on a project with Microsoft in Seattle. But now he was back home and, truthfully, he never missed the big city life. Instead, he was content to be back among family who, for generations, had lived along the narrow roads he was now driving, between the border villages of Derrylin and Kinawley. He knew every house and family along the route. The school friends with whom he'd grown up, played football and worked alongside. All that had been possible because of one phone call from the man who had gone on to become like a second father, a mentor, to him; the businessman who changed his life.

Sean Quinn.

As Kevin made his way home, he passed farmers taking advantage of the late summer sun to get a final cut of grass in. He thought of his wife, Bronagh, preparing the dinner for seven o'clock as usual – he was a man of routine, as she often said. They had known each other since their schooldays and married three years after he returned home from Dublin. They had since raised a family of six. The eldest boys were entering their teens now and he knew that Bronagh had a whole new level of worries about them. They both did. It would only be a matter of time before they'd want to go out on a Saturday night into pubs that Kevin and Bronagh worried were full of dangerous hotheads with too much drink in them. Nowadays, simply being a son of Kevin Lunney's could cause a row.

If Kevin had looked in his rear-view mirror at that moment, he might have seen that the driver of the black Audi was on his mobile phone, telephoning ahead, confirming that the target was a matter of minutes away. They'd scouted the route and identified the weakest spot for Kevin Lunney: a section of road near his home from where he couldn't easily escape. The driver's accomplices were already in position. Kevin Lunney was driving straight towards them.

Kevin turned left off the main Derrylin road and onto the home stretch, the Stragowna Road. Ahead of him he could see Molly Mountain, where he'd lived as a child. One of his brothers still lived up there on the family farm. The wind farms on Doon Mountain were also in view. They were now owned by a French firm.

Kevin often pondered on his life since his return to 'Quinn Country'. He'd never actually thought of anything he'd done since returning to work for Sean Quinn as for himself. It was always for the big man, the boss, the chieftain. Kevin could still clearly remember that day in

Dublin, when he was working at Andersen Consulting. Out of the blue, he got that call from Quinn, inviting him up to see him the next time he was home. Kevin was amazed that Quinn knew who he was and had called him personally, never mind his shock at the role that Quinn later offered him when he did travel north. That had been in 1995, with the Celtic Tiger in full throttle and the country throwing a party. Having left Fermanagh almost fifteen years before, Kevin was going home to become the general manager of Quinn Insurance, which had only opened its doors the previous January. Quinn told him that the company was going to become the biggest of its kind in Ireland. And Kevin Lunney would be the person to make it happen.

And he did.

But now, as the Stragowna Road narrowed and the uncut hedges tumbled out onto the road, that time felt long gone for Kevin Lunney. Sean Quinn was now a king without a kingdom and, as Kevin was back at the company as chief operating officer after Quinn's departure, his former mentor was now telling the world that Lunney was a traitor. Dozens of 'Wanted' posters with Kevin's face on them had appeared all along the border, alongside the words 'Cromwell's men are here again'. There had been threats against him and some of his colleagues, but for Kevin, Quinn's anger felt much more personal. The threats had already led to violence, as he was still recovering from a vicious attack by a young boxer while he'd been eating his lunch in a local café. It had left him in hospital with multiple facial injuries, including a broken nose. He still felt tender around his right eye and face. But he'd made his choices and refused to be forced off the land of his ancestors, even if he knew there was a clear and present danger from those who wanted their king back on his throne, or at least on the red chair Quinn used to sit on in his old office. Those who refused to believe that this was no longer Quinn Country.

The driver in the Audi called ahead again to say that the prey was only moments from the trap. Kevin Lunney pulled off the Stragowna

Road, passing Carn Cottage on his right, a new bungalow built by his neighbours. He steered the jeep past the short stone wall on his left and around the bend and up the lane, which hadn't much more than a foot's clearance on either side of his 4x4. He was less than 200 yards from home.

Kevin had failed to notice the Audi during the short journey and remained unaware of it as it took the same turn, reversing up the lane to box in Lunney's Land Cruiser and allow for a speedier getaway. But he couldn't miss the large white vehicle now obstructing the lane in front of him.

It was unusual but not unheard of for a 'townie' to get lost in the multitude of vein-like roads – many of them little more than tracks – that ran through the borderlands. Still, Kevin approached with caution. If by the time he reached them they had yet to move, he decided to stay in his own car rather than to get out. For a moment, the white vehicle sat still. The only noise on the lane was the sound of a late summer evening: birds buzzing, distant tractors, grass being cut. In truth, Kevin's mind was still primarily on the evening ahead – dinner, the possibility of cutting his own lawn – not really on the car in front of him.

Without warning, the white vehicle burst into life. It reversed straight for Kevin, wobbling over potholes and bouncing off the ditches as the driver struggled to keep it on the lane and on target.

There was no time to avoid the inevitable. Within seconds, almost in slow motion, Kevin saw the front of his Land Cruiser crumple as the vehicles collided. From nowhere, two men in balaclavas pulled at the driver- and passenger-side doors of his jeep, which Kevin had instinctively managed to lock. They were shouting, but he couldn't make out a word they were saying.

He reached into the pocket of his suit jacket for his phone. Bronagh and the kids. Call Bronagh. Panicked, he struggled to get the code into the iPhone.

Bang.

The driver-side window crashed in, showering him with fragments of glass. As one of the men grabbed at him, Kevin retreated to the back seat, away from his grasp. Now the man was inside the car, followed by the other one. Kevin kicked and pulled at their balaclavas, but was soon overpowered and hauled outside.

Though disorientated, Kevin was still aware enough to notice that a third man, heavier than the other two, was now behind him. Then he saw it for the first time. The red, old-style Stanley knife. It was in the hand of the third man. The blade flashed in the late summer sun, as the man thrust it towards Kevin's throat. He then used it to slice away his watch from his wrist. Amid all the head-spinning confusion, he understood a command: 'Get in there now. We want to talk to you,' one of the attackers shouted.

But he'd no idea what the 'there' was.

He knew the accents too – they weren't northern but southern, with a mix of brogues. The guy with the knife was clearly from Dublin. If they wanted to rob him they'd come a long way. If they wanted the jeep, why wreck it by smashing the windows? None of it made sense.

One of the men was holding what looked like two milk cartons. What was in them? 'Get into that or we'll kill you,' said the man with the knife.

'Jesus Christ almighty,' Kevin screamed.

What could possibly warrant such viciousness? They hustled him towards the back of the black Audi, which he saw now for the first time. Kevin contorted himself, trying to pull free, but his captors held on tight. It was clear that they had a destination for him.

The boot.

He kicked at the car as they tried to force him inside. They were all shouting again, at him, barking orders at each other. 'Get in there or we'll kill you.' One shoved his head while the other two lifted his feet from under him.

His face was pushed tight against the rear of the back seat as the rest of him was stuffed inside. Before he could turn over and make a bid for freedom, the boot lid slammed shut. The summer sun, the dinner with Bronagh and the kids, cutting the lawn, the prep for the board meeting, were all gone.

Replaced with an all-consuming dark.

1

The Dig

As he walked the road close to the border, a young Sean Quinn knew every hole in the hedge. At one such opening, he glanced over his shoulder and jumped through the whin bush. He poked his head back through another of the holes to check if anyone had seen him. It was the day of his 11+, important exams that decide a student's transfer from primary education to a grammar school or other secondary schools. However, awaiting the bus to ferry him to the exam, Sean had come to a decision. He was finished with the type of education that a school could give him.

He knew he was making a life-changing decision, but as he pulled his coat tight around the blue suit his father had bought especially for his exam day, his instincts told him that he was doing the right thing. By now, the other students had arrived and were waiting by the side of the road. He could hear their chatter. His defiance only grew as he heard the bus approach. The driver stopped and welcomed the others aboard, knowing all of his passengers by their first names. Then the door swung shut, the diesel engine growled, and the bus drove away.

Sean waited until he could no longer hear the growl before climbing out onto the road. He was barely eleven years old, but Sean Quinn had just defied authority for the first time in his short life. And he was very proud of himself, even if he was nervous about telling his parents of his decision.

Looking back on that decisive moment now, Quinn reflected, 'School was never of any great interest to me; I was always more interested in getting involved in something.' His sister Bernie went to the same primary school. 'He was nearly too fond of the fun and in the classroom he was always witty, he was always quick with his responses,' she recalled. 'There was a group of them and there was great craic, you know, they entertained us. I would never have at that stage anticipated that he was going to go on to be a successful businessman. He nearly seemed too relaxed and too laid back for that. But I suppose he showed his determination in that he just didn't turn up for the bus the day he was supposed to go to the transfer exam. He wasn't going to go down that path. And maybe that was the first insight we got that he was his own person and was going to do his own thing.'

Quinn still remembers the moment his parents realised he hadn't taken the bus. 'When I went home my mother wasn't very happy, but my father said, "Leave him alone, he'll be all right, he'll help me with the land, he'll be grand." My father left school when he was six or seven, so I beat him by a good margin.'

For better or worse, Sean Quinn had decided to forge his own path, one far away from the classrooms and school yards of rural Fermanagh. He would forge this path in an area rife with sectarian tension.

***

Sean Quinn was born in 1947, just twenty-six years after Ireland had been partitioned in 1921 and two years before the twenty-six-county Irish State became a republic and the British government reacted with the Ireland Act of 1949, which set down the status of the six counties of Northern Ireland as being part of the United Kingdom – a status that would only ever change with the consent of a majority of its population, which, in the 1940s, appeared a mathematical impossibility.

The Quinns lived just two miles on the northern side of the border with the new Republic, in the one-horse town of Derrylin, Co. Fermanagh. Those in the North who wished to remain a part of the UK, called 'unionists', were of the ruling class and were also largely Protestant, while those who wanted the North to rejoin with the rest of the island of Ireland were termed 'nationalists' and were mostly – though not exclusively – drawn from the Catholic underclass.

The tension between both groups had been simmering for decades prior to Quinn's birth, often threatening to boil over. The unionists regularly resorted to desperate measures to maintain their control over the six counties. Fermanagh, for example, suffered from unionist gerrymandering in its councils, meaning that, despite the fact that the county had a Catholic majority averaging 55 per cent since the turn of the century, unionist figures maintained control of these councils. The year before Sean Quinn was born, a local unionist councillor told a meeting that the nationalist majority in Fermanagh must be 'liquidated' and, over the following years, it did indeed drop, as detailed in Margaret Urwin's authoritative book *Fermanagh: From Plantation to Peace Process*. This was due mainly to the fact that Catholics faced widespread discrimination in housing and jobs and therefore had to leave the county to find work.

On a parliamentary level, Derrylin and the south Fermanagh region was actually represented at Stormont – the political base of power in Northern Ireland, found in East Belfast – by a nationalist, Cahir Healy MP. Born in Donegal in the late 1800s, he'd been interned twice and argued against Fermanagh and Tyrone being included in the new northern state. In 1945 he helped establish the Anti-Partition League (APL) and was returned to Stormont in 1949 in the so-called Chapelgate election, after fundraising collections were organised around the North by the APL.

Yet even these minor successes were met with a fierce backlash. Unionists reacted to this latest threat by increasing discrimination of Catholics, making it even more difficult to get jobs or council housing (to include flats). For example, between the end of the Second World War and 1968, a mere fifteen council houses built in Derrylin were let to Catholic tenants. Furthermore, just a few miles away in Lisnaskea, a predominantly nationalist town, 108 council homes were built during the same period, yet only twenty-eight went to Catholics. Fermanagh Council even went so far as to create the new village of Donagh in an attempt to move Catholics out of Newtownbutler, four miles away, so unionists could gerrymander a majority vote in the area.

A 1972 report by the Fermanagh Civil Rights Association called it out: 'Between 1945 and 1967, 195 houses in Fermanagh were allocated to Catholics, while 853 – over four times as many – went to people of other denominations. Approximately 54% of the population, and that containing by far the greater number of those in need of houses, received only 18% of the Council houses.' The report, titled 'Fermanagh Facts', went on to accuse unionists of attempting to 'eradicate' the Catholic majority in Fermanagh.

Given the prevalence of this practice throughout the six counties, it would be of little surprise that housing discrimination proved to be one of the sparks that lit the fire of conflict in the North. A conflict that would cause Sean Quinn's neighbours along the border, and even in nearby Derrylin, a lot of hardship over the years.

The village of Derrylin – or *Doire Loinn*, meaning 'Oakgrove of Floinn' or 'Oakgrove of the blackbirds' – sits on the main road that runs from Fermanagh's county town of Enniskillen all the way to Cavan town on the southern side of the border. With Upper Lough Erne to the east and Slieve Rushen Mountain to the west, the village's population has never peaked beyond 650. In the mid-twentieth century, farming provided the only source of significant employment.

Heading south-west out of Derrylin, you cross the border onto the A205 and one mile into the Republic you find Ballyconnell. Sitting on the Woodford River at the foot of Slieve Rushen (or Slieve Russell) Mountain, it's in Co. Cavan but its natural hinterland is Co. Fermanagh. Because of its proximity to the border, it was the scene of a number of attacks by both Anti-Treaty and Free State forces during the Irish Civil War of 1921–3, culminating in an Irish Republican Army (IRA) column sacking the town and killing two men in February 1923. Sean and his siblings would grow up with Derrylin in the North and Ballyconnell in the South as the two compass points in their lives.

It was, according to many, a unique area. 'There was an English professor visited Derrylin because, he said, Elizabethan English was still being spoken there. It was trapped by Lough Erne to the north and the mountains to the south, so it was an enclave largely untouched by the twenty-first century,' says former headmaster and local historian Bryan Gallagher in an interview, adding that the people of the area were very aware and proud of their distinctiveness. 'The accent of the people in Derrylin was different from those who lived on the far side of the lough. There, the accent was more northern but in Derrylin, or Teemore where Sean Quinn was from, the accent was broader, more of a brogue. The people are known to preserve folklore and the history of the area.'

And it was from this distinctive region that Sean Quinn emerged, like his parents before him.

***

Although there were ten years between them, Hugh Quinn and his future wife, Mary Clarke, knew each other from a young age, growing up on neighbouring farms in south Fermanagh. Mary's parents, Arthur and Ellen, had both emigrated to New York and married in Manhattan's grand nineteenth-century neo-Gothic St Patrick's Cathedral before returning home when they inherited a family farm, a decision that their grandchildren would come to appreciate. Hugh Quinn and Arthur Clarke became friends, the older man becoming something of a father figure to Hugh during his teen years. In his memoir, *The Outsider*, Sean's older brother, Peter, told how his father had 'appeared to act as Arthur's minder when the older man got drunk and started rows, which was a regular occurrence'.

At the time of Sean's birth, his parents lived in a small two-bedroom house in the townland of Gortmullan, which runs right up to the border. As well as Peter, Sean had an elder sister, Miriam, while the baby of the family, Bernadette, or Bernie, was born two years after Sean. By that time, Hugh Quinn had bought a twenty-three-acre farm in the neighbouring townland of Knockategell and built a larger home, a typically austere two-storey farmhouse.

Many years later, Sean Quinn reminisced on his father's shrewdness. 'My father was able to buy the farm in 1950 for £2,000 and paid cash for it. He couldn't read nor write, but he was quite clever and he could count money and he would know a good animal from a bad animal.' He added, 'He was very astute, you know. He would know what was going on.' In his book, Peter also recalls his father as being exceptionally good at mental arithmetic: 'I discovered that if I told him that an animal weighed eight three-quarter hundredweight and we were getting £7.15.0 per cwt (hundredweight) he could work out the price in his head faster than most people could do it with pen and paper.'

Peter Quinn explained his father's business philosophy as being 'one learned by doing and *only* by doing'. He recalls being shown how his father's system worked at a young age. 'He decided that I needed to learn how to buy and sell, or "deal" as it was called in the farming community. For a thirteen-year-old, that sort of experience was a much better way of learning than reading books or anything I did at university later. And his philosophy, that "now" is always the best time to learn what one does not already know, is still valid. He may have been illiterate, but he was also wise in the ways of the world and intelligent enough to know that experience teaches even the greatest fools. He did the same with my brother, when his time came to learn the art, or science, of trading, and I have to admit that despite a few mistakes, he made a much better use of the lesson in his business dealings in subsequent years.'

While his father had a strong intuition and head for numbers, Sean recalls how it was his mother who had the book smarts. 'My mother was quite bright and a lot of the local farmers used to come in to ask her to fill in their farm documents, whatever it may be, their herd numbers. She was quite brainy as regards figures and she could write a good letter back sixty, seventy years ago. So, from an education point of view, she wore the trousers and my father done whatever he was told. He done the work and she done the arranging.'

Peter concurred, saying that his mother, 'became what would be described locally as "widely read" and her ability to retain information was phenomenal. She was very articulate both in speech and on paper and could be equally caustic through both media. At her funeral, the priest indicated in his homily that being relatively new to the parish he hadn't known my mother until the last six months of her life. However, he continued by saying that, from what he had heard of her, "... she could have trimmed hedges with her tongue". We thought that his comment was entirely apt.' She 'had dreams and ambitions and saw a world full of opportunities and potential'. Sean spoke fondly of his mother, although he remembered there being disputes. Peter describes their mother as being a bright woman but 'a very cross mammy', only realising much later in life that she'd likely suffered from recurring, mild depression.

Subsistence farming is a tough life, and like with any family there were ups and downs. Sean recalled: 'It wasn't always friendly. There was plenty of rows but lovely times as well. I suppose we didn't know any different. We didn't have a car. We didn't have a tractor. We didn't have anything in those early years; I think maybe I was ten or twelve when my father bought a tractor. And then maybe I was fifteen, sixteen when he bought a car. There were no telephones, no television, no running water. There was very little.' Yet, overall, they made the best of their situation: 'They looked after us very well. We were always very well fed and dressed and we felt that we were as well looked after as any other family in the area.'

Bernie also remembers the Quinns' upbringing as being no different to any other family in the area. 'It was subsistence farming. We had all our own produce, we had all our own potatoes, vegetables, fruit. Mammy was a good baker, a good homemaker. Everybody learnt how to milk and everybody helped out with that. Mammy made her own bread, her own butter; her boxty was very popular. Now, we didn't always enjoy it. We would prefer to get away from the work but I suppose it was good training.'

She remembers good times away from the daily grind, nights of humour and gentle gossip. 'Ours was the céilí house so all the elderly men in the area would have come, sometimes nightly, but certainly weekly, to play a game of cards or just have a chat in the corner with my mother and father and the rest of us. There was never any division within our community, you know. One of our callers came every single night, but during the day he would have had all his non-Catholic neighbours visiting and he'd be telling us about what they were doing and we knew them that way, as if we were living with them and we were living among them. And our postman was from across the fields, and he would have brought Daddy all the news of what was going on in the area. And there was never any feelings of difference.'

Yet differences remained in the area, particularly around issues like land ownership, as the Quinn boys found out when their father looked to buy more land. With two sons and only one farm, Hugh Quinn felt that he had a problem. As he saw it, Sean and Peter were both destined to be farmers and in order to avoid any future dispute, their father decided to buy a second farm of land at Cranaghan, on the southern side of the border. The seventy-six acres were a mile south of Ballyconnell and three miles from the homestead on the Mountain Road. The land had once belonged to the Church of Ireland Estate and was now being sold by a Protestant farmer who Hugh Quinn knew and respected. He offered to pay £30 per acre, or a total of £2,250, but when he went to seal the deal, there was an issue. Some local Protestants, angry that the farmland was being sold to a Catholic, attempted to prevent it from going through. A meeting was convened in a local hall to discuss the proposed deal, but, according to Peter Quinn, one of their own Protestant neighbours told the gathering that 'Quinn was the highest bigger, it should be left with him.' Only then was the sale agreed.

At a later point, Hugh tried and failed to buy another Protestant farm in Teemore, even though he was again the highest bidder. Peter Quinn recalled: 'Someone had learned the lesson from a decade earlier and "the mistake" was not going to be repeated.' It was over forty years since partition, but Hugh Quinn's plans for his family were being blocked by the invisible sectarian walls that ran across the borderlands.

Still, Hugh was likely happy to finally own land on both sides of the border, even if the very notion of partition was something with which he disagreed. In his book, Peter Quinn writes that 'even though he was not politically minded, my father never really accepted the validity of the border. He felt, as did most of his nationalist neighbours, that Fermanagh should have been part of the Free State.'

The Quinns, like every other family on the Mountain Road, Protestant or Catholic, looked on Ballyconnell as their local town, no matter about the border. 'It was where groceries were bought, where cattle, sheep, pigs, donkeys and horses were bought and sold on the monthly fair day, where pints and half-ones were consumed and men got drunk, where politics was discussed and, mostly importantly of all, where most of those who lived along the Mountain Road expected to be buried,' Peter said. 'The creation of an international boundary could not break that link. Indeed, in many ways, it has still not been broken.'

All the Quinn siblings would agree with Peter's conclusion that, as a result, the family grew up with a 'bipolar perspective'. He explained, 'We were in Teemore, but we socialised in Ballyconnell; we were in Fermanagh, but we were aligned economically and socially with Cavan; we knew west Cavan much better than we knew most of the rest of Fermanagh – in fact, we barely knew anyone in north or west Fermanagh at all. We lived in the newly established "North" but we thought and acted as if we were in the Free State, as it continued to be called in south

Fermanagh. We had relatives in various parts of Cavan, but very few in Fermanagh, beyond the boundaries of our own parish. In fact, most of the old people from south Fermanagh had more relations in New York and the other parts of the United States, than they had in other parts of Fermanagh; that was certainly true in the case of Catholic families because the dreaded emigration did not apply as an equally consistent imperative to those of other religions.'

In many ways, it was the border that created the character of Sean Quinn. His identity was carved out of his upbringing on the Mountain Road. There was a duality at the core of his existence, a cognitive dissonance that came from living on the line between two states: twin cultures, two currencies, two governments of mutual suspicion, two religions and two political aspirations. Difference was his normal. In business, he would come to ruthlessly exploit those differences.

For all the effort that Hugh went to in order to purchase this patch of land south of the border, it did not stay in the family for long. Bernie explained that the land was sold, 'Because they [Peter and Sean] were going through Ballyconnell, I think my mother and father thought that Sean might get some bad ideas or bad habits there. So eventually they sold it, the land.' Perhaps the more likely reason was that Hugh already suspected that his sons were not destined to be farmers.

Many years later, Sean Quinn would buy back the same parcel of land to build a hotel.

***

Growing up, the main focus for the Quinn children was the Teemore Shamrocks pitch just north of their home off the main Enniskillen road. The club's history stretched back as far as 1888, though they only formed officially in 1904. They won the Fermanagh championship three times in the 1920s and again in 1935, though local rivals Rosslea Shamrocks and Lisnaskea Emmetts dominated Fermanagh football in the 1940s and 1950s. As the Quinn boys progressed through underage levels, they dreamed of bringing success again to Teemore.

For Sean Quinn, football became the sole focus of his teenage years. 'It's funny, there was no history of football in the family. My parents didn't play or nobody belonging to me played football. But it probably just came from the fact that the football pitch was only 200 metres away from our bedroom. And I used to be running from the byre, from milking the cows, straight across, jump the wall and across to the football pitch. And that happened maybe five, six evenings a week, you know, we'd be there. It was the only thing we knew.'

Of course, there was little else to occupy his spare time in those days. 'There was no cinema, we didn't go to the pub, we didn't go anywhere, we didn't have any way of going apart from a bicycle, so the football pitch was our home. And we used to have good fun there. So that's how it started, and of course then when you played for a few years you want to get better at it and you want to get bigger at it, and you want to try to win trophies.' So with his already customary resolve and work ethic, he set out to make his boyhood dreams a reality.

During the sixties, the Quinn brothers established themselves in the team alongside stalwarts such as goalkeeper James Cassidy, who had won an All-Ireland medal with Fermanagh in 1959. Their manager was Teemore curate Father John Maguire. Teemore hadn't won a championship in a generation. By 1969, however, that wait was about to end. Things began well when Sean convinced Cassidy to play one last championship. They went on to beat Ederney St Joseph's in their first game before coming up against Devenish St Mary's in the semi-final, who'd beaten the Shamrocks in the championship in two of the previous three years. 'Seán made the difference,' wrote team captain Peter Quinn, 'driving his body through flying boots to score the game's only goal with his fist.'

The final was against Irvinestown St Molaise, who hadn't won the championship since 1952, but had the edge as the game was played on their home pitch on the far side of the county. Sean Quinn, who played full-forward, scored a point in the first minute. The game was tight but in the final minutes Teemore were awarded a free forty yards out. Peter Quinn wrote about the conversation he had with his brother before he struck the ball. '"It's up to you," said Seán, "point this and it's our championship." I hit it and it got over the crossbar by about three inches.' Peter had scored but he admitted that it was in fact a 'great defensive intervention' by his brother that ultimately ensured the Shamrocks won their first championship since 1935. 'The ref blew it up,' Peter told *The Irish News* many years later. 'Ah it was pandemonium! I remember Paddy Drumm came over, he was a small fella but he lifted me clean off the ground!'

In the aftermath, Peter would return to his fledgling career in Belfast, while Sean, who had just turned twenty-two, remained at home, a hero in the local community. He remembers the occasion fondly. 'If you're asking me for any one event that meant more than anything else, it was winning the senior championship with Teemore. It was one of my better games and there was great rejoicing in the whole area and we all went to Ballyconnell and drank orange. I think maybe I was drinking a little bit more than orange at the time, but most of the guys were still pioneers and there wasn't much alcohol being consumed. But it was really, really big and for people that lived in the area and had played football thirty, forty years earlier, I think they got more of a kick out of it than we did. That would be my best memory from the GAA.'

Bryan Gallagher was the founding principal of St Aidan's Secondary School in Derrylin. He would become well known for his writing and broadcasting and rich depictions of life along the border. He remembers well the team led by the Quinn brothers. 'Seán Quinn's team were legendary. I don't know how to say this delicately, but they knew how to win matches, let us say. They would make threatening speeches beforehand, "the first man that questions the fourteen-yard line gets his leg broke",' says the historian.

Teemore would go on to win three more county titles in the 1970s, but their 1969 victory would always be best remembered by Sean Quinn. He went on to captain Fermanagh and, in his fifties, when his life and commitments had changed dramatically from his early playing days, he was still coaching at Teemore. 'Football would have taught me, of course, that it can be a hard life and you have to be resilient and you don't say no. You know, when things get tough the easy thing is to lie down, but I wouldn't lie down. I'd have learned a lot of that from my football days, that when you lose a big county final, you would be very down for days and maybe weeks after it, but you have to get back up. And I suppose that would have helped me in life. I was always very resilient and the football would have helped me in that respect.'

The Championship victory at Irvinestown was a moment of huge celebration for the tight-knit families of Teemore and the parish. But for the Quinns it was bittersweet, due to it coming after eighteen months of changes at home, changes that began with a tragic event just before Christmas 1967.

***

By December 1967 all of Sean's siblings had left for university. When not on a football field, he was working the farm with his father, whose health had diminished in recent years. 'My father had a bad heart. He had a heart attack in 1950 and had an operation. He was fairly seriously ill, but he recovered and he was told never to work again, but of course he worked as hard as ever,' said Sean.

Bernie takes up the story of that fateful Christmas: 'Peter [had already] gone to college, Miriam similarly, although she would have worked on the farm too. It was my first year in college, and I came home for Christmas. It was the Sunday night before Christmas, we [Miriam and Bernie] were debating whether we'd go out to the showband dance in Belturbet. And Miriam was kind of stalling and saying we'll not go. And Daddy said, sure Bernadette's only home for a couple of weeks, you might as well go.'

Eventually, it was agreed; they would go to the dance. Upon their return, however, they were greeted with a terrible scene. 'When we came back the priest and the doctor and the neighbour were there and my father was dead. Sean was also out and when he came home he was met with the same story.'

For Sean, the death of his father was a life-defining moment. Even if he wanted to, it meant he could never leave home. 'It was a huge shock for the family, a serious shock. Peter had already left at this stage. He had the brains. There was never a discussion about who was going to own this or who was going to own that. I stayed at home on the farm while Peter went to university and my two sisters went to university as well, and they became teachers. So I was the dunce that stayed at home milking the cows,' he said self-deprecatingly.

Bernie described him in kinder terms. 'Sean was the worker, the farmer. He was the one that was at home and did everything. And when we got into difficulties, like when I crashed my car, he was the one that I called on to see what he would do, and he was the one sorted out the insurance – he was probably the one bought the car in the first place! He was always at home, I suppose. The rest of us left home. He was always at home.'

And this was how, as the year 1968 began, Sean Quinn found himself in charge of his family's land. Next he needed to decide what he was going to do with it. Whether he would continue in the farming footsteps of his father, or strike out for new terrain.

***

Money had always been a concern for the Quinns. Their own farm barely produced enough to keep the family fed so Hugh Quinn, while alive, earned extra income working for neighbours. Shortly before his death, however, he discerned another way of bringing in a few more pounds.

Throughout the 1950s and 1960s, there had been three local families who started to dig down into the land, rather than farm it. Hugh Quinn saw an opportunity to profit by selling land to one of these families.

'Pat Curry, who was very well respected in the area, was the first man to start to dig the gravel in the area. And my father sold him a field of gravel. So we knew the gravel was there. And thankfully he didn't sell him any more fields, he just sold one field. I remember the price of it, it was £900. I was fortunate he only sold one field,' said Sean Quinn, who would greatly benefit in years to come from his father's prudent decision to hold onto the vast majority of his farmland.

It turned out that gravel – an integral material for the making of concrete and road construction, among other uses – was bountiful in the region. As the ice melted at the end of the last ice age, sand and gravel deposits formed on top of bedrock by melting water, typically in valleys. Fermanagh had two main geographical areas of 'glaciofluvial deposits': north-east of the village of Brookeborough stretching out towards Tempo was one, but the largest deposit was in the five-mile radius that fanned out from Hugh Quinn's farm.

Bryan Gallagher recalled how during the Second World War, American soldiers stationed in the North made use of the sand and gravel from the area. 'There was one lorry on the road when I was growing up. It was extremely dangerous work at the time. There were faces of sand exposed and I remember two men being killed when they undermined the sand and it fell on top of them. During the Second World War, when the Americans were building the airport at St Angelo, north of Enniskillen, a lot of the gravel they used came from Derrylin.' Not that the locals didn't make the most of the situation. 'It was a while before the Americans found out that these Irishmen were not as innocent as they first thought. They would spray the load of gravel with water to double its weight and one man claimed that he drove to the airport through one gate and drove back out another, with the load still on board, and did that six times in one day!'

Clearly gravel was a potentially lucrative business opportunity. Local farmer Bernard McCaffrey opened his business at Drumderg, Teemore, in 1968, though his family had been involved in sand and gravel along the border since the war years. Another neighbour, Robert Mitten, went into business a year later with a single pit. Both families are still trading today. And then there was Pat Curry, to whom Hugh Quinn sold a portion of his land. This, in turn, was likely when Sean Quinn first took notice of the gravel business. This interest only grew after his father's passing, particularly as Sean, now alone on the farm with his mother, came to realise a fundamental truth about himself: he disliked farming with a passion.

Looking back, he freely admits it. 'I wasn't big into the farming. I had farmed along with my father but we farmed poorly. After he died, we didn't have a lot of money. I bought a tractor and trailer and a bailer and a few things like that and tried to do a bit of work in the local area, that was as far as I got. I felt that farming wasn't for me and I didn't enjoy it at all. Farming was too slow for me. There's an old saying in farming, I think it's a true one: "in farming you live poor and die rich", because the farm's worth a lot after you're dead. But you live poor. So I formed that opinion very early on, rightly or wrongly, that farming wasn't for me. Maybe, as it turned out, wrongly.'

Bernie vividly recalls Sean sewing the seeds of change. 'After the funeral and Christmas, I went back to college. Sean and mammy were the only two at home and they had to pick up the pieces. And things reverted, as far as was possible, to normal and Sean took over the running of the farm. I suppose it gave Sean a greater independence. He'd already gone away from simply working his own farm to doing bailing in the country and using his tractor and trailer for other people and making a few pound on the way.'

Decades later, Bernie can still recall the first time Sean brought up the idea of entering the gravel business. 'And I remember Miriam and I being out talking to Sean in the front street when he says, you know, "I'm going to start this, I'm going to start my own sand and gravel business." We kind of looked at him. He said, "well, it's like this, if Pat Curry could buy it off my father and make money of it, why couldn't I, if I've got my own sand and gravel?"'

Bernie and Miriam both sounded unsure, but Sean knew that their opinions ultimately didn't matter. His mother would be the key to whether his plans moved forward. 'It was his mother then he had to persuade,' Bryan Gallagher concurred. 'Because it was going to be awful to see the good farm with the good grass, the fields where they'd grown their own potatoes and vegetables, dug away from under them.'

Sean could see the reasons for their reluctance; in some ways, he shared them. 'I suppose we were all frightened of the expenditure that was involved in it, because it seemed almost an impossible dream,' he said, explaining the initial worried reaction from his siblings – and his mother when he eventually told her. 'I had mentioned to my mother, once or twice, that I was thinking of starting to deliver gravel. And she said, "sure you're crazy, Sean, you have no money to start gravel, what would you know about it?" They all had big doubts: Is Sean mad? I suppose that was always the question was asked, you know, where is he going with this? Or will this work? And they weren't sure that I was doing the right thing. They were saying to themselves, is this thing all going to blow up?'

After a while, though, they came onside. Then there was no going back. Sean Quinn was getting into the gravel business.

***

1968 was a year of dramatic change around the world. In the US, Robert F. Kennedy was shot dead and there were riots in Chicago at the Democratic Convention. The Prague Spring saw mass protests on the streets in Czechoslovakia against Soviet rule, and in the North, Prime Minister Terence O'Neill started the year in meetings with Taoiseach Jack Lynch to discuss cross-border co-operation. However, by October, when

Royal Ulster Constabulary (RUC) officers beat civil rights marchers off the streets of Derry, there were growing concerns of trouble ahead. But, as Sean Quinn mused on the year of his first moves in business, the song at the top of the Irish charts was 'Daydream Believer' by The Monkees.

Like so many great businesses, it all began in a very small way. There was no money to invest, so Quinn used the tractor and trailer and the other equipment he'd purchased for the farm to draw off loose sand and gravel from the family's land. His mother, rather reluctantly at the outset, manned the phone and, on weekends, Bernie and Miriam would help him balance the books. He worked on his new venture by day, as well as maintaining the farm, while the evenings and the weekends were devoted to Teemore Shamrocks.

Quinn quickly realised that the fact he was so immersed in football at club and county level had potential benefits for his fledgling business. 'I remember a Cavan man by the name of Pat McIlweeney, who'd rang me as soon as I started the gravel. I asked him after, why did you buy it off me, Pat? Why did you not go to McCaffrey? He says I seen you playing football in Ballyconnell a few times, I always wanted to meet you. That's the sort of thing would have helped me at the start.'

He needed every bit of help he could get, given the climate in which he was trying to make a success of his business. The area was an economic wasteland, with continuing high levels of emigration, no heavy industry and an almost complete reliance on the land. The rate of unemployment in Fermanagh was 14 per cent for Catholics and 7 per cent for Protestants, with the small number of jobs that were being created found mainly in Enniskillen and the bigger towns, causing some farming families to up sticks and follow the work.

Realising he could draw heavily on all his GAA networks proved to be beneficial in those early years. And he did begin to make progress. However, just as he was getting on his feet, 'the Troubles' erupted, as feared, following the RUC officers' brutal attack on peaceful civil rights marchers in Derry in October 1968, with the violence quickly spreading to Belfast. It was a long way from the Fermanagh border, however, and, for a time, life continued as normal in their more remote corner of the North. But when British troops were sent to Northern Ireland in August 1969 after sectarian violence in Belfast and the Battle of the Bogside in Derry, the landscape around Derrylin changed. Since partition and the Civil War, a generation had emerged that lived in relative peace. Now soldiers patrolled the roads, camped in the fields and were based in the police stations in each of the border villages.

During the early years of the conflict, Fermanagh escaped without a single death. But in 1971, death came close to Sean Quinn's doorstep. The Ulster Defence Regiment (UDR) had been formed the year before, with many of the members of the Ulster Special Constabulary, or B Specials, transferring across to the new British Army unit. Throughout the conflict, the UDR would be accused of harassing Catholics at road checkpoints. Whether they were full- or part-time soldiers, they tended to be stationed in their home counties, as a result quickly becoming targets for the IRA. Private Johnny Fletcher, who was forty-three years old, was the first UDR man to die in Fermanagh, shot twenty-two times in front of his wife at their home in Garrison. Following his murder, many of the serving UDR men in the area abandoned their border homes. Still the attacks continued. In September of that year, Private Frank Veitch, a twenty-three-year-old part-time member of the UDR, was shot dead outside the police station in Kinawley, which was just ten minutes north-west of the Quinn home on the other side of Derrylin. The following month, in the same village, Corporal David Powell, a member of the Queen's Royal Lancers, was killed in a landmine attack. A garda inspector, Samuel Donegan, also died when he stepped across the Cavan–Fermanagh border to examine what he thought was a hoax bomb.

The killing by the IRA of fifty-three-year-old Thomas Bullock and his fifty-year-old wife, Emily, in September 1972, as they watched the television news, shocked the community and led to a series of attacks that are etched in the memory of all those who lived at the time. The IRA shot Emily Bullock as she attempted to protect her husband, who was a private in the UDR. The gang escaped across Aghalane Bridge, which spanned the Woodford River, and back into Co. Cavan. The bridge would be an open sore for locals throughout the Troubles and a costly problem for Sean Quinn.

As the violence worsened, Sean Quinn focused on growing his business, displaying no interest in the politics of the North. Of the twenty-two acres on the family farm, he reckoned there were ten acres of sand and gravel. That would be enough to keep him going. Having made do with the farm equipment he had purchased after his father's death for the initial few years, he now knew that it was time to invest. He drove to Belfast to buy a lorry and an industrial shovel capable of scooping up three tonnes of gravel.

Reflecting on this decision, Quinn sees it as a turning point. 'I suppose the big moment for me was in 1972 [when] there was a lot of trouble in the border region and there were people being killed. I headed off to Belfast and when I came back late, the cows hadn't been milked and my mother was shouting that the cows are roaring in the byre and asking where I'd been. I said I was away in Belfast and she said, "sure you're crazy, Sean, you have no money",' said Quinn, laughing. 'But when I took that spin to Belfast to buy that catch shovel, I suppose that was the day that everything changed. It didn't change on the day, but it put in place a mechanism that was going to change my life.'

Before long, he would start to see his gamble pay off.

***

In 1972 Sean Quinn made a profit of £10,000. Through nothing but grit, he'd proven to his mother, to his siblings, and, most importantly, to himself, that he wasn't going to be the dunce who stayed home milking the cows. While his brother and sisters studied in Belfast and Dublin, he'd got on with making money. Fifteen years earlier he'd made his decision about the value of education when he hid in a hedge rather than take the bus to attend the 11+ exam. Now, without any qualifications or meaningful education, he was earning more money than any of his siblings could expect to make once they graduated and qualified in their chosen fields. Furthermore, he was making good money without having to follow the emigration path of so many of his generation to London, New York or Boston. Instead he'd remained at home and won a senior championship with Teemore Shamrocks and was captain of the county team.

Still, he wanted more. He had already built an operation that could challenge the Mittens, the Currys or McCaffreys, but that wasn't enough. In fact, he hadn't even started. 'Education wouldn't have done me any harm. Maybe if I had have been better educated I wouldn't have walked into the hole that I did forty years later. But maybe a lot of people who are over-educated wouldn't have had the success that I had. So it's hard to know how that would have went, or what difference it would have made. They might not have been as successful in the early part of their lives as I was, but they might not have made the mistake that I made in the latter part of my life. I don't know. And I never will.'

After further thought, he conceded, 'And I suppose I was just greedy.'

2

Trouble at a Border Bank

By the spring of 1973, all Sean Quinn was worried about was the need to invest further in his business and his future. He did this by purchasing his first brand-new lorry. After the purchase, he made sure that the supplier put his name across the headband above the front windscreen – an early example of his appreciation for the importance of building a brand. Sean Quinn wanted everyone to know that he'd arrived.

He fondly recalls the vehicle. 'It was a wee Bedford lorry and it cost £1,800. The registration number was AIL 8023, we bought it from Lochside Garage in Enniskillen. I drove it home myself and I hadn't a clue how to drive it. I got stuck in the middle of the town; thankfully there was only 10 per cent of the traffic that there would be today, but I had trouble getting it home.'

By the end of that year, he'd bought another two lorries and had four employees, three men and one woman. Things were coming together. 'You mightn't know exactly from day to day what you were doing, but I always tried to create a plan. And you'd work the plan and you'd renew it at the end of the year and you'd think through it and you'd say, am I on target, or am I off target, and what'll I do next year? It was my own plan, nobody helped me with the plan. Now, did it always work out 100 per cent? No. But was I always there or thereabouts? Yes. I never set the expectations too high as it was always the idea that you would finish up the year with a better figure than you had budgeted on,' he explained of those early years in business. 'So then at the end of the year what was the position? The position was we made money.'

Things were going well, though issues along the border threatened to undo all his hard work.

After partition, a customs barrier was created along the border in 1923, which economically separated the Free State from Northern Ireland. Bureaucratic arrangements were made for the regulation of people and goods crossing the border that were both onerous and time-consuming. Paperwork had to be completed and duties paid ahead of any planned crossing, as what were called small, one-or two-roomed 'customs huts' appeared at crossing points with signs placed in the middle of the road to warn motorists of the need to stop.

The governments in London and Dublin agreed a series of fifteen officially designated 'Approved Frontier Crossing Points' along the border, which were to be used during approved daytime hours. Anyone taking goods for personal use or sale had to make an appointment to use the approved crossing points and have their goods and permits checked. The two governments identified over 200 road crossings along the 310-mile border, although community groups along the border say there are closer to 275 routes. Customs checkpoints were placed on the fifteen approved customs crossings, and cars and motorbikes were banned from using the unofficial roads – any motorist using the unapproved roads faced being fined. The customs checks were a feature of everyday life for those living along the border.

After the troops arrived in 1969, temporary military checkpoints, which soon become permanent, were set up on the northern side of many of the approved and unapproved roads. Heavily fortified buildings and soldiers supported by armoured vehicles appeared on the border landscape. The military set about making the unapproved roads that didn't have checkpoints unusable by either blowing them up, or by placing heavy spikes or bollards across them – all designed to prevent nationalist paramilitaries from being able to escape across the border.

To Sean Quinn, the border was invisible. He had no interest in aligning with one particular party or other, but he was a nationalist and didn't recognise partition, believing there should be a United Ireland. As a result, the customs and the military posts were a constant reminder of the wrongs inflicted on Ireland by the British. Now, in 1973, the permanent structures were also a significant obstacle to his business.

'The road between Derrylin and Ballyconnell was unapproved at the time so we weren't allowed to take goods on it and if we did, first of all, you had the army in the northern side, and they would cause you all sorts of trouble, and did on many occasions. And then you would entered the South, the customs were liable to pull you up. The customs were out on the road practically every day, and if they caught you bringing a load of gravel up the road, you had to off to Swanlinbar to pay a fine of maybe fifty or a hundred pounds. There was no duty. You just had to fill in these forms to say you were bringing the goods into the North or the South. There was no duty, it was just so stupid it doesn't even bear thinking about,' he recalls. 'It just made absolutely no sense. You had the army one side, the customs the other side and the only main road close to the quarry we couldn't use. It was ridiculous.'

Things had gotten even worse following the IRA murders of Thomas and Emily Bullock, when Aghalane Bridge, now an unapproved route linking Fermanagh and Cavan that had been used by the IRA to escape after the double killing, became a particular focus for the military. There had been two separate bomb attacks on the bridge following the callous murders, both of which were blamed on loyalists but were more likely the work of the British Army. In December 1972, Cavan County Council, trying to save the economy of the town of Belturbet, which had effectively been cut off from its natural hinterland of southern Fermanagh by the destruction of the bridge, installed a temporary Bailey bridge. But four days after its opening, loyalists used it to launch a bomb attack. They drove a car bomb into the centre of Belturbet, which exploded without warning, killing teenagers Geraldine O'Reilly and Patrick Stanley.

Following the attack, the Bailey bridge was removed but the crossing point remained a flashpoint for the rest of the conflict, local people spending their weekends building temporary crossings only for the British Army to remove them.

The quarry at Teemore was five minutes north of Belturbet along the main A509, as long as you could cross Aghalane Bridge. With it gone, Sean Quinn's lorries, along with everyone else, had to take a detour north through a British Army checkpoint, where you could be held up for anything up to an hour, then cross the border at Swanlinbar and take a route along the narrow main street of Ballyconnell, which was hardly wide enough for two lorries to pass at the same time, to reach the same destination. It was a twenty-eight-mile round trip, which was costly both in time and money for Quinn. The daily inconvenience was also destructive to local life and caused the shuttering of many businesses in Belturbet and the surrounding area.

It also meant that frustrations regularly boiled over for both Quinn and his drivers. 'There were different soldiers and regiments in all the time, and they might be there for a month or two and then all of a sudden there was new guys. And you'd feel you had something sorted out and then it wasn't sorted out. So it wasn't good. And there were soldiers who'd think "Quinn has got Catholics working for him and he has green lorries and we'll give him a hard time." It was a nasty time,' he said, also admitting that, as the Troubles escalated, attitudes on both sides hardened, leaving no room for an accommodation or resolution that worked for both locals and the security forces.

***

Despite the challenges caused by the border, Sean Quinn's business continued to grow. By 1974 he had seven lorries on the road, and with a brand new washing plant he purchased a year later, began manufacturing and selling concrete blocks from his Derrylin base. Next to come on-stream was ready-mixed concrete. He later explained to *Export & Freight* magazine how his relationship with his customers was 'possibly more important than price. If someone rings for a delivery of blocks at eleven in the morning, he will have them by two or three o'clock the same day; it would be a rare occasion that he would be disappointed. The very same goes for the builder, North and South. What he wants is reliability first of all, then he looks for a good competitive price.'

Not that work was the only thing on his mind during this period. Sure, Quinn worked six days a week, but on a Saturday night he'd sometimes go to a dance in Dublin. It was there that he met his wife, Patricia. 'Patricia had just moved from Galway to Dublin a few months earlier and she was doing secretarial work. We met in one of the ballrooms and I remember I'd a few drinks in me! And she thought I was too old for her – she was right – but she was foolish enough to allow me to bring her home and that was the end of that, or the beginning of that,' he laughed.

They were married within a year. In 1975 their first daughter, Colette, was born. Four more children – Ciara, Aoife, Sean Junior and Brenda – were to follow over the next ten years. 'When we got married we lived with my mother, Lord have mercy on her. We lived in the home house. She had her section and we had our section! The two eldest girls, Colette and Ciara, were born in Enniskillen [at the Erne Hospital], because we were living in the North. Then we built our own home outside Ballyconnell and Aoife, Sean Junior and Brenda were all born in Cavan Hospital. So two of our children were born in the North and three in the South.'

His business life intersected somewhat with his personal life when, in June 1977, having married a Galway woman, Sean Quinn went west again – this time to expand, buying a quarry outside Williamstown. Industry magazine *Plantman International* reported on the purchase, saying that although Quinn was 'only in his mid-thirties there can be little doubt as to his ability and foresight in the sand and gravel industry'.

As well as washed sand, the Williamstown site produced small stones used for drainage. Quinn, just as he was doing back on the border, immediately invested heavily, purchasing new machinery that would significantly increase production. The ready-mix plant, according to the same article, was 'the most modern available' and its blockmaking was 'completely automatic, producing 30,000 blocks per day if required'. It concluded, 'Hard work and dedication has been rewarding for Seán Quinn and his company give a first-class service.'

'It was just probably the best deposit of gravel I've ever seen at the time, and quality is everything,' said Sean Quinn of his first investment outside his home county. 'I met the man that owned it and we talked and chatted and I finished up buying it for £110,000. I never saw a mystery to running a business, I never thought it was difficult. Running a business always came easy to me. I never sat up at night and said "this thing can't work", that wouldn't be in my vocabulary at all. But it started from very, very little. But, yeah, we were successful early on.'

The Williamstown plant had thirty employees, with another twenty employed indirectly. It was a sizeable operation that was almost seventy miles and two hours by road to the main focus of his business in Derrylin. With this in mind, Quinn allowed the existing local foreman and general manager to get on with running the quarry, which would remain a part of his company for the next thirty years.

His business was growing, but the dichotomy of life along the border meant that while life was never better for Sean Quinn and his young family, for many of his neighbours, their experience was very different.

***

Throughout the years it took Sean Quinn to properly establish his business – from 1973 to 1979 –almost fifty people died as a result of the conflict in Fermanagh and along its border with the Republic, with many more perishing across the North. With troops on the streets and in the hedges, life had become abnormal in both urban and rural areas. Fear was omnipresent for both unionists and nationalists. Sean Quinn and his family were avowed nationalists, although business obviously came first. But while Sean tried to bury himself in his business, he couldn't completely escape the pain and trauma that continued to be inflicted all around him.

Lieutenant Colonel George Saunderson was the headmaster of the Earl of Erne Primary School in Sean Quinn's Teemore. He had joined the Royal Inniskilling Fusiliers and served in Palestine and the Middle East and with the Parachute Regiment in the Second World War. In April 1974, six months before Sean and Patricia Quinn were married, he was shot twenty times in the kitchen of his school while he was drinking a cup of coffee during his morning break. The evening before, six gunmen had forced their way into a house in Teemore and stolen the family's car; after the murder of Saunderson they then hijacked 'a sand lorry' and a car and used them to form a roadblock while they escaped across the border, smashing through a garda checkpoint in Ballyconnell. Another car used in the attack was found burnt out in Cavan.

On a Saturday night, two weeks after George Saunderson's murder, a well-known local mechanic, Jim Murphy, was working late in his garage, fewer than six miles from Teemore on the northern side of Derrylin. He repaired vehicles and sold petrol and diesel from the garage in the townland of Corravehy. Jim, who was forty-two years old, had been interned without trial for six months during the IRA Border Campaign (a guerrilla warfare campaign carried out by the IRA between 1956–62 with the aim of overthrowing British rule in the North) and in the late 1960s had joined the Northern Ireland Civil Rights Association, a peaceful campaigning group focused on ending gerrymandering and discrimination in housing. Shots were heard in the area after 11 p.m. but it was the early hours of the morning before a priest and the local doctor arrived at Jack Murphy's home to break the news that his brother had been found shot dead. It appeared that Jim had been bundled into a car and shot elsewhere, his body later dumped on the forecourt of his garage.

Jack Murphy and many locals were suspicious that the security forces had colluded with the killers, if not been actively involved in the murder. The *Fermanagh Herald* later published a letter purporting to come from the Fermanagh Ulster Freedom Fighters (UFF), confirming that they had murdered Jim Murphy in retaliation for the killing of George Sanderson. Jim Murphy was the 1,000th victim of the so-called Troubles.

Sean Quinn wasn't oblivious to the violence that was all-pervasive in the community. He'd grown up aware of the bloodshed from partition and was old enough to remember the IRA's Border Campaign. It was brutal, but it wasn't new for the borderlands. 'There was a lot of trouble in the region and there were people being killed and there was a lot of hassle. At the time there was a lot of hatred and I suppose a lot of people being killed, a lot of Protestants and Catholics. The whole thing was a mess,' he said.

Throughout all the violence, his business proved a constant distraction. Even when he had his own problems.

***

Sean Quinn was in trouble with the bank. As he hared through the village of Belturbet towards Cavan, he was already imagining how the meeting ahead of him would go. It was going to be tricky, as his bank manager was not in full receipt of the facts and would, at the very least, be a little concerned when he learnt of Quinn's actions earlier that morning. The young businessman was breaking new ground. Now, he had decided, it was time to expand his operation.

Of the twenty-three acres he'd inherited, only ten had any gravel deposits, which limited his capacity for growth. The other quarry businesses in the area stuck to sand and gravel, but Sean Quinn, now in his mid-thirties, had much more ambitious goals. He was going to produce ready-mix concrete and blocks. But to do that he needed a key ingredient his own quarry didn't have: limestone. So, when a neighbouring farm was put up for auction, Sean Quinn went along. He didn't know how much the land would go for but it didn't really matter because he had no money to buy it. Not only that, he was already overdrawn at the bank.

As he reached the edge of Cavan town, he knew he was in for a tough conversation with his bank manager. He would tell him the overdraft would be paid off in full by the end of the month, which he hoped would calm him down. But then he'd have to admit that he had just come from the auction where he'd paid £40,000 for the land; £40,000 he didn't have.

It was 1978 and this was the first but not the last time that Sean Quinn would have a difficult conversation with the manager of a bank.

Quinn still has a clear memory of the meeting. 'As soon as I went through the door he says, "can I have a word with you, Sean?" I said, "you can, of course." So we went down to a wee room at the back, and he says, "you're overdrawn in the bank, you know that?" I says, "a wee bit, but sure, we're going in the right direction, our profits are increasing all the time." I knew that he didn't know I'd the farm bought. I looked at him and I said, "I just bought a farm of land." "You what?" he says. I says, "I bought a farm of land this morning." He says, "who's going to pay for that?" I said, "I don't know."' Quinn laughed. 'He was scared.'

Quinn didn't even know if the farm he'd just bought would provide him with enough limestone to realise his ambitions for the business. There had been no time for a geological survey of the fifty-five acres. Quinn had simply acted on raw instinct, an inborn impulse that would serve him well in the years ahead.

But first of all he had to find the money to pay the farmer for his land. He had somewhat placated the bank manager in the meeting, but he still wasn't going to lend him the full amount. So every night for a week, Sean Quinn travelled around the border to borrow the rest of the money from family and friends. In the end, he managed to scrape together the amount required. And his gut instinct regarding the land did ultimately prove correct: 'It was difficult enough to quarry because there was various types of rock in it and some of it was very heavily contaminated with clay. But it done the job and we got through it.'

Quinn's business was moving to the next level.

But success came at a cost and for Sean Quinn in the 1970s that meant getting used to being in front of a judge. His quarry sat on a stream that ran into Drumderg Lough close to Garvary Primary School, where he'd spent his only years in education. As he grew his business, he initially paid little attention to the fact that effluent from the sand-washing plant was running into the stream and lough. He was forced to pay attention, however, when he faced court four times in the space of three years, charged with polluting the stream. Over the next forty years, campaigners would continually raise concerns about the damage his businesses were causing to the local environment.

Appearing before a resident magistrate in Newtownbutler Court in March 1979, Quinn faced a charge of discharging effluent in June the previous year. According to the *Fermanagh Herald*, Mr John Fyffe, for the Department of Public Prosecutions in the North, told the court that a sample of water taken from the stream showed that it exceeded the amount of 'suspended solids' allowed. He said that despite Quinn's previous convictions in 1976, 1977 and 1978, nothing had been done to stop pollution at his quarry. The prosecutor said that the sand now lying on the bottom of Drumberg Lough was killing 'all the aquatic life that fish could feed on'.

However, a solicitor for the defendant, Mr T. Gibson, said that his client had put in place a procedure to discharge water from the plant into filters, thereby reducing the amount of suspended solids entering the stream. He also outlined how his client had made continuous efforts to deal with the problem. The prosecutor countered that, having looked back on the files from the previous court appearances, Sean Quinn had 'put up the same excuses' before. Fining Quinn £60, the RM said that, although his record was a bad one, he recognised that he was making efforts to remedy the situation.

Two months after his final court appearance of the 1970s, Sean Quinn (Quarries) Ltd, was first registered. Sean was listed as the managing director and his wife, Patricia, was company secretary. The husband and wife were the only members of the company's board of directors.

By then, the company required a proper base and Quinn put some of his own materials into building its first headquarters at the Gortmullan quarry on the Ballyconnell to Derrylin road. This would have workshops and stores on the ground floor covering almost 10,000 square feet. Above would be 2,400 square feet of space, with an office for Sean and a meeting room. The building was split level, with the main office entrance opening onto the main road and the workshop opening to a yard at the rear, which was below road level. It mirrored the times and local geography: modest and unappealing but practical. In the border region, it was a statement of intent.

Quinn meant business.

***

Despite all the challenges – the geographic disadvantage, the conflict and the attendant military presence – by the end of the 1970s, Sean Quinn had a hundred employees working on the quarry in Teemore. From making a £10,000 in 1973, he'd doubled profits each and every year that followed. He'd invested heavily in plant and machinery and had added two new quarries. With so much achieved in such a short time, he'd every right to think things were going to continue in the same direction.

But Ireland in 1979 was entering an economic crisis, largely brought on by the shortage of oil following the Iranian Revolution. By the end of the year the country had a new Taoiseach, Charles J. Haughey, who, despite himself being over £1 million in debt at the time, as later outlined in *The Irish Times*, made a startling address to the nation on RTÉ within weeks of taking office.

I wish to talk to you this evening about the state of the nation's affairs and the picture I have to paint is not, unfortunately, a very cheerful one.

The figures which are just now becoming available to us show one thing very clearly. As a community we are living way beyond our means. I don't mean that everyone in the community is living too well, clearly many are not and have barely enough to get by, but taking us all together we have been living at a rate which is simply not justified by the amount of goods and services we are producing. To make up the difference we have been borrowing enormous amounts of money, borrowing at a rate which just cannot continue. A few simple figures will make this very clear ... we will just have to reorganise government spending so that we can only undertake those things we can afford.

In an interview for the RTÉ documentary series about Quinn, author and *Irish Times* columnist Fintan O'Toole described the country's new leader as 'flagrantly corrupt'. He elaborated, 'Haughey is a really talented, brilliant, very energetic, domineering kind of politician, I mean, really good at his job. But he's on the take in a big way.'

Sean Quinn didn't know it in 1979, but he would soon go head-to-head with one of the new Taoiseach's chief advisors.

3

Stone and Shite

Sean Quinn was born an outsider, but in his home county in the early 1980s he was beginning to appreciate the benefits of trading on his status. His geographical position in Teemore meant that for the first ten years in business he largely operated below the radar, with only the local community around him on either side of the Fermanagh–Cavan border aware of what was going on, along what locals call 'the Mountain Road', the main cross-border route from Derrylin to Ballyconnell, in the shadow of Slieve Rushen. And even then, it was mostly gossip and speculation as to what Quinn was really planning.

Fintan O'Toole saw it as him creating his own territory: 'I think one of the extraordinary things about Quinn is that he does stay outside of the system. And I think he gets this from his border existence, you know – that he's both inside and outside the Republic of Ireland and Northern Ireland. He's not really anywhere in a way, you know, he's in this kind of space that's his own space. And he creates his own territory. He creates his own thing. And I think nobody quite knows how to deal with him.'

His business was growing fast and so too was his family. In October 1981 Patricia gave birth to Aoife, a baby sister for Colette and Ciara and Sean Junior. It was a turbulent year against a backdrop of a hunger strike by republican prisoners in the H-Blocks at the Maze Prison protesting against conditions. Ten of them would die before the protest ended. In April IRA prisoner Bobby Sands was elected as a Member of Parliament to represent Fermanagh and South Tyrone when he polled over 30,000 votes in a by-election, beating the Ulster Unionist candidate, Harry West, in an election which brought Westminster's most western constituency to the world's attention. Sands' death a month later sparked a fresh wave of violence, death and destruction.

In June, Ronnie Graham was delivering groceries to a house in Lisnaskea, fifteen minutes north-east of Teemore, when he was shot dead by the IRA. Graham was a member of the UDR who played football for Lisnaskea Rovers. In the same month that the Quinns welcomed baby Aoife into the world, Ronnie's brother Cecil and his wife welcomed their own newborn. But on 11 November Cecil was shot dead by the IRA when he visited his Catholic wife and their baby at her parents' home in the village of Donagh, minutes away from the Quinns' house.

The unrelenting nature of the violence caused further polarisation in the border community, with many Protestants believing the IRA was intent on driving them out of the area. Protestant and Catholic communities, not just along the border but across Fermanagh, turned in on themselves, seeking comfort and reassurance from their own people. Predictably, this led to further mistrust that would seep into the soil for another generation.

While the hunger strike in the North acted as a centrifugal force that saw the Troubles spiral into an even more vicious cycle of violence, in the South of Ireland, the slowdown in the world economy continued to send shockwaves through the country. Mass emigration was back as unemployment spiralled. 'People were just trying to get out because it felt hopeless,' Fintan O'Toole remembered. 'And that was true for different reasons on both sides of the border.'

All this turmoil made Quinn's continued growth and success all the more remarkable. As O'Toole said, 'So you can imagine the impact that somebody like Sean Quinn has in a particular part of that terrain, where there is nothing and where for most people it's not just [that] there's nothing now, it doesn't look like there's going to be very much in the future. And here you have the extraordinary energy of Sean Quinn coming into that, saying: "You know what, I can do this. We can make stuff." You know, it's perfectly understandable why people would see him as almost a magician to be able to defy all of that pessimism and to do stuff that you could see on the ground. They were getting those jobs. Those jobs were allowing young people to stay in those communities. And doing all of this in the bleakest possible environment. I mean, the man must have seemed like a god.'

***

For his next trick, Sean Quinn looked to Europe. Accompanied by his lofty, mop-haired electrician, Gerry Reilly, who would become a very close friend, standing beside him through thick and thin, he went on a research trip to figure out the next stage in his business.

After considering all the different manufacturing options open to him, he decided that he was going to build a 25,000-square-foot roof-tile plant at Gortmullan. 'By the end of 1981 we were becoming a bit restless, thinking that maybe we were running out of steam and not keeping up the pace of development of previous years. We looked at various possibilities and decided that the area we are in was fairly freely available for a tile plant,' Quinn was quoted as saying in *The Impartial Reporter* newspaper, the highly respected and most popular weekly paper in the border area.

Quinn had identified that there wasn't a tile plant within a ninety-mile radius of his quarry. 'The nearest plants [are in] Belfast, Antrim, Dublin and Offaly so we could see that we had the north-west of Ireland pretty much to ourselves as far as roofing tiles were concerned.'

Given that he'd no idea what was required to make the tiles, he decided that another visit to the continent was necessary; this time to visit some of its biggest tile manufacturers.

By the time he began manufacturing in March 1983, the new factory, which was built by his own men in the 'Sean Quinn Building Division', was being described as one of the most modern plants in Europe. It was the first clear signal of the way in which Quinn would go about his business. He wasn't just going to open a tile factory, it was going to be *the best* tile factory in Ireland, maybe even Europe. He wasn't in business to compete, he was going to win. And he wanted his staff, and the local community, to know that what he was doing was bigger and better than anyone else in the country, if not the continent. He wanted them to be proud of what he was doing.

Throughout this period, articles began appearing in trade magazines, in local newspapers and, soon, in the national media about the tile factory being built on the border. While Quinn would go on to develop a reputation for being media shy, the archives tell another story. He was always interested in good press, in promoting his success.

In the *Impartial Reporter* article, Quinn talked of his trip around Europe with Gerry Reilly. They'd visited several sites, looking at different types of machinery before settling on the Vortex Hydra system. 'Automation is the key word in the factory, making precise quality control.' He'd eliminated the possibility of human error in the manufacturing process and quality was constant. 'Once the sand is tipped from the lorry into the batching plant, the entire process is automatic until the tile is delivered at the other end,' Quinn told the paper in a report that went into incredible detail about the processing of roof tiles.

He'd decided it was time to let everyone know he'd arrived. A 1982 November–December edition of *Export & Freight* magazine carried a spread across several pages on Quinn's plans. Despite the headline, 'Planning to Put a Roof over the West of Ireland', Quinn announced that he viewed his market as stretching from Belfast in the east to Donegal. 'In theory, we could deliver our tiles as far away as Belfast but I don't know whether that will happen. By the same token, I hope buyers in this area will no longer see the need to go to the other side of the province for their tiles,' adding that his 'patch' included Donegal, Sligo, Fermanagh, Leitrim, Cavan and Monaghan.

By this point, he'd four sales staff – Terry Curry, Michael Gilleece, Hugh Murray and Jerome Maguire. But his most significant appointment to date was John Lee, his general manager, who'd become a key confidant over the years to come. The splash in *Export & Freight* raved about the fact that he'd added a chartered accountant, Con Dolan, to their senior staff and installed an Olivetti computer system, which dealt with invoices, wages and products. The company also had a typist, Rositta O'Reilly. Quinn was investing heavily in machinery, in staffing and in his own base business instincts.

Within weeks of opening the roof-tile plant, he also began to manufacture floor tiles, a production line coming on stream in just a few months. Despite the recession that gripped both ends of the island, by the summer of 1983 he'd established a limited company structure that was not just about able to service the markets he was already in but would act as a foundation for whatever he decided to do next.

And, somewhat predictably by now, Sean Quinn had big plans. 'I suppose the big spread was the roof tiles and the floor tiles in Derrylin; that widened us out. Because up until then we were working with maybe a thirty-mile radius. And then we were working more like a 100-mile radius or up to a 150-mile radius in some cases. Because the value of a load of roof tiles was a multiple of a load of gravel or sand or whatever the case might be. So you could afford to draw it that much further. That brought us more into the national scene,' Quinn said, looking back on this incredible period of growth.

***

Personally, Sean Quinn had little respect for banks or banking. But, by this point in his life – he was now thirty-seven years old – he had also little worry about his bank balance or overdrafts. He was beginning to see very serious returns on his efforts. Apart from opening two new factories, 1983 was also the year Sean Quinn became a millionaire. In just over ten years, he had turned a small plot of poor farmland into a business that was now throwing off profits that were significant by any standard. He'd already made it; he'd succeeded in business. But in terms of personal drive and ambition, Quinn still had huge tanks of propulsion that would continue to fire him forward for many years to come. He simply didn't have it in him to be content with his achievements. As if still on the football pitch, he was determined to compete to the final whistle, to win as decisively as possible.

Speaking during an interview with the author in 2018, Quinn contemplated wealth and his becoming a millionaire. 'It's like everything else, it grows on you and, you know, people would say to me, when did you realise you were wealthy? I never realised I was wealthy, because right from day one I always saw the problems. I didn't worry about the problems, but I always saw issues to be dealt with tomorrow. And as long as you have issues to deal with tomorrow, you're never complete, you've work to do,' he said, providing some insight into his state of mind at the time.

Even if he took a minute to consider his wealth and what it meant, his brain wasn't wired to consider how he might deserve to treat himself. Granted, he was now driving a top-of-the-range car – a Mercedes-Benz 450 ECL – but he was still living in the same house he'd built for his family. There was no second home in the south of France, or even on the west coast of Ireland. Quinn was ploughing every penny of profit back in the company.

He was also showing early signs that he was deriving significant satisfaction from the impact he was having not only on his own life, but on the lives of the border people around him. There were no wine bars in Ballyconnell for the wealthy to mix in. There were no golf clubs. Instead, Quinn sat on the same high stools in the town's Woodford Arms as those he employed. He had a talent, a business acumen that would allow him to accumulate great wealth, but he never lost touch with the local people around him. Indeed, he wanted to be treated and seen as one of them, although knowing that he was very different and someone they should look up to.

It was that same instinct and business acumen that led him to his next key decision. In the same month that he opened the tile factory, Sean Quinn did something he'd never done before – he diversified. Up to then it was all about the quarry and the associated businesses. But in March 1983 Quinn became a publican when, out of the blue, he purchased the Cat & Cage pub in Drumcondra in North Dublin.

The *Irish Independent*'s property supplement reported on the moment that the relatively unknown quarryman made his move in a room full of Dublin publicans. 'Sean Quinn, a businessman from Ballyconnell, County Cavan, emerges as the man who was the top bidder for the Cat & Cage Public House in Drumcondra. Mr. Quinn, who has extensive quarries in Fermanagh and Galway, had the pub knocked down to him for £640,000 this week at a public auction conducted by Tony Morrissey of Daniel Morrissey & Sons. Bidding opened at £200,000 and moved along smartly with two £100,000 bids and two £50,000. The spree slowed as five bids took the figure to £600,000. New owner Sean Quinn has no experience of bars from behind the counter and he said last night he may seek a tenant for the popular hostelry,' read the report.

The *Independent* report also suggested that Sean Quinn bought the pub in his own name. Later in his life, there would be confusion over who exactly owned what, whether property belonged to them personally or were owned by the company, of which they were the shareholders. It was clear that Sean Quinn saw the limited company's money as his own and at the time there was no denying or disputing that fact. Only later would such entanglement cause him great pain.

It was during this period that he first became concerned about inheritance. When he bought the Cat & Cage, Sean and Patricia Quinn had three daughters and a son. As the money kept rolling in, he made a calculation that his daughters would not want to go into the quarry business, so he began to make plans for their futures. The girls would have the pubs, he decided, while Sean Junior would stay at home to take over the quarry. At the time, it made complete sense to both Sean and Patricia, who had no idea that their children could possibly grow up to have their own opinions on their futures, just as Sean and Peter Quinn had defied their father's plan for their lives.

'I knew what I was doing in buying the pub. In a lot of businesses, family rows can have a major effect on the business, second or third generation. At the time I thought that if they all had a pub or two, and then the quarry, you know, we had three girls and one boy; we just thought that it was necessary to have a diversification plan. And we were diversifying with very little human input. I knew that if we bought a pub in Dublin we could lease it and we could get a decent return from day one. I done a bit of investigation on it and just checked out and, I mean, it was the dearest pub I think in Dublin at that time in '83. And we leased that pub out for ninety thousand [pounds a year]. So we were getting a brilliant return from day one. We got a good tenant and put a bit of an effort into the refurbishing of the pub, [and in return] you got your monthly rent for five, ten years whatever it was. It was one of the best decisions I made,' said Quinn, looking back.

Within months, he'd bought another North Dublin pub. This time it was McGovern's, which was also on the Drumcondra Road and close to the GAA headquarters at Croke Park. In this instance, Quinn hadn't just diversified; he was sending out a clear message. Between the two bars, he'd spent a reported £1.4m, a huge sum of money at a time of recession. Business was booming.

In early 1984 Sean Quinn (Quarries) Limited reported a £1.7m profit on a turnover of £5m for the year 1982/83. The new plant was producing 30,000 tiles a day. He'd built up the business, he'd diversified through the pubs, and he still had huge amounts of cash. The question now plaguing Sean Quinn was what to do next. The investment in the pubs were for the next generation, his children. With all he had achieved, he wasn't lacking confidence nor ambition.

And soon a fresh idea was planted in his mind, providing another opportunity to feed that growing ambition. It came during a chance conversation with an old friend, Bertie Hanly, who, along with his two brothers, had been running a quarry at Elphin in Co. Roscommon since the late 1960s. 'At the time back in the mid-eighties, cement was very hard to get. There was a scarcity of cement, and all of the quarries were on allocation, so you had to order a couple of days in advance and you might get 50 or 60 per cent of what you needed to get. And we were at a meeting one day in Longford Arms in Longford, and we were all talking: where can we get cement? What's the story with cement, and this, that and the other. And I didn't even know what cement was made of. And I said to Bertie Hanly, who was sitting beside me, and I said to Bertie, what is cement made of, Bertie? And he says, "it's made of stone and shite". And I said, we have stone and shite! We started investigating the chemistry then of what it was. The shite is clay, it's a form of clay, but this was Bertie's description of it. So when we investigated that [it] took us maybe six, twelve months to look into it all. None of our raw material was perfect but at least it went a long way to where we needed to get to, and we made a decision, yeah, we'll go for it,' recalled Quinn of a meeting and a decision that would set him on a high-risk path that would be more challenging than anything he'd ever done before.

He was going into the cement-making business, a path that would put him on a direct collision course with Ireland's political elite.

***

Quinn's rise against the odds defies description. However, moving into the manufacture of cement was the business equivalent of a gambler putting every last cent on red at the roulette wheel. The odds were firmly stacked against him, as he went up against a company with a rich and long history in the cement business.

The first patent for cement was obtained in 1824 by Joseph Aspdin, a native of Leeds in the English midlands, who called his product 'Portland Cement' as it looked very similar to Portland stone. According to *Grace's Guide to British Industrial History*, Associated Portland Cement Manufacturers Ltd (APCM) was formed in 1900 by the amalgamation of twenty-four cement companies, including the two cement plants, Robin's and Swanscombe, that first manufactured Portland cement in the 1840s.

The first plants in Ireland opened at Drinagh, Co. Wexford, and Ringsend and Rialto, Dublin, but these had all closed by 1925, when the only cement plant on the island of Ireland was in Co. Antrim. Later, a new company emerged, Cement Limited, which began production in Limerick and Drogheda in 1938 and had the Irish market to itself. One of its biggest customers was a Dublin gravel company called Roadstone, owned by two brothers, Tom and Donal Roche.

Like Quinn, Tom Roche's father died when he was still relatively young. In 1932, when he hadn't yet turned sixteen, Roche left school and bought a coal and sand business for IR£800. The *Irish Times* obituary on his death in 1999 told how Tom Roche 'found himself running the business with three employees and a 1.5 ton truck'. Along with his brother, he then established Castle Sand Company, a gravel business, in 1944 and only five years later the brothers took the company public under its new name, Roadstone.

By 1970 Roadstone was the largest single consumer of cement, buying up to 200,000 tonnes a year from Cement Limited, who insisted on a thirty-day payment schedule and would offer them no discount whatsoever for bulk purchases. Then, in February 1970, when Cement Limited was crippled by an industrial strike that lasted three months, a strike that blocked all importations of cement, Tom Roche seized on an opportunity to make the most audacious move of his business life. Despite not having the finance in place, he decided to make a move to take over what was described as the 'gilt-edged' Cement Limited company.

Roche offered shares in Roadstone but was frustrated when Readymix, based in the UK, made a counter-offer. According to *The Irish Times*, Roche responded by playing 'the green card'. The State-controlled Irish Life Assurance had a 10 per cent stake in both Cement Limited and Roadstone. After an approach from Roche, then Taoiseach, Jack Lynch, made it clear to Irish Life that he backed Tom Roche's offer. Shortly afterwards, his bid was accepted and, by the end of 1970, Cement Road Holdings (CRH) was born.

As part of the deal, Cement Limited and Roadstone would have four directors each on the board of the new company, with Taoiseach Jack Lynch putting forward the name of his predecessor, Seán Lemass, as chairman. Also joining the board was a North Dublin accountant called Des Traynor, a critical appointment with significant repercussions for Traynor's friend, a ruthlessly ambitious member of the Irish parliament called Charles Haughey.

As well as now being the sole producer of cement in the country, with Traynor and Lemass on the board, the new company, CRH, was bolted into the political elite. Roche's move on Cement Limited created an industrial monster company with friends at the highest level of government. When Ireland entered the EEC in 1973, CRH expanded onto the continent, acquiring a Dutch builders' merchant. Five years later it established a foothold in the North American market when it bought out a concrete producer in Utah. The early 1980s saw further acquisitions in the US. All of this against the backdrop of holding a vice-like monopoly on the Irish market through its wholly owned subsidiary, Irish Cement Ltd.

Tom Roche was enjoying his retirement by the time Sean Quinn was beginning to make his own audacious moves. Moves that would make an enemy of Des Traynor's ambitious friend – and now Taoiseach – Charles Haughey.

***

Charles Haughey was born in Castlebar, Co. Mayo to parents from Swatragh in Co. Derry. His father served in the Irish Republican Army and the Free State Army after the War of Independence. When he left the army, the family moved east and settled in Donnycarney, one of Dublin's northern suburbs. Haughey went to University College Dublin where he met his future wife, Maureen Lemass, the daughter of a future Taoiseach, Seán Lemass, who was a veteran of the 1916 Easter Rising and a founder of the Fianna Fáil party.

In 1969 Charles and Maureen Haughey bought Abbeville, an eighteenth-century country house in the parish of Kinsealy, North County Dublin. Haughey had been elected as a member of Dáil Éireann (TD) in 1957 and by the time he bought the palatial pile in Kinsealy, he was the Minister of Finance, supposedly living on a relatively modest government salary. Throughout his career, there were questions about his finances and where he was getting the money to service his opulent lifestyle. It turned out that his friend and accountant Des Traynor was playing a key role in this regard.

Des Traynor had been a mover and shaker in the Irish capital since the 1960s, when he joined the boards of some of the country's highest profile companies. In her book *Political Corruption in Ireland 1922–2010 – A Crooked Harp?*, Elaine A. Byrne documents how the introductions, contacts and clients, provided by Haughey, allowed Traynor to become a highly skilled and networked accountant during Dublin's property development boom of the swinging sixties. This led him to the door of the city's oldest merchant bank, Guinness & Mahon, where he became a director in 1969 and later its 'de-facto Chief Executive'. During his tenure at the bank, Traynor set up a secret financial service where he lodged funds, opened offshore trusts and took out loans for wealthy clients in a Cayman Islands bank, Ansbacher Cayman Ltd. (A tribunal of inquiry later set up to investigate found 200 investors held Ansbacher accounts. One of them belonged to Charles J. Haughey. Eight members of the board of CRH were also among the investors. It was estimated that the Ansbacher accounts cost the Irish revenue over IR£120m.)

It was also later revealed that when Des Traynor became chairman at CRH, he was 'skimming' accounts to support Haughey's extravagant lifestyle, or, in other words, he was drawing money off the company for the benefit of the politician. In a column for the *Irish Examiner* in 2014, Michael Clifford set out the close relationship between Haughey and CRH: 'One of the more controversial deals CRH was involved in was the purchase of 147 acres in Glending, Co. Wicklow, the location of a quarry. The lands were bought for IR£1.6m without going to public tender, and were soon discovered to be worth a multiple of that. The sale occurred while Haughey was Taoiseach and Traynor chaired CRH.'

'Haughey was part of an extraordinary scheme which was run out of a particular merchant bank [Guinness & Mahon] through which very large numbers of the sort of the wealthy business class were able to completely avoid paying tax,' said Fintan O'Toole. 'So they would lodge their money in this bank in Dublin. It would ostensibly lodge the money in the Cayman Islands and then they would borrow their own money back from the Cayman Islands, so they wouldn't pay tax. Haughey's bag man runs the scheme [Des Traynor] and one of the beneficiaries of the scheme is likely a senior member of the board of the central bank. This is very much at the heart of the establishment itself and the message really is, you know, if you're within the system, it's good for you. If you want to be outside the system, well, it's at your own peril.'

It was this corrupt establishment that Quinn was about to take on.

***

In the spring of 1984 Quinn found himself on another European tour, this time of cement plants and meetings with engineering companies. During this trip, he visited the headquarters of Fives-Cail-Babcock, based outside Lille in northern France, whose origins go back to 1812. The company initially gained worldwide renown for building the first steam and electric locomotives. The Alexandra III bridge in Paris and the metal framework for the city's Orsay train station all bear the company's name, as well as the elevators for the Eiffel Tower. After a positive meeting, Quinn came away convinced that they were the company to build his cement factory on the Irish border. He signed a contract with them at the end of 1984.

While Fives-Cail-Babcock began working up plans, Quinn began raising the money to pay for the project. Up until now financing hadn't been an issue. The tile plants cost him between £3-to-4 million sterling and the pub acquisitions another £1.2. Borrowing for those hadn't caused any problems. Raising £16 million required for the factory wasn't going to be easy, however, particularly for a product destined for a heavily monopolised industry. But none of that was going to put off Quinn. 'We thought it was fifteen, sixteen million, but it turned out to be twenty-one, twenty-two million. So it was a challenge raising the money and getting that whole thing done. It was probably the hardest financing I had to do. There was never anyone who came along and said, I'm writing you a cheque for twenty million. That never happened,' said Quinn.

Quinn had rolled the dice by contracting with the French before putting the finance in place, but knew well that the huge hurdle he'd face wasn't going to be raising the money, but taking on CRH in the South and their counterpart in the North, Blue Circle. Initially called Associated Portland Cement (APC), and formed at the turn of the twentieth century, it had supplied the cement for the British trenches on the front line in France in the First World War and gone on to control 80 per cent of the British market for the next six decades, formally changing its name to Blue Circle in 1978.

North and South, Quinn was taking on monsters of industry who were not going to give up their stranglehold on the market without a fight. As far as CRH was concerned, that meant doing whatever it took to protect its control of the Irish market through its wholly-owned subsidiary, Irish Cement.

Furthermore, the figures were stark. CRH had a global turnover of

IR£700m and was annually turning profits around IR£50m alone in Ireland, while Blue Circle was importing cement into the North through its base at Larne in Co. Antrim, and also repackaging and selling Irish Cement at a much cheaper price, to the frustration of the building industry in the Republic.

Some importers had emerged, though they also faced an onslaught from the establishment-backed company. One brought in cement from Spain, but found that CRH had gone to their suppliers and buyers and used a mixture of bribes and threats to try to put them out of business. Another cement importer, Noel O'Brien, whose company was based in New Ross, Co. Wexford and had a tiny share of the market, selling less than 30,000 tonnes of cement annually in the early 1980s, told how Irish Cement had sent spies to monitor cement coming off ships in the harbour. 'It has seriously affected our business and offended many of our customers,' O'Brien said at the time to RTÉ. One of O'Brien's customers told how his lorries were followed onto building sites by CRH and intimidated into stopping their use of imported cement. When Belfast-based company Lagan Holdings, owned by Kevin Lagan, won a contract to supply tarmac for the new nine-kilometre Lucan bypass west of Dublin, he found that he couldn't buy the stones he needed in the South – all the suppliers in the area had been warned off by CRH. In protecting their monopoly, CRH also had the help of government, who had helpfully came up with tighter restrictions on the importation of cement.

It was against this threatening backdrop that Quinn pursued his intentions of opening a plant that at full capacity was set to produce half a million tonnes a year, meaning he could service over 20 per cent of the Irish market, North and South. It was a direct attack on CRH and Blue Circle. But he understood fully what he was taking on, even though he didn't fully appreciate how it would impact on his plans to finance the building of the factory.

He was about to find out.

***

The new plant was in Northern Ireland, which allowed the quarryman to turn to the North's Industrial Development Board for support. At the time, local businesses could expect grants of up to 40 per cent of capital costs. But after much back and forward, Quinn was offered only 20 per cent of what was required, just over £3.3m. He wasn't happy. State Papers released by the Stormont administration in 2014, and covered by the BBC, revealed the depth of his anger. Historian Eamon Phoenix, reporting for the BBC, said that 'The difficulties faced by Fermanagh entrepreneur Sean Quinn in developing his border business in the 1980s are outlined in this year's Stormont files. In particular, they highlight the formidable political and commercial opposition to the launch of his cement industry. There were also serious allegations by the nationalist businessman of political and sectarian discrimination.'

Sean Quinn turned to the leader of unionism, James Molyneaux, for support but he rejected his approach, telling him that there was already an overcapacity in cement manufacturing in Europe. On 15 April 1985 he wrote angrily to John Hume, in a letter seeking the SDLP leader's intervention with the then Northern Ireland Commerce Minister Rhodes Boyson. Quinn contended that a 40 per cent grant was justified in view of the attractiveness of the project, the jobs he'd create in an area of high unemployment, and the fact that Blue Circle, a long-established monopoly company, accounted for only 62 per cent of usage in Northern Ireland.

In his view there were a number of real reasons for his unfavourable treatment. Primarily, Quinn saw the dead hand of unionism at work, not realising that CRH were putting on enormous pressure behind the scenes. He told John Hume in the letter that unionists were working with the Industrial Development Board against the interests of the people of south Fermanagh, simply because the county had a nationalist majority. This, he said, was a form of 'religious discrimination' and he alleged that the IDB's refusal to give him a 40 per cent grant was nothing more than a concession to the political and commercial lobbying against him by those who did not wish to see strategic economic investment in south Fermanagh. He said this could be because they saw it as having a potential impact on jobs in unionist constituencies.

In the North's Public Records Office, Eamon Phoenix found that Mr P.T. Bill from the Industrial Development Board had written a confidential memo in response to the quarryman, admitting that hostility from the cement industry was 'a factor in the decision to deny Quinn a larger grant'. In particular, Mr Bill said Quinn's plans could mean that the Blue Circle cement base in Larne might close. This, he told the Commerce Minister Rhodes Boyson, meant that the IDB had 'gone to its limit' with its offer.

Up to this point Quinn had been working on the basis that he would ultimately acquire the 40 per cent funding from public monies. The rest would come from his own resources and borrowing. Moving to a back-up plan, he turned to the Northern Bank in Belfast and Security Pacific in London, only to find that CRH had gotten to them too. The banks wouldn't support his plans.

Quinn was unsure what to do next in order to get the project fully financed. Even as he struggled, CRH were desperate to find other points of attack. In August 1986, as the cement factory began to emerge out of the ground, Quinn noticed that the helicopters flying overhead weren't the usual British army's Gazelle or Chinook that everyone in the border area could identify by their distinctive engine noise alone. Private planes were also spotted in the air. Later, it transpired that CRH had sent them up in an attempt to find evidence that Quinn was not sticking strictly to his planning agreements.

They'd already attacked his private funding by going to the banks, now they moved again on the public funding. CRH took a case to the European Commission, arguing that the Industrial Development Board grant of 20 per cent would distort the market. They also said that Quinn's plans would not create employment but instead would cause layoffs at Irish Cement's plants. In response, the Industrial Development Board reduced its offer to Quinn to 12.5 per cent of the total capital cost of the new plant. The quarryman was suffering from a military-style pincer movement, cutting off his sources of public and private funding.

While Quinn was focused on resolving his troubles, he was reminded again of the fragility of life on the border. It was November 1987, the month of one of the worst atrocities in the conflict when the IRA exploded a bomb at Enniskillen's Remembrance Day service, killing eleven Protestants (a twelfth victim, headmaster Ronnie Hill, never recovered consciousness) and injuring over sixty. The bombing was condemned outright by political leaders from around the world, while the IRA, struggling to explain the rationale behind such a viciously sectarian attack, blamed the British security forces for inadvertently detonating the device. It was a hopeless time for both communities in Fermanagh.

Some respite arrived for Quinn when, four months later, RTÉ's *Today, Tonight* programme broadcast an excoriating investigation into CRH. In the programme, Quinn, filmed on a bleak winter day at his quarry, revealed that the 12.5 per cent grant he'd been offered was now in doubt. 'So we [may] have to finish the factory without grants. We think that we have been unfairly treated,' he said with some understatement. The then managing director of Irish Cement was interviewed by presenter Olivia O'Leary and made no attempt to deny the allegations against his company. Indeed, he unashamedly admitted during a performance dripping in arrogance that they had gone to Quinn's banks, saying they were discussing matters related to the market and 'Sean Quinn's advent was a major event in the market. We're keeping the banks informed, all major companies do it. They must know what's going on in the market place,' said Doyle, without a hint of self-awareness but with an overconfidence that only CRH's political and financial muscle could instil.

Still, despite all the obstacles and roadblocks that the establishment could put in his way, Quinn ultimately pulled the finance together with the help of an Englishman who would become a lifelong friend. 'Val Flynn had good contacts within the financial industry. And probably only for Val I would never have got it financed. He would have helped me a lot [but it] was a tough one,' he recounted. Val Flynn, who spent a lot of his career working with Irish clients and businesses, helped Quinn raise £12.5 million, while Quinn himself put up another £12.5 million with the last of the final cost of £30 million coming from the Industrial Development Board's reduced grant.

It had cost him almost twice what he expected, but as he sat down to his Christmas dinner in 1988, Sean Quinn knew he'd won a major victory. He'd built a cement factory. He wouldn't have time to dwell on his turkey, however, as the French engineers and the locals he'd employed to run it were still attempting to iron out the last of the teething problems. Everyone would hold their breath a little longer, but still one thing was beyond doubt – Quinn had taken on the establishment, north and south, and won a battle that would change his life and those of thousands of families along the border.

Though the truth was that CRH had yet to give up the fight.

4

Monopoly

Sean Quinn often joked that there were people in Ireland who thought the IRA had provided the money to build his cement factory. Behind the flippant comment, however, he was admitting that there was a suspicion, particularly by those in positions of power, about the scale and speed of his success. But was it really about the pace of his progress, or because he came from the border? The fact was that such was the meteoric growth of his company that, unless you were a local and personally witnessed the physical manifestation of his entrepreneurial skills, you could be forgiven for raising an eyebrow.

By the late 1980s, over and over again, the daily newspapers repeated the story of the boy who left school at a young age, inherited twenty-three acres of poor farmland, and yet was making a name for himself, despite the Troubles and his being based in an industrial wasteland. He became almost a mythical character whose backstory was one any Hollywood writer would have been proud of creating.

The locals in Ballyconnell and Derrylin and along the Fermanagh–Cavan border had bought into his success, were indeed beginning to benefit from it, and now it was the turn of those from beyond his natural hinterland to get to know the quarryman. He was fast becoming a national figure, due mainly to his audacity and courage to take on CRH.

But in the first dark, bleak days of January 1989, Quinn had no time for public relations. He was spending every waking hour with his sleeves rolled up at the new factory, working alongside teams of engineers, chemists and mechanics. There was always another problem, another gremlin in the system of the machinery that the skilled French engineers installing the plant had to identify and solve. Soon they'd return home, leaving Quinn's team – most of them drawn from the border area – to manage the £30m plant without having any real experience or understanding of the technological monster he'd created on the side of a mountain.

While he'd miscalculated on the cost of the build, he fully appreciated the challenge of a start-up cement manufacturing business and how important it was for him to be seen to lead from the front, which, to the benefit of all involved, came to him naturally. 'We were very amateurish, and it took a huge effort from all of us to get that thing up and running. We had a very inexperienced team and it was a lot of hard work. It was twenty-hour days. I was in that factory until twelve o'clock at night and, at times, until two or three o'clock in the morning, just trying to motivate the staff,' said Quinn. 'It was a huge effort. But it worked and it was the starting ground for us becoming a much bigger business.'

While he was focused on getting the cement factory up on its feet, Quinn was already well ahead with plans for another major move in the hospitality side of the business. Sean's sister Bernie had married a local farmer, Brian Maguire, and they lived with their family just along the border. They were close to Sean, indeed he was their daughter Noreen's godfather. Bernie remembers a day when Noreen was let in on Sean's latest plan, after showing her some vacant fields near their home. 'Noreen came home very excited, she was a very small, wee girl at the time, and she said, "Uncle Sean lifted me across a gate today and he said, Noreen, you'll have your wedding reception in there some day." She was very excited. She still remembers that distinctly, him lifting her up on the gate and saying: "You'll have your wedding reception in there." He'd shown her a blank field.'

Noreen had been given an exclusive glimpse into the future, into the plans her uncle had for that field. He had been working away on a project that would astonish even his closest friends and family.

In the late 1970s, just a few years after they married, Sean and Patricia Quinn had built a relatively modest two-storey home on the site of the farm that his father had originally bought for his brother, Peter, south of the border in the townland of Cranaghan, five minutes south of Ballyconnell. His father had sold it a year before he died, in 1966, when Peter made clear he was not going to be a farmer. But it came back into Quinn hands when Sean began buying up land, most of it around the quarry. The family archive has a handwritten note from 1982, the only record of the deal between Sean and a local farmer. 'Sale of farm (30 acres) at Knockategal, 28/6/1982, between Sean Quinn and Pearse Martin. Price £35,000. Signed Pearse Martin.'

This was the site for his next move – the development of a hotel that would challenge almost everything anyone knew about tourism in the border region.

'Quinn moves into another major deal' was the *Sunday Press* headline on the story, revealing the hotel would cost £3.5m and would open in mid-1990. 'The hotel will have 50 bedrooms, it will have swimming pools, snooker rooms, jacuzzis and all that sort of crack,' Sean Quinn was quoted as saying. 'We are getting a grant of £400,000 from Bord Fáilte. There is also a lake nearby and it is a possibility that we may include an 18-hole golf course.' The story went on, in an unsurprisingly sceptical tone: 'The border is not generally considered to be a tourist area but Quinn confesses to being an optimist. "It is good shooting and fishing country and there is of course good business in the local catchment area. I do not think that people will be reluctant to come to the border. Indeed, I think a lot of people who come to Ireland want to go to the border to see where the trouble is."'

Sean Quinn's confidence couldn't have been higher.

***

By Monday 16 January 1989 the last of the teething issues at the cement factory had been fixed and Quinn was ready to make his first sales of bulk cement.

The £30m structure he'd built, which could be seen from up to fifteen miles away, had changed the face of the south Fermanagh landscape to the extent that one local newspaper, the *Fermanagh Herald*, described it as being 'so colossal, like something from a Space Mission launching zone that even before it began production, there was a steady stream of visitors on Sundays stopping off to inspect the works'.

Quinn was happy to see the press on both sides of the border reporting on his success and fed them detailed information about the plant and its operation. Like the tile factory before it, the new operation was ranked as 'one of the most modern in Europe'.

Just because the factory was up and running did not mean that his conflict with CRH had gone away, of course. The industry expected a price war to now open up between Quinn and CRH's subsidiary, Irish Cement Ltd, in the South, and with Blue Circle in the North. CRH certainly feared what the wildly unpredictable gambler from the border might do. Quinn had a big decision to make. Should he undercut the monopoly or go into the market at the same price? Undercutting would provide him with significant immediate market share but he'd also be diluting his profit levels and therefore his ability to repay the loans he'd taken out. On the other hand, if he sold his cement at the same price, he might not achieve the required percentage of the market that he needed, though it would at least keep his margins high.

In the weeks before he began distribution, very few of those around Quinn really knew what option he'd choose. The Irish *Sunday Independent* declared in one headline: 'Blood and cement in concrete war' with the article predicting a 'bloodbath' in the coming months, with CRH the first victim. Reporter Martin Fitzpatrick, wrote: 'A price war that could change the face of the Irish building materials industry is looming. If it comes off, the dominant company in the business, CRH, risks seeing its domestic profits slide dramatically and there is likely to be parallel reductions in the earnings of many lesser concrete companies.'

Fitzpatrick revealed that in preparation for Quinn's arrival, CRH had gone North and bought up a series of silos in Belfast Port from cement importer Kevin Lagan, the very businessman they'd attacked after he won the contract for the Lucan bypass. Lagan would have the last laugh, however, by using the profit of the sale to build brand-new cement silos on a site next to the one he sold. CRH hadn't seen the Lagan move coming and could do nothing to stop him. For Lagan, revenge was a dish best served cold. Meanwhile, in the South, CRH looked to protect its prices through its political connections. At its behest, the Dublin government introduced a certification scheme, which effectively banned the importation of cement from north of the border. Again, Quinn took them on, this time through the European Commission, which ultimately forced the Department of Industry and Commerce to accept European national standards. It was another vital win for Quinn, though it also helped that his luck was in.

Napoleon was once quoted as saying, 'I know he's a good general but is he lucky?' Sean Quinn's business in general was showing a habit of fortuitously hitting the sweet spots in each of the markets he entered, and cement was no different, as it just happened to coincide with a pick-up in the Irish economy.

Prior to that, almost ten years of economic crisis, high unemployment and recession had seen spectacular increases in national debt, largely due to borrowings by Haughey's government. Taxation reached rates of 60 per cent and by 1987 the country owed more than it could produce through goods and services. That year's budget presented by then finance minister Ray MacSharry attempted to control excessive spending and manage the debt. The same year saw the Programme for National Recovery (PNR), which brought about an historic agreement between the new Fine Gael Taoiseach, Garret FitzGerald, and the Irish Congress of Trade Unions, which included limits on pay increases for three years, with the unions agreeing not take industrial action that would increase costs for employers.

As a result of this social contract, the Irish economy began to recover in 1988 and improved again in the following two years. Economists would later argue as to the real impact of the PNR but by the end of the eighties, Ireland was suddenly seen as an attractive country to invest in, with American corporations in particular choosing it as its preferred European base. Even the country's football team provided something to cheer about, when Englishman Jack Charlton led them to a famous victory over his home country at the 1988 European Championships in West Germany. Quinn's confidence and determination aligned with the improving mood of the country. They were both raring to take on the world. He just had to decide at what price he would sell his cement.

The existential fear for Quinn was that CRH and Blue Circle would cut their prices to try to put his lights out before he could even get on his feet. When pressed by Kyran Fitzgerald of the *Sunday Tribune*, CRH Finance Director Harry Sheridan refused to reveal what the company's pricing strategy would be but warned that Quinn was 'entering what is a complicated chemical process industry. He could have problems in making a consistent product and would be unable to produce "anything near 300,000 tonnes" per annum,' he told the paper.

The Dublin newspapers warmed to the growing dispute and talked up that the risk was all Quinn's and his bankers. For his part, Sean Quinn continued to threaten to undercut his competitors, telling the *Sunday Tribune* that he was prepared to sell his cement at 50 per cent off the market price. He also said that there would be an initial price reduction of between 4 to 5 per cent. 'If CRH meets this price, we can do down a lot lower,' he said, claiming that even if he had to sell cement at £25 a tonne, he could still make a profit. Just like he'd done on the football pitch, Quinn wasn't afraid to go toe-to-toe. 'The consumer will benefit. Over the past twenty years we have seen annual price increases of 35 to 40 per cent. Not just the consumer but the nation will benefit [from Quinn Cement],' he told RTÉ.

Behind the scenes, Quinn got ahead of his competitors by cutting a deal with the Independent Concrete Manufacturers Association, which, at the time, was led by a fellow-Fermanagh man, John Maguire, who had gone on the record for *The Irish Press* newspaper to say that 'for the good of the industry and because of what has gone on in the past, there is a need for responsible competition in cement supply'.

Quinn spotted an opportunity to work with the underdogs, the businessmen with whom he could identify. 'John and I were good friends and John was proud of my success in the area, and I was proud of him and very, very supportive of him,' he said. 'We worked well together. CRH and Blue Circle were given a very competitive price to the big players in the island of Ireland, I'd say the top half-dozen customers for cement. They were getting cement 10 or 15 per cent cheaper than the smaller guys. So I went to John and said, look, there's a lot of independents here, small guys who are paying through the nose for cement. I'll make a commitment – if they can give me a bit of support, I'll charge them the same price as I'll charge the bigger guys. And we'll try to grow the smaller market. So John called a couple of meetings and he got tremendous support, and the small players in the cement, the small cement customers came to me and they honoured their agreement, and I honoured mine.'

As production ramped up at the plant, reaching close to its capacity within weeks, Quinn announced that he was going to sell his cement 5 per cent cheaper than CRH. In response, CRH, somewhat surprisingly, accepted this, opting to live with the fact that the border businessman was now a bona fide competitor. There would be no price war; instead, détente was reached. This was something of a shock, given all the acrimony that had led to this point. Indeed, some in the industry suspected that Quinn and CRH may have reached some sort of behind-the-scenes agreement to no longer hurt each other by any means, fair or foul.

Quinn told the popular weekly paper in Cavan, *The Anglo-Celt*, that there was now a new reality in the cement business in Ireland. 'Our competitors are now accepting us. They know it is now a fact that we exist. They also know the fact that we are going to work well and take our market share.' He elaborated to *Irish Construction*, an industry magazine: 'It is a fact of life, it is different and I have not heard any complaints. The existing firms have their market share and all they can do is lose it. If there is a war, we would be losing on [market share of] 20 per cent but our competitors would be losing on 80 per cent and that would not be intelligent from their point of view.' He added: 'We have established our market niche and we are very happy with it.' Quinn finished off by saying that he was already selling in twenty-four of Ireland's thirty-two counties.

He'd gambled that through his now-established networks he could sell his cement without having to significantly undercut his competitor. Sure enough, within six months Quinn had taken close to 20 per cent of the market across the island. 'You mightn't have the money in your pocket but you'd know your debtors had increased dramatically. We felt secure within six months, that this thing was very profitable and that there was good margins in cement, better than there was in anything else we were doing.'

Bernie remembers the moment she realised what he had achieved. 'He took Brian and me up to the very top of the tower up there [part of the factory] and just looking round and thinking, holy God, he did this, you know. It was a huge achievement, and it was overpowering [in] its immensity at the time. It was, for a little place like Teemore and Derrylin, it was, people just couldn't come to terms with this, you know, and yet there was a modesty there and he was round chatting to everybody with the same kind of way that he always had. And just a pity you couldn't meet some of the eighty- or ninety-year-old ladies in the countryside who would still be in awe of all his achievements and so loyal and so supportive to him, because he changed the whole face of the area.'

To achieve all this, having bested the establishment, likely made the success all the sweeter. 'You have to really admire the courage of this, you know,' said Fintan O'Toole. 'He's a tough man, right. And I think he does it because he has this absolute sense of himself. So he doesn't feel he needs to suck up to anybody, you know, because nobody's given him very much and so he doesn't really feel that he needs to grease palms or that he needs to be an insider. He's happy to take them on. My impression is that Sean Quinn is kind of seen as a wild card, but a wild card that's, you know, full of aces. It's not just that he's throwing shapes and threatening the establishment, he just takes it on. He says, okay, you've got a monopoly in this very valuable commodity, which is cement. I'm going to make it cheaper, and I'm going to break your monopoly, and he does it.'

In an article for *Irish Construction*, published soon after production began, Quinn was bullish, condemning the failed economic policies of successive Dublin governments. 'Their attitude to borrowings was scandalous and if I had run my business the same way, the banks would have shut me down,' he said.

He also remained confident that his policy of now allowing more than a third of his profits to go towards interest payments was the way to do business. The fact was that with his success, Quinn had shown that he was not afraid of ramping up huge borrowings. His enterprises were all cash-based, and there was no shortage of it by this stage. He was using the deposits he had at the bank to leverage borrowings. From the early days when he impulsively bought a farm despite being overdrawn at the bank, Quinn had continued to see banks first and foremost as there to support his ambitions, and with his quarry and tile businesses throwing off huge profits, he didn't see himself as anything close to a risky bet. Apart from the £25m he'd borrowed for the factory, he'd also financed the purchase of the Dublin pubs.

Without explanation, Quinn told the *Sunday Tribune* newspaper before he opened the factory that he had taken out new borrowings from a Scandinavian bank. In the *Irish Construction* magazine article, it was clear he still felt sore about the lack of support from local banks for the financing of the cement factory. 'Much to his chagrin, Irish banks were unwilling to take the risk and he was forced to go overseas for support. Although it still annoys him that the banks here lacked the imagination to bank his entrepreneurial spirit, the feeling is probably outweighed now by the satisfaction that he has had the last laugh.'

This, of course, wouldn't be the last time he would have trouble with Irish banks.

***

While the cement factory was taking up most of his time and attention, Quinn refused to take his eye off the growing hospitality side of his business. After buying the Cat & Cage and McGovern's pubs in Drumcondra, he went back into the Dublin market, this time to pick up Parkes Hotel in Stillorgan, South Dublin for close to £2m.

He had leased the bars with little time or investment, and decided to follow a similar model with the hotel, though this time he wanted to put significant investment into the premises. The 'Pillars of Society' column in the *Phoenix Magazine* recorded the opening night. 'The huge yuppie contingent that surfaced in Parkes Hotel in Stillorgan for the grand re-opening were blissfully unaware, for the most part, that they owed their presence there to a forty-two-year-old Border County entrepreneur with an excitingly low profile, named Seán Quinn. The lavish £1m "Studio Circus" nightclub was filled to capacity as was the exotically-named bar/restaurant, "La Café" courtesy of the redoubtable Louis Murray, [who later owned the famous La Stampa restaurant in the city] for so long synonymous with such happenings. Murray is actually leasing the place from Quinn, the new owner who paid a respectable £2m for it last May.'

Quinn had put a lot of money – £1m on the nightclub alone – into refurbishing the hotel. However, it soon became clear that he wasn't seeing the returns he wanted. He sold it again for a reported £4m, making a very healthy return on his initial investment, but the venture could still be viewed as a rare failure for Quinn. By his own admission, it was his worst investment, he was quoted as saying, while refusing to be drawn on what exactly had gone wrong. At the time, he was stung, but amidst the shock, and aware of the cement factory and other acquisitions, the Parkes Hotel became little more than a footnote.

Soon Quinn was moving on to the next project. It was always his family – four girls and a boy now after the birth of Brenda in 1987 – that remained the driving force for his hospitality acquisitions. He had legacy on his mind. Perhaps that is why he decided to put the family name over the door of what was formerly McGovern's pub in Drumcondra. Never one to miss an opportunity to promote himself and his business, he had himself filmed going into 'Quinns', which was only a couple of hundred yards from Croke Park, for the RTÉ *Today, Tonight* programme in 1987. The camera was turning as he sat on a stool at the bar and ordered himself a pint of lager and told the barman to set up drinks for the locals.

He clearly enjoyed the limelight and wanted people to know that he was both wealthy and successful, but also that he wore the pressure that came with running a multimillion-pound business with apparent ease. 'I felt no pressure with any of those things, whether cement or whether pubs in Dublin or hotels or anything, I didn't feel any pressure with those, because I told myself early on that those things all looked after themselves provided you had good leadership, provided you have a good structure in place for all of your businesses, they will look after themselves,' he said.

***

Sean Quinn was now a national figure. He had carefully cultivated his life story for the public, but was happy to share it with anyone who showed an interest in him.

The author Colm Tóibín was an unlikely visitor to Quinn's border offices during this period. He was writing a book that would be called *Bad Blood: A Walk Along the Irish Border* when he explored the communities, life and legacy in 'a bleak and desolate landscape'. Speaking in New York in 2019 for an interview for the RTÉ television series on Quinn, Tóibín recalled the haunting life experience of the 1980s along the frontier. 'You were going into places like Castlederg … you felt a sectarian thing I think much more intensely in somewhere like Castlederg, that Protestant/Catholic thing was actually strangling the society, but you didn't feel it in the same way in Strabane. There were differences as you moved from place to place. Sometimes the sectarian thing didn't matter and sometimes it really poisoned the air – especially if you were a guy from the Republic wandering around thinking you owned the place – that people were really watching you.'

Tóibín first encountered Quinn's lorries passing him as he made his way towards the Fermanagh–Cavan border. 'It was written into the landscape, Sean Quinn lorries, and obviously the thing for me was, the thing I wanted to do was to find the man himself and to see what he was like.' So Tóibín set off for Derrylin, hoping to meet with this quarryman.

'There was no other Sean Quinn figure along the border area, there was no one operating on both sides of the border. There was no one investing. People were divesting, people were getting out, to hell out of the place. The idea of investing in the borderlands, you know, between Monaghan, that sort of area, into, or Leitrim, into Fermanagh, was something that just could not have happened, no one else was thinking of it. I mean, you could find the IRA if you were looking for them very easily, the thing I never saw which I looked for a lot was the IDA, which was the Industrial Development Authority, which was the group which was authorised by the Irish government to actually build infrastructure and create and connect industry to certain parts of Ireland. They certainly did very well in places like Galway and in the whole area around Dublin. I never saw them up there.'

In other words, according to Tóibín, what Quinn was doing in the area was unique. 'Sean Quinn was operating in a way which was strangely, strangely solitary; in other words it wasn't as though he was helicoptered in there to do this. I mean, his roots were the GAA. And he started small and people could trust him, people knew him. And so he realised he did something that people really thought was funny, which is using the stony grey soil, the very thing that was causing a lot of this trouble – there was so much bad land. I mean, part of the problem in the North was there was very bad land beside very good land, and in Fermanagh the Protestants in general had the good land. The Catholics just sat there on their twenty, thirty acres of stony grey soil wondering what hit them, you know? And Sean Quinn started to make money from the very thing that had caused the poverty, which was the sandy nature of the soil. And so people talked about him with a sort of awe. And then people, I mean, there was a sense, you know, of him as a mythological figure, as someone who had come with an idea that had been staring everyone in the face but that no one had had the courage to think of, which was that there's money in sand. And so he was talked about, in that way that you can hear, I suppose, in many poor countries, as the idea of the big man, the idea of the figure who is different from us, whose vision is different from ours. And he certainly was that figure.'

When he arrived at the offices for the meeting, Tóibín was met by an assistant who 'came to fill me in on the background', i.e. the backstory of the man who inherited twenty-three acres but was now a millionaire. Tóibín wrote: 'He had benefitted enormously from the early years of [Margaret] Thatcher, when there was a hundred per cent, tax-free allowance on profits which were re-invested. There were no trade unions in his business, nor was any employee paid a salary. Everyone was paid according to productivity.'

After a time, Tóibín came face-to-face with Quinn. 'Eventually, the great Thatcherite himself came in. He was a dark, good-looking, gruff man in his late thirties, wearing an old grey pullover. He talked with an off-hand precision; the accent was straight Fermanagh. He didn't act like the boss. And he certainly didn't look like a millionaire.'

Yet he was, many times over by now. While his mystique was growing, he certainly wasn't growing the business alone.

*****

In the months before the end of what had been quite an astonishing decade for Sean Quinn, he made a significant appointment. The former manager of County Cavan Council, David Mackey, became Quinn's right-hand man, taking the title of general manager. It placed a very reliable pair of hands on the rudder of a company that needed them. Quinn would be the 'rainmaker', leading from the front, but Mackey would ensure that everything was kept tight and under control at the Derrylin headquarters.

There were others around Quinn by now who would remain at his side for decades. Tony Lunney's lifetime at the company began in 1982 as a mechanic. There were fewer than a hundred people working there when he started. Lunney's boss at the time was in a wheelchair from a car accident and Sean had kept him on working in the garage after this. 'Gerry Reilly was the technician. John Lee was operations and works manager,' said another of those working there at the time: 'Sean Quinn was based in the quarry office and you'd see him around, [but] he mainly focused on sales. There was a good buzz about the place. The factory was starting up, lorries were busy. At the time, all the farmers were getting European grants to do concrete lanes. Sean did well out of this. The cement factory was another level. The locals couldn't believe the size of it – they didn't appreciate the scale of it until it arrived.'

Another starter joined in 1987. 'I went to school in Derrylin, I went on to Enniskillen, done a building course there. And then in the summer I worked in the Quinn Group in the quarry section. I then took my first full-time job in it, in the pre-cast factory in the office. Sean was always around, well, I wouldn't say always, but we would have met him in the pubs maybe at the weekend. He would have went to all the local Teemore matches. And there would have been a big rivalry I suppose between Teemore and Derrylin at the time. Some of us supported Derrylin, Quinn and his crew supported Teemore. So there was always a bit of a rivalry there, you know. But certainly he wasn't mythical by any sense of the imagination, you know. He was well known.'

While some didn't view Sean Quinn as a mythical-type figure in the area, an incident that occurred around this time at one border crossing only added to the public impression of Quinn as a hard man who had little respect for any law.

'I was going to a funeral, a man by the name of Paddy McGovern who had died,' said Quinn. 'I remember the name because I remember the incident. And this soldier took the wheels off the car and oh, he done everything to annoy me. And the fella was driving down the road, John Gilleece was the name, who worked at Quinn's, and John was driving down in a wee white van, and I was standing there for maybe forty, fifty minutes at this stage. And I said, well, to hell with this, and I went and tried to jump into the van and said, keep the oul' bloody car, whatever you want to do. And the soldier didn't allow me to [leave].'

In response, Quinn punched the soldier. 'There was a wee bit of a dust-up all right,' he recalled. 'I remember when the police were called, this policeman got the call and he was told that there was a confrontation with some of Quinn's [men]. But he was sure it was some of the lorry drivers. And he arrived up and I had known him reasonably well, I had met him a few times anyway, and I said, well, officer, how are you, whatever. He went inside the checkpoint and he came back out and said, "Mr Quinn," he had to be official, he says, "Mr Quinn, I'm taking you with me," and such and such a one, he had a colleague with him, the policeman, "and he's going to take your car down to the office." So I said, that's fine. And I hopped into the car with him. And he said, now, "if you struck that soldier", he says, "I have to arrest you. But," he says, "if it was self-defence I don't." So I thought he was a gentleman,' said Quinn, who never heard anything more about his assault of the soldier.

Colm Tóibín heard the story when he was on the border. 'I think Quinn felt that he deserved a certain amount of respect in the area. And of course the one place you would never get that was from the British Army, because they came and went, didn't know who anyone was. And also, even if they did know who they were, they could just be bolshie on that day or be under orders to stop everybody. I mean, he was a chieftain, he was somebody who was employing large numbers of people, investing large amounts of money, and, you know, he obviously had to cross the border, it was part of his job. I mean, it's a real good example of how that border caused such an amount of grief.'

Still, despite the continued headache of the border, Quinn could undoubtedly be happy with his lot as the 1980s neared their end. The past ten years, and the success he'd achieved, had changed not only Sean Quinn's life but was beginning to make a difference to hundreds of his fellow border people, who now had stable, well-paying jobs on their doorstep. He'd achieved all this while showing neither respect for nor fear of authority, be it an establishment-backed company protecting a monopoly or a British soldier preventing him from attending a funeral. Given his success, many would expect him to rest on his laurels, yet he remained as hungry and ambitious as when he started out in business.

And in another instance of fortuitous timing, the world was changing, as was Ireland, both North and South. Sean Quinn was to benefit richly from the opportunities that were about to open up on both sides of the border.

But he knew that he also needed to change to keep up. David Mackey was putting in place new governance structures in the company. Until then, Quinn had operated as a one-man band for almost twenty years, personally taking the major decisions. Now, in order to grow effectively, he knew he had to put people around him who could stand up to him. The question remained: was Sean Quinn prepared to be told he couldn't do something?

The episode with the soldier may have provided a hint of the answer.

5

Cavan's Versailles

With the dawn of a new decade came a swagger to Ireland's stride. The misery of the 1980s was gone, replaced with a growing confidence among an up-and-coming generation that economist David McWilliams described in his book *The Pope's Children* as 'the huge new Irish middle class: young, sassy and successful. They are the dynamo of Ireland's economy, politics and culture, and they will shape its face in the twenty-first century.'

In the first six months of the 1990s, as if to underline this newfound confidence, Ireland held the presidency of the European Union, allowing Charles Haughey – who had become Taoiseach for a second time in 1987 – to take a central role as the world came to terms with the monumental events of the previous December, with the fall of the Berlin Wall and the move towards the reunification of Germany. Haughey saw it through the lens of his own partitioned island. 'I have expressed a personal view that coming as we do from a country which is also divided, many of us would have sympathy with any wish of the people of the two German States for unification,' he told Dáil Éireann.

Change was also evident in Ireland and the first year of the new decade saw the political glass ceiling shatter with the election of the country's first female president, Mary Robinson. Then there was the success on the football pitch, as Ireland's soccer team reached the quarter-finals of the World Cup held in Italy. On top of winning games, they won hearts and minds, those at home feasting on the team's success and turning the country into a sea of flags and bunting in the national colours.

All of this was creating a buzz, but back on the border, Sean Quinn was focused on one thing and one thing alone: business.

He began the decade as he'd left off, with the pedal flat to the floor. With the Slieve Russell only emerging out of the ground, Quinn invested in another hotel just twenty-five minutes down the road in Cavan town. The Kilmore Hotel had opened in 1983 but had already changed hands three times by the time Sean Quinn took possession of the keys in the first days of 1990. *The Anglo-Celt* reported on the auction sale: 'Ms. Adrianna Sherry, Chief Negotiator for the sale for Jim Farrell and Associates, who were joint agents in conjunction with P. V. Gunne, told *The Anglo-Celt* that the bidding was brisk. Taking less than a minute, six bids of IR£100,000 each brought the hotel to the sale price of IR£1.6 million, approximately IR£400,000 more than Indian business tycoon, Yash Malhotra paid for it in March, 1988.'

In a marked change from Sean Quinn doing all the talking, General Manager David Mackey was the one sent out to sell the company's intentions for the premises. He told the paper that they intended spending another IR£500,000 on external and internal renovations, including new car parking, improved decor and layout. 'Sean Quinn will provide this,' he said. The intention was that the Kilmore would be complementary to the Slieve Russell, as Quinn also intended to make it a hotel of which the town and county could be proud. 'As with his existing enterprises, Quinn will be aiming for three distinct goals – quality product, first-class service and competitive prices,' reported the paper.

Mackey said that Quinn believed that there would be a boom in Irish tourism in the 1990s and he felt that it was up to central government to work in partnership with the private sector to maximise potential in Co. Cavan. According to *The Anglo-Celt*, 'Mr. Quinn, who has been living in Cavan for thirteen years, believes that the wonderful tourist amenities are not being adequately exploited.'

Quinn was not only putting his money where his mouth was in terms of the hospitality sector. With quotes such as this, he was showing that he was also comfortable with pushing government to match him. The CRH experience had taught him that there was nothing to lose by going public, by pulling back the curtain to reveal his personal opinions on what government was or wasn't doing. Just by purchasing it, Quinn had made a statement, but by pushing government to do more for the area, he was presenting himself as someone invested in the county who wasn't afraid to speak their mind. Quinn was displaying an acute awareness of sentiments felt by many locals that the border area generally – and Cavan specifically in this case – had been overlooked by successive governments. He was prepared to call them out for it.

The same report recorded that Quinn was impressed by the British government's commitment of £46 million to be spent across the border, bolstering Fermanagh's tourism economy. Quinn's message was clear – he wanted to see the same level of investment on the southern side. And given that he was spending millions on two hotels that were a journey of over two hours on poor roads from Dublin or Belfast, Quinn knew that he needed government support if he was going to attract large-scale tourism to the area.

After all, a heavily militarised border with British troops on the ground, helicopters constantly in the air and checkpoints on the main crossings north and south did not exactly produce the kind of attractive images likely to entice tourists. The killings continued to affect what passed for normal life at the time in the North, but green shoots of change were appearing. For example, the British government's decision to enact the Fair Employment Act, which became law on 1 January 1990 and introduced measures such as the Fair Employment Tribunal, was a landmark moment. Data available at the time served to highlight the disparity in the Northern Ireland workforce, which was 65 per cent Protestant and 35 per cent Catholic, despite the available Catholic labour force being closer to 40 per cent. It was clear that, in many instances,

Protestants were being favoured for jobs ahead of Catholics. At the time, the North's police force, the RUC, for example, was over 90 per cent Protestant, totally unrepresentative of the community it served. The new law was designed to redress the imbalance. Employment would now be monitored closely and sectarian favouritism would face the full force of the law.

On the border, Sean Quinn's workforce was a mirror image of the surrounding community – i.e. overwhelmingly Catholic – but even so it was possible that, moving forward, he too, just like the RUC, would face scrutiny for his employment practices. Still, the new law gave a sense that Northern Ireland could be changed, that the status quo could be challenged.

And this was far from the only development at the time. Known only to the very few, the leader of political nationalism in the North, John Hume, was already in talks with Sinn Féin president Gerry Adams. Both the British and Irish governments were also secretly reaching out to republicans, testing the waters on how to end a conflict that was still very real in the lives of Sean Quinn and his employees. In December 1989, for example, the IRA had launched a sustained and deadly attack on a British Army checkpoint just twenty miles along the border from Quinn's home. A team of almost a dozen IRA volunteers armed with an assortment of weaponry, including two Russian-made DShK heavy machine guns and a flamethrower, drove their armoured Bedford lorry into the Derryard checkpoint north of the village of Rosslea. After opening fire, they drove a van laden with explosives into the base. Two soldiers from the King's Own Scottish Borderers regiment died in this attack.

Despite setbacks such as this, Hume's talks with Adams offered hope of a very different future.

***

By the early 1990s Sean's brother Peter was becoming a well-known figure who would play his own instrumental role in the changes that were helping to create a more positive environment that could end the conflict. Peter and Sean had grown up together on the football pitch. Alongside his brother, whom he described as 'a natural leader' on the pitch, Peter went on to win four championship medals with Teemore before becoming a key figure in the administration of the sport, first at his own club, then later at Fermanagh and Ulster level. He recognised early on that because of a childhood illness, he would never be as good a footballer as his brother and wouldn't match his business successes either. But having studied at Queen's University in Belfast and qualified as an accountant, he still became a highly successful finance and business advisor, spending time abroad before returning to his home county of Fermanagh. At times, he advised and worked with his brother, even setting up a business together at one point, but Peter was always determined to follow his own path.

The GAA was where his heart lay, and in 1991 the opportunity opened up for him to lead the GAA, by becoming its president. However, after much consideration, he decided not to run for election. That was, until his brother called him, as recollected in his autobiography:

'What are you doing about this Presidency thing,' he asked.

'Nothing,' I said, 'I'm not running.'

'You're what?' was the sharp response.

'I'm not running,' I said.

The silence on the other end of the phone was prolonged and deafening. Then it was broken by a decorated outburst, which I had never, in my wildest dreams, expected and which was certainly not normal from Sean. He lambasted me, 'You've wasted most of your bloody life on the GAA when you could have been making yourself a wealthy man.' He finished with 'go out and fight for it and win the bloody thing.'

Peter Quinn duly took his brother's advice and did in fact win 'the bloody thing', becoming president in April 1991. He would later argue for the lifting of the contentious ban on members of the security forces playing GAA, a move that was seen as a major contribution to attempts to break down barriers caused by the Troubles.

Still, as he prepared to take on the role, he felt that some changes needed to occur with the RUC before they could consider lifting the ban. 'It was obvious to everyone who was close to the situation that, unless there was some movement on the political front and major changes in the structure and membership of the RUC, our members in the North, and a significant proportion of those in the South, just would not vote for the removal of the ban,' wrote Peter Quinn in his book.

In an RTÉ interview the night before he took up the office, he was asked about the ban on members of the security forces playing GAA games. Quinn's interview with RTÉ was attacked by sections of the out-of-touch Dublin-based media already sceptical of the Hume-Adams initiative, accusing him of being too hardline and not going far enough to indicate how he'd use his presidency to bring the two communities in Northern Ireland together. Peter Quinn, as his brother would also come to deeply appreciate, was suddenly very aware of the anti-Northern bias in many sections of the Republic's media.

'That was the first salvo in a personal campaign against me by sections of the national media. I was being branded as a northerner, first and foremost, but, worse than that, as a republican who was militantly anti-unionist and who was operating to a political agenda,' he wrote. Warming to his theme, he continued, 'The northern badge was enough to raise the hackles of the liberal media in Dublin. Even the hint of a republican opinion was enough to make me persona non grata with those bigots. It is easy to be brave, fighting from a distance of a hundred miles, with a pen. I hate all cowards, but I consider cowards who use pen, print and paper, or electronic media, to be the worst of the lot.'

After a bruising experience with the Dublin media, Peter Quinn believed he had been defamed and began legal action, which he later withdrew, but he was left with a bitter taste, believing he had been targeted by those opposed to the political changes ongoing in the North. 'Like the Mounties, the media always get their man. There is no story if there is no scapegoat and I became the scapegoat. I would not be the last Quinn to fill that role. I also learned that, despite their desire to portray themselves as liberal, fair and anti-establishment, journalists will always support the establishment. The establishment will survive any individual. Thirdly, I learned that when one media organ targets an individual, the "herd instinct" takes over; the target becomes fair game for them all. And, finally, I discovered that "outsiders", including northerners, are especially fair game for the Dublin scribes – just ask John Hume about how he was treated by some of the self-serving organs of right and liberalism,' he said, referring to the bitter attacks on the SDLP leader for daring to talk to Gerry Adams.

Still, his lasting legacy as president would be the redevelopment of the GAA headquarters, Croke Park, as he took the brave decision to greenlight the multimillion-pound project that would transform the venue into one of the greatest sporting stadiums in Europe.

While his brother was firefighting with the media and redeveloping a stadium, Sean Quinn was basking in the continually positive headlines he was creating. Every move he made was scrutinised, but at the time there was very little negativity in the Irish press, other than the aforementioned institutionalised anti-northern bias to be found in any reporting of events in the six counties. In fact, Sean Quinn had become a dream story, especially now that he was the David that had slain the Goliath of CRH.

With the cement plant now humming along and the company under the general management of David Mackey, Quinn spent much of his time scanning the horizon for new opportunities. He snapped up another Dublin pub, The Rathmines Inn, for IR£1.1m. 'Situated in the heart of flat land, Rathmines, it has proved to be a popular meeting place over the years and is also a well-known venue and many of the top bands in Dublin play there. It is not yet decided whether Mr. Quinn intends to continue with the music at the venue,' wrote *The Anglo-Celt* under the headline, 'Quinn Group Purchase Another Dublin Pub', which only spoke to the obvious opacity in who exactly owned the properties. Was it the Quinn family or the company? It wasn't a question that was being asked at the time.

Back on the border, the reports of Sean Quinn's purchasing of pubs and his victory in the battle with CRH had elevated his reputation to the point that rumours of his next move were always the source of conversation around kitchen tables, in the street and in the pubs of Derrylin and Ballyconnell and much farther afield. However, when he was said to be somewhere in one European city or other doing his next £1m deal, he'd actually be on a bar stool in The Angler's Rest in the company of his closest friends and colleagues. He was an omnipresent figure. Mysterious, aloof, yet present and approachable. Denzil McDaniel was the highly respected and well-known editor of the weekly *Impartial Reporter* at the time. 'You know, his reputation had spread throughout the county, and there was very much a presence, there was very much an awareness. And it didn't become Seán Quinn, it became Quinn.'

And, for 'Quinn', his next major project – the Slieve Russell Hotel – was the very manifestation of everything that he had become, and what he meant to and for the people of the borderlands.

***

It turned out that hotels had been on Sean Quinn's mind for a long time. He says he first thought of building a hotel twenty years before the Slieve Russell opened. Then, he said, he was walking into Ballyconnell for a pint when he'd been struck by the idea of opening his own hotel. If his memory is correct, he was thinking about going into hospitality before he even started up his quarry business.

It would take until 1986, however, before locals got the first indication of his intentions, when he applied for planning permission to Cavan County Council. At the time he was largely preoccupied with building the cement factory but had already bought the Dublin pubs. He proposed a £2m, thirty-bedroom hotel with function rooms and an 'underground complex' with snooker and pool rooms. (Irishman Dennis Taylor had just won the Snooker World Championship, beating Steve Davis in a black-ball finish. Over eighteen million people had watched his victory into the early hours on television. Snooker was now a very popular sport.) 'The project will be of 15 months' duration and we will be open for business by June, 1988. We envisage employing 20–25 full-time staff plus a number of part-time people,' he told *The Anglo-Celt*, his initial original ambitions much more humble than those he'd later have for the project.

This version of the hotel never materialised. Then, in 1989, he told *The Sunday Press* that the hotel was going ahead and would now cost IR£3.5m and have fifty bedrooms. Behind the scenes, he was working out the financial model for the venture, which was a first for County Cavan and just about every other county in the country. By December 1989, with work already underway at the site, Quinn announced that the hotel was actually going to cost IR£7m and would now have 140 bedrooms. He wanted it to be unlike anything the border counties had seen before, something that would draw people into the area.

Like every other aspect of the business, Quinn was making the big decisions and, generally, making them on the hoof based purely on his own instincts. But he had attempted to mitigate the risk he was taking by bringing in one of the country's most respected hotel managers to help. Michael Governey, a native of Co. Carlow, had trained at the Russell Hotel on Dublin's St Stephen's Green under the celebrated French manager, Hector Fabro. He had also managed the Royal Hibernian Hotel in Dawson Street in the city. He had been working with the Doyle Group before coming on board with Quinn as a consultant. Within months of his appointment, the plans had been scaled up beyond anything Quinn had initially envisaged. The project was now the largest the Cavan tourism industry had ever seen.

Quinn explained his rationale: 'There was no hotel between Enniskillen and Cavan town, and there was a big lump of country here with very high levels of employment, and I just thought that a hotel might work. And then I said, okay, what sort of a hotel works? Does a forty- or fifty-hotel bedroom hotel work? And the answer was, no, not so easily. It has to be a 'go-to' hotel. It's not a hotel where people walk down the street and go into. It's a destination hotel where you have to drive to and stay. And I said, okay, if it's going to be a destination hotel, then we have to do it big time, we have to do it right. We need the swimming pools, we need the golf course. And it was a big challenge because it was built to a very high standard.'

With his own cement works and factories just up the road, he could manage the building costs by keeping much of the work in-house. David Mackey led the management team that also included project engineer Sean Feehan and site manager Joe Donegan. What they had to do was simple: get the hotel built to the highest standards and have it ready to open by the summer of 1990, or within twelve months of breaking ground.

David Mackey set out the vision for *The Sunday Business Post*: 'Sean Quinn has great faith in the potential of the leisure industry in Ireland in the 1990s.' The paper reported that the 'leisure element of the development is being regarded as exceptionally comprehensive. The complex will include a 20-metre swimming pool, two squash courts, sauna, solarium, steam room, jacuzzi, gymnasium and a snooker room. A bowling alley is also being considered. For nocturnal revellers a night club-cum-discotheque is also part of the development. Externally, a children's playing facility is being planned, as well as a crazy golf course and for the serious golfer, an 18-hole championship golf course. Two lakes on the property will be stocked and the extensive woodlands will be stocked for shooting.'

It was little wonder the locals were in awe, if not a little sceptical. One of his managers at the time recalls the local reaction to his boss's latest project: 'When he was going to build the Slieve Russell Hotel we used to go to the pub on a Friday evening after work and we used to think he was mad building a hotel in the middle of nowhere. But it turned out to be a great decision. Indeed, I was married in it!' Quinn's own sister, Bernie, was acutely aware of how the project was being perceived: 'There were so many people who would have thought this was going to be a white elephant.'

Whatever the concerns about this project, it was clear that Quinn's overall business was going from strength to strength.

**

Quinn's business was now being lauded in *The Impartial Reporter* newspaper as the 'second most profitable in Northern Ireland'. In 1987 he had recorded profits of £3m on a turnover of £8.1m. Two years later, in 1989, his turnover had increased to £14.5m and he'd made £4.5m profit. 'When it comes to profitability, Sean Quinn has the Midas touch,' reported the *Impartial*'s Chris Donegan in August 1989. However, within a year, the success of the cement factory was showing on the bottom line as he returned profits of £7.4m on a £26.3m turnover. In the short space of four years his turnover had increased by 150 per cent and his profits by 140 per cent.

In the company accounts, there was also evidence of Quinn's willingness to borrow to support his ambitious plans during this period. In 1987, when construction began at the cement plant, he had borrowings of almost £10m, which rose to over £14m the following year and by almost 150 per cent to over £20m for the following two years, when he was also buying pubs and hotels and building the Slieve Russell.

Despite his success, his relationship with some of the banks in the Republic remained problematic. It was reported in 1992 that Quinn had problems in particular borrowing from Dublin banks. 'Irish banks, with the exception of the National Irish, have never been very enthusiastic about the Sean Quinn Group,' he told *The Phoenix*. 'They have never supported us even though we have always kept to our projections and have grown our turnover and profits every year since we started. I think they are scared by people who they think are climbing too quickly but they do not seem to realise that people who are climbing too quickly are not usually left with 20% net profit as we are.' However, in seeking financial support for the Slieve Russell, he did manage to form a relationship with a small Dublin bank that, like himself, had huge ambitions.

It was Anglo Irish Bank, which was run by Seán FitzPatrick.

Seán FitzPatrick was, like Quinn, the son of a farmer. Born in Co. Wicklow two years after Quinn, he differed from the borderman in pursuing an education, gaining a degree in commerce at University College Dublin before qualifying as a chartered accountant. He would later say that he wasn't the brightest student but was bright enough to recognise it. 'I have always been keenly aware of my own limitations,' he said. In his 2011 book, *Anglo Republic*, journalist Simon Carswell told how FitzPatrick joined the Irish Bank of Commerce despite having 'no idea of banking' and, six years later, in 1980, found himself managing director of 'Little Anglo', as it was known in the industry, which at the time had assets of less than IR£500,000.

FitzPatrick had four staff but was soon making a name for himself as the bank's profits increased, even though culturally it had a small-bank mentality, something which would help explain events some twenty-five years later. The bank had traditionally lent to small-time builders, publicans and professionals, such as solicitors and accountants, but by the mid-1980s they were becoming much more aggressive. FitzPatrick turned his bankers into salesmen and went after the 'sexy end' of banking – the market for loans to professionals and businessmen.

By 1986, the bank was reporting profits of over IR£800,000 and had established itself as a very different type of finance house to its much more muscular competitors. It was sharp and nimble, while its competitors,

Bank of Ireland or Ulster Bank, were stuffy and bureaucratic. It would take decisions on loans in hours, while the opposition would labour over them for weeks. FitzPatrick made his staff see the bank as a business, with a bottom line, and incentivised them to help it grow.

It was little wonder that Sean Quinn liked everything about Anglo Irish Bank and FitzPatrick. But 'Seanie', as he became known, came from a different world to Quinn. He was always suited and booted, liked fine dining in Dublin's city centre and to be seen as a man about town. He spent weekends at Greystones Golf Club and having gin 'n' tonics with his old rugby teammates, with his pastel-coloured sweater nonchalantly draped over his shoulders. But while they may have inhabited different worlds, both men got out of bed in the morning for one reason: their love of the deal.

And in the early 1990s, their success and dealmaking, indeed greed, already had them on a path of mutual destruction.

**

Despite having his own team look after the construction of the Slieve Russell and Michael Governey advising, Quinn couldn't help but get his hands dirty. He visited the site most days, making some radical changes in the final stages. He didn't like the finished fit-out of the hotel's centrepiece, the Kells Bar – named after the Book of Kells – and ordered that it be stripped out and replaced, sucking up the huge costs involved. He also had a replica of the Book of Kells created at a cost of over IR£11,000 and placed in the grand lobby of the hotel. This wasn't a hotel or a pub in Dublin, this was on his doorstep and he aimed to impress locals and visitors alike.

By the time he opened its doors at the end of July 1990, the hotel had already cost IR£14m to build. It had 150 bedrooms – ninety of which were available to book on opening day, including thirteen suites – a jacuzzi, a swimming pool, saunas and a gym. There were two conference suites, one big enough to hold 1,000 delegates, a disco and a 240-seater restaurant. And that was only the first phase. In the following twenty-four months, he opened up more bedrooms, bringing the total to 222.

The eighteen-hole championship golf course was also finished on the now 300-acre site. Over 4,000 trees were planted around the course and 200 golfers were able to use the course each and every day, paying annual subscriptions of IR£700 and green fees of IR£30. Initially, membership was limited to a hundred golfers. Just like everything else he did, Quinn didn't want *a* golf course, he demanded to have the best golf course, the best grass, the best tees, the best greens, more trees. He had ambitions for the Irish Open to be played there and to bring the European PGA Tour to the Slieve Russell. He even built pathways into the course for spectators. Everything had to meet his standards. Once opened, Quinn brought in a former general manager of the world-famous St Andrews Golf Club, Raymond Maguire, to manage the Slieve Russell Golf Course. The head greenkeeper was local man, Finbar Cooney, who had twenty-eight full-time staff working alongside him. In the end, the total cost of the hotel was IR£17m – 250 per cent over the budget originally set by Quinn himself. He'd made yet another bold statement.

But now that he'd built it, would the visitors come to Cavan? 'We decided to change the goal posts, which doubled the cost of the development. But it meant we could market the hotel as a top of the range product,' he told *The Phoenix* in 1992.

The response was overwhelmingly positive, if not a little haughty. 'The world is full of rich people who have taken a bath over their pet project,' Howard Rose wrote in *The Sunday Press*, 'in the case of Fermanagh quarryman-turned-hotelier Sean Quinn, the doomsayers have had him spiralling down the plug-hole since he started building the first bedrooms and bathrooms in his own personal dream, the Slieve Russell Hotel. Already described as "Cavan's Versailles", the Slieve Russell is the jewel of the Midlands, a grand hotel in the old style, a five-star oasis in a desert of bed and breakfasts geared to blue-collar German and English anglers. First reports of the Slieve Russell, back in February, were treated with a sniffy disdain. Sweeping marble staircases? Luxury 10-seater settees scattered through a cavernous lobby? A fountain in the driveway, spouting water 30 feet or more, seemingly just waiting for the carriage-and-fours to sweep up and disgorge their passengers into the county ball? In Cavan? But it's all true. Looking nothing so much as a 17th-century grandee's country home for a well-endowed seminary than the pride of Cavan,' opined Rose, saying the hotel had the 'gawp factor'.

Quinn himself saw the hotel as a way to help market the core business. 'The plan we had for it is exactly what turned out – a destination hotel, done to a high standard. We knew it would work in this area and it would bring a lot to the Quinn Group. Every Christmas, for example, we would give the customers presents and the presents would be for a weekend or whatever it might be in the Slieve Russell, compliments of the company. So it did build relationships with a lot of people.'

Howard Rose may have dubbed it 'Cavan's Versailles' but the locals had their own name for it. 'It was called the "bejesus hotel",' said Quinn, 'and the reason it's called the bejesus hotel was because if you were coming down from Dublin, you drove along these old back roads and you see nothing, and then all of a sudden you drive round the corner, and you see oh, Jesus,' he says before adding to the business case for building such a big hotel. 'I suppose, the fact that we were very successful in the business down the road, and the manufacturing business was going very well for us, and we had a lot of loyal customers and a lot of loyal staff,' he reasoned. Speaking to David Nally from the *Sunday Tribune*, Quinn admitted that he had done some market research but that the decision to build the hotel had ultimately, once again, been made on pure instinct.

After it opened, the hotel quickly began to make an operating profit. He admitted to Nally that he didn't know from where the guests were materialising – 'I don't know who they are, to be honest. I've no idea where they're coming from' – but was full of belief that his gamble would pay off. 'I don't consider it a risk. It's only a risk if we don't run it the way it should be run.'

Bernie summed up the pride of the family at the opening of the hotel. 'I remember him taking Brian and ourselves up to the very top of the tower of the Slieve Russell and just looking round and thinking, holy God, he did this. While I was not actively involved or couldn't participate in any of his other enterprises, to have the Slieve Russell to go to was just unbelievable. And our mother was in her seventies at that stage, and she regarded it as her achievement too. She had her friends bring her up there on a Sunday afternoon and she'd sit in the foyer of the Slieve Russell and she'd watch the people coming and going and she would chat to them. And sure it gave her a whole new dimension to her life in those last fifteen years.'

Quinn was once again proving his doubters wrong. In terms of the bottom line, the hotel was soon operating ahead of his own forecasts. During the first year of operation, the occupancy rate was 30 per cent, which doubled when Quinn opened up another sixty rooms. The weekend rate, he reported, was 100 per cent.

The 'gawpers' were coming through the doors alright, but he had to get them to spend money in the bars and restaurants, and stay the night. When he was interviewed eighteen months after it opened, it was clear that he was beginning to understand the nuances of running a hotel of the size he'd built and, crucially, its customer base. 'Around 50% come from Dublin with a large proportion of the rest coming from Northern Ireland. People come mainly for midweek or weekend breaks. I like to think we have built a good reputation in that area,' he told *The Phoenix* magazine.

He looked to take advantage of that reputation by buying another hotel in Cavan, the Kilmore, and then adding another of his competitors in the border region, the Hillgrove, in Monaghan. He paid IR£1m for the seven-acre property, which had 42 bedrooms and a large dancehall. He immediately closed the hotel and ploughed a further IR£2.5m into upgrading it. Less than an hour east of the Slieve Russell, he was consolidating his position in the hospitality sector along the border.

'Sean Quinn was talked about a lot more because the Slieve Russell Hotel really wowed everybody,' said Colm Tóibín. 'I mean, this could not have been imagined, that you came around a corner on a damp old road where the ditches hadn't been cleared for a very long time and there was this. And it was like something, it was like something in Vegas, a sort of, you know, pink palace of a thing.' Tóibín could plainly see why it proved to be such a success. 'Of course, it was absolutely marvellous to have it there because it meant you could have weddings, a big wedding locally. You could have all sorts of events. And it began to be used, and people from Dublin started to go up there for the weekend and boast about it when they came back down, saying the Slieve Russell's food had been amazing, or the spa or their bedroom or the sheets. You know, there was some sort of sense of, that he didn't just build this, he had some vision that people would come to it if it did one more thing than offering just comfort or value for money. If it filled the imagination, which it certainly did,' summed up the author.

***

The year the Slieve Russell opened, there was little fuss about the new hire who began working at the accounts department in the company. Yet, of the 7,500 people he would eventually employ, it was one of the most significant appointments Quinn ever made.

Liam McCaffrey was a twenty-seven-year-old accountant with Coopers & Lybrand, who, at the time, were Quinn's auditors. Quinn saw something in McCaffrey and, acting on instinct, immediately offered him a job. Another manager at the time remembers him joining. 'He would have been at the monthly meetings that we would have attended. A very astute individual and would have been very close to Sean. At any of the meetings I would have been at, I suppose they didn't have that much experience at that time in production, it was more the accounts. Sean very much led the meetings when it came to production, factories, manufacturing, the general workforce. Liam was very much in the office looking after the financial side of things.'

McCaffrey was not the only one getting work within the company. With the opening of the hotel, some of the Quinn children were also getting jobs. The two eldest girls, Colette and Ciara – who were still at school – worked in the hotel at weekends. Their father was determined that they would learn that 'the only way to make money is to work hard for it'.

He also came to a realisation about their legacy. He now saw that his property business would be much more profitable than the cement factory and subsidiary businesses he'd built along the border could ever be, even though they were making him millions in profit each year. Finance was cheap and there was plenty of opportunity in the local Irish market for investors looking for a decent return on their money. His initial 'instinct' had been to buy the pubs and bars for his daughters, while his son, Sean Junior, would inherit the cement factory. But as he kept buying, with the Slieve Russell now the jewel in the family's crown, he could see that his legacy would be in the property portfolio he was building, not in the quarry business.

In fact, the opening of the Slieve Russell was the start of a golden decade in which nothing got in the way of the one-man business bulldozer that was Sean Quinn. By 1995 he was employing an incredible 1,000 people across five factories in Derrylin, Galway and Longford, as well as six hotels and nine pubs. In one week alone he spent IR£3m on The Harp Bar on Dublin's O'Connell Street and The Ambassador Hotel in Kildare, adding them to the group. He also picked up his first award, winning the 'Person of the Year' award from the Cavan Association 'for his contribution to job creation, tourism and the economy of the whole region'.

But it wasn't all plain sailing for Quinn during this period, as a decision he took caused significant controversy in Ballyconnell, with some locals warning that it could come back to haunt him in the years to come. The quarryman had continued to buy up land to feed the hungry machine he'd created on the Mountain Road. In purchasing a parcel of land in the townland of Aughrim, which ran right up against the southern side of the border off the Ballyconnell to Derrylin road, Quinn had inherited a megalithic tomb, or, as locals knew it, a fairy fort. According to experts called in to inspect it, the tomb had been built between 1800 and 2000 BC and had protected status, which meant it couldn't be touched without approval.

But it was now a problem for Quinn as it was bang in the middle of his quarry's insatiable onward march through the countryside spanning the Fermanagh–Cavan border. He contacted the Office of Public Works in Dublin and requested permission to move it.

The chief archaeologist at the time, Peter Danaher, agreed and his staff supervised as Quinn had the tomb excavated, moved and reconstructed, under the supervision of archaeologist John Channing, at the Slieve Russell Hotel. Indeed, Mr Danahar said the move was 'a reasonably good result'. He admitted to *The Anglo-Celt* that he would have preferred it not be moved at all, 'but in the circumstances, it is in as good a place as any'.

Some superstitious locals were not on board with the tomb's removal, however. One, John Forrest, told the same newspaper report that moving the tomb set a dangerous precedent and said it should have been relocated on the mountain or along the Ballinamore canal. Local historian Bryan Gallagher said the tomb was a fairy fort that shouldn't have been touched at all. 'Everybody said it was unlucky. You should not do that. You should not touch it at all. As the man Packie Gilleece says, "ah sure you wouldn't believe in fairies, but they're there just the same."'

The fairy fort, or tomb, became a visitor attraction at the Slieve Russell, with the Quinn Group general manager, David Mackey, telling the local paper that it was '10,000 times more accessible now than it was before and those who want to view do not have to go into the hotel to do so'.

Many years later, the same locals who had protested its movement at the time would say that Sean Quinn's downfall was all because he'd tampered with that fairy fort.

For now, however, Quinn didn't give it a second's thought. It had been a problem and he'd found a solution. Although very aware of local customs and with good friends who were believers in fairies and forts, he'd little time for superstitions. He was not dwelling on the past, only the future, and he believed his best days were ahead of him.

He wasn't wrong.

6

Border State of Mind

If there were a specific day or a month when Ireland began to feel like it could do no wrong, it was definitely somewhere within the year 1994. A mix of having the fastest dancing feet the world had ever seen in *Riverdance*, a soccer team with the habit of creating celebratory hangovers and an economy that was nothing less than a miracle were all part of the alchemy that made Ireland unrecognisable to the nation of the previous decades.

The icing on the cake was the IRA ceasefire in August 1994, ending the twenty-five-year-old conflict in the North that had cost the lives of over 3,500 people. Loyalist paramilitaries followed suit six weeks later. With the ceasefire, a genuine hope burst forth that violent acts such as these were at an end. And that hope proved contagious. 'There's a real economic boom that really begins to get under way around 1994,' said Fintan O'Toole. 'There's a sense of optimism, which is very powerful, psychologically. You have globalisation really beginning to take off. You have had the fall of the Berlin Wall, the opening up of China. You have the huge tech boom going on in the United States, vast amounts of money being made, looking for investment. The single European market had happened in 1992, and from 1993, 1994, that's beginning to kick in. All those barriers to trade in Europe are coming down. So you've a lot of money looking for a place in Europe, and here you have Ireland, where wages are still relatively low, a very young population and an incredibly well-educated population. You've got a very favourable tax regime in the Republic.' As a result, 'You have a genuine economic boom.'

Ireland was changing fast, O'Toole observed. 'You have women coming into the workforce in huge numbers because of social change for the first time. So you have a lot of these factors working at the same time. I remember what it felt like to be in Ireland in those years. You just thought, I don't recognise this place, you know. The sense of optimism, the sense that all that dark history, you know, both in terms of the North and the Troubles, but also the dark economic history of mass emigration, all that hopelessness, is behind us.'

It was an exciting time to be in Quinn Country, too. On the border, the new wind of opportunity was blowing in his direction. In 1992 Ireland's first wind farm had been erected at Bellacorrick, Co. Mayo. Within months, Sean Quinn was awarded a licence under the North's first non-fossil-fuel legislation and applied for planning permission to build his own wind farm on the northern side of Slieve Rushen, also known as Slieve Russell, the mountain he was quarrying behind his headquarters, and which had provided the inspiration for the name of his hotel.

The wind farm would produce a rather meagre five megawatts of energy, but Quinn was prepared to start off small in order to test whether a farm could be built on the difficult terrain. Initially, he wasn't interested in selling the electricity he created back into the grid, but believed he could make the cement and tile factories below Slieve Rushen self-sufficient. The ten 500-kilowatt wind turbines, each with a thirty-nine-metre rotor diameter, were the latest technology, designed in Denmark with a German gearbox by the world-leading Vestas company, and they could produce enough electricity to power 4,000 homes. It cost him over £2m, with the EU pitching in a 30 per cent grant with the aim of encouraging more Irish entrepreneurs to slipstream behind Quinn.

Once erected, it was one of the first wind farms to appear on the horizon in the North and the electricity generated did only supply the cement factory, at first, helping to cut his production costs, before later going directly into the local grid.

Quinn enjoyed being at the cutting edge of technology and the wind farm had the 'gawp factor', just like the Slieve Russell. The transit of the huge blades, making the final leg of their journey from Denmark through Derrylin and out to the mountain, had caused a stir in themselves, locals coming out to see them pass by. Quinn was bringing more change to the place, reshaping the horizons of what was by now known the length and breadth of the island as Quinn Country.

***

In 1995 the Sean Quinn Group recorded its highest-ever net profit of £9.1 million on a turnover of £36.2m. Quinn himself was now being described as a 'multi-millionaire'. Not that you could tell. For some years, neither he nor his wife, Patricia, had taken a director's salary or dividends. The family continued to live in the house that he'd built for them and, despite his success, their living costs had not increased significantly. There were still no second homes abroad or ostentatious displays of wealth. The family drove cars – he was usually seen driving a Range Rover – purchased through the company.

However, in many ways, this was further evidence of the continuing blurred lines between Quinn the family and Quinn the business. The company was Sean and Patricia's, and its profits were their profits. That's how he saw it, anyway, and as long as there were no other shareholders seeking their dividend, there wasn't an issue.

The company remained very much a family affair. In his unique style of diversification, Sean had put the Slieve Russell Hotel in the ownership of his youngest daughter, Brenda, who was just four years old at the time. It was a signal of his intentions for her, his way of securing her future. On his children's inheritance, he told *The Sunday Press* at the time: 'I don't want to be in a position that they'll all be fighting for my legacy. I don't think there'll be any likelihood of that now,' he laughed.

Later, in an interview in 2018, he expanded on the plans he had at that time for the business and the family. 'With having four daughters, I thought that hotels might suit, or pubs, might suit them better than quarries or cement factories and stuff like that. So there was a bit of that, but also [there was] the diversification idea. I always felt that, it was never my idea to go round Ireland or England or whatever it was, and open twenty, thirty, forty, fifty quarries. Because they are very hard to manage, and there's a certain expertise needed to manage those quarries, and to make them efficient ... Whereas if you buy a hotel, and put in a good manager there, and leave him or her responsible for the income or outcome, and you pay them a good bonus for success,' then he believed that the hotel's success would be guaranteed. He added, 'And in the pubs, of course, it's easier again because you just leased it. So I just thought that putting too many eggs in the one basket wasn't the right thing to do.'

He wasn't interested in opening more quarries, but Quinn had plenty to keep him busy. Visitors to the Quinn Group headquarters in Derrylin were used to the informal way he conducted meetings, usually with his shoes, covered in quarry dust, kicked off to the side and him doing business in his socks. He was ubiquitous: in the hotel one moment, then on the floor of the tile factory the next or in the cement factory, dropping off rock samples he'd found on the mountain. 'I suppose I was a bit unorthodox in that respect,' he conceded.

As the boss, too, he was able to keep his own hours. 'I never had a starting time nor never had a finishing time. I was available 168 hours a week, and that was the way it was then and that's the way now and that's the way I'll die or until the old brain goes entirely. That's the way I am. I never use a clock, I never, maybe three or four mornings a week that I had to be up at five or six o'clock, Patricia would waken me or something, but apart from that I got up when I wakened and had my breakfast and I went to work, and that could be at seven o'clock or that could be at ten o'clock. I would come home at five o'clock and I could come home at ten o'clock. I will come home when I'm finished, and I'll go when I'm ready, or if there's something important, if I have a meeting I won't be late for it, I'll be there for it. But I'll try not to have them at half seven, eight o'clock in the morning.'

One manager, who was helping to manage the roof-tile division at the time, said Quinn was very much present. 'When I first joined I wouldn't have seen that much of him on a daily basis, but you were always aware of his presence. He used to be about, he would come in just unannounced and walk the factory floor. He could just hop into the office at any time and he'd have a quick chat for you and he'd be out again. I always found he was most content when he was out and about the quarries chatting to the guys at the coalface basically, looking at the rock being crushed, going into the factory, seeing the end product coming out. I think he got a great kick out of that. Always found him more comfortable out and about than he was sitting in a boardroom, I think. I think most people that worked there would have thought the same, you know.'

The manager added that, despite the changing nature and scale of the business, it retained a family atmosphere. 'Sean would stop and chat to guys. So it was a very, I suppose, homely atmosphere in ways. Guys worked hard, don't get me wrong. I remember in '87, '88, we started at eight in the morning, probably worked late at night. On Saturdays we would come in at eight o'clock and work until four or five, but in fairness we were always well paid for that. We used to get a Christmas bonus, which we always looked forward to. And it used to come with a letter signed by Sean, and to be honest I think in 1988 or 1989, it was £500. At that time it was a lot of money. But then when I look back now, I certainly earned it!'

According to Bernie, Quinn was very aware of the value to the local area of the wealth he was creating. 'I know that personally he got great satisfaction out of everything he did,' she said in a 2018 interview. 'I'm not saying he was a regular visitor in our house at that stage when he was very busy, but say he came down, there was a new house built. Who built that house in such a place? Does he work for us? And he just loved to see the people building good houses, being successful in their lives as a result of what he had done. It was both sides of the border, people of all ages just appreciated the jobs that were there. And I suppose you'd be very unreasonable if you lived in that [area] not to have loyalty to it. Nobody else in the centuries before that had created too many jobs there. There was a factory in Lisnaskea, it closed; factory in Enniskillen, they all closed. You know, there was definitely a huge indebtedness to him,' she said.

Quinn now had gathered a very close-knit team around him who had his sworn loyalty. 'When I started there was John Lee and Gerry Reilly, they would have been his close lieutenants,' explained the manager, 'they were on the ground. They were local men as well. Tony Lunney was the production manager and was a very hard worker. They knew all the workers and they enjoyed the respect of the workers. David Mackey probably brought a more corporate feel to it. He was very professional, very well connected, introduced more structures into the company. But we all worked well and respected Sean, [we] brought a lot to the business, helped him grow the business.'

This team was helping Quinn to push his business on to new heights.

***

After spending so much time and money in hospitality acquisitions, Quinn's focus returned to the core business of cement in October 1995 with the opening of a new £9m state-of-the-art concrete block plant. The new autoclaved, aerated concrete block to be produced at the plant, which was to be marketed under the brand name 'Quinn-Lite', was described in *The Impartial Reporter* as being the 'optimal building product for modern construction, offering outstanding strength, fire resistance and thermal insulation at only one-third of the weight of conventional concrete blocks'.

Quinn was creating a further sixty jobs in what was the first factory of its kind on the island of Ireland. Built with the help of a German design team, he installed a sophisticated computer-process control system, which he said was the 'most modern of its type in the world', according to the Fermanagh-based paper. It was just a line in a press release, but it was an indisputable fact. This reinforced the standards that Quinn had set for himself: Sean Quinn didn't just build factories or products, he created the best in Europe, if not the world. That's what made him different, that's what set him out from his opponents. It was what really motivated him to get out of bed in the morning. It wasn't about the money; it was about being the best. The fact was that he was in competition with no one but himself.

The new block plant was significant in and of itself. However, Quinn used it, in effect, as something of a tease for his next big play.

He'd built the block plant on the northern side of the border and had been given a grant of almost £1m from the North's Industrial Development Board, whose chairman, the highly successful pig farmer John B. McGuckian, travelled to Derrylin to meet Quinn and inspect the new product. Alongside him on this visit was the chairman of Fermanagh District Council, the respected Ulster Unionist councillor Sammy Foster. In his remarks, quoted in the following Thursday's edition of *The Impartial Reporter*, McGuckian said Quinn had 'confounded his critics with another dimension to his burgeoning industrial complex'.

Still, despite their help, Quinn was using the block plant to send a message to the IDB and its counterpart in the South, Forbairt. By now, the cement factory, the tile factories, the site of the new block plant and even the wind farm on Slieve Rushen were stretched out along the Derrylin to Ballyconnell road. But, despite the way he felt he'd been treated by the IDB during the construction of the original cement factory – when they significantly reduced funding – everything he'd built so far had been in the North: only the Slieve Russell was in the South. But he was planning on rolling the dice one more time in a huge gamble and was going to need all the muscle and support he could muster. Behind the scenes, Quinn was talking to both the IDB and Forbairt, seeing what each could bring to the table for his next project. For this development, it really didn't matter what side of the border it was on; whichever group offered him the best deal would win.

Taking on monopolies was a game to which Sean Quinn was very attracted, as seen with CRH. Now, in the mid-1990s, he had found another monopolised industry to take on, one vulnerable to the challenge of a border businessman with little or no concern about risk. 'I never had any great strategy, just impulse,' he had once said. For all that the people of the border region were becoming used to Quinn's surprises, even they were taken aback when he announced he was going to build a glass bottling plant.

Given that its raw component was sand, of which he had an endless supply, it made a lot of sense. But those who gave the glass industry any thought really had to know one thing: the Irish Glass Bottle Company already supplied all the bottles the country needed. They had a monopoly.

As with his other endeavours, there was a fair amount of surprise and an expectation of failure. Quinn's sister summed up the local reaction: 'Who would have thought about building a glass factory in Derrylin? I don't know what made him do that. I can see the cement to some extent, even though it was a huge investment and it was objected to and it was difficult to do, I can understand that. But a glass factory, that was completely off the radar. I don't think anyone else would have even dreamt of building a glass factory in Fermanagh, far away from the airports or from the docks.' However, there was hope too. 'I think that was the pride in the local area too, you know, it'll be jobs for local people. It will increase the population maybe locally, it will keep them at home.'

Speaking to the *Belfast Telegraph* at the time, David Mackey said Quinn had been working on the plans for over a year: 'When the plant is completed there will be employment for 200 people but that figure will rise to 350. We are very excited about it. The plant will manufacture glass containers such as jars and bottles as well as pharmaceutical containers. Irish Glass [Ardagh] in Dublin is the only firm making these types of glass products, so we will be a new challenger on the market.'

And being a new challenger meant new adversaries.

***

'The Cooler' wasn't at all pleased at Quinn's plans. Having graduated from Trinity College Dublin, Paul Coulson had made serious money in the aviation industry, leasing aircraft from his base in Dublin. He'd also gone into stocks and shares and, just as Quinn was getting his own glass ambitions in hand, Paul 'The Cooler' Coulson bought a minority stake in the Ardagh Group.

Going back to the 1920s, there were two glass bottle companies in Ireland – Irish Glass and the Ringsend Bottle Company. Both companies closed in 1930 but, two years later, the Irish Glass Bottle Company took over both operations. In 1989, after over half a century of enjoying a monopolised position in the local market, Irish Glass was rebranded as 'Ardagh' and within months Coulson made his move, quickly setting the company on a path to make it a multibillion-dollar, multinational company.

However, when Quinn announced he was building a glass plant, the business he'd invested his money in faced nothing less than a full-on crisis. Coulson knew that a modern plant would outstrip his thirty-year-old production lines in terms of both efficiency and costs. And Ardagh had a lot to lose. On top of its virtual control of the southern market, the company had 90 per cent of the £5m market north of the border, which represented 15 per cent of their total output.

Ardagh weren't alone in struggling to come to terms with the threat posed by Quinn's plans. In Sheffield, the leaders of the British Glass Confederation (BGC) quickly circled the wagons to protect their market share in the UK. They decided the best form of defence was to go on the offensive. They picked up the CRH playbook, alleging any jobs Quinn created would cause considerable job losses in the UK. Furthermore, worried that Quinn would pick up an IDB grant for his plan, BGC director-general Bill Cook warned in a press statement targeted to be picked up on both sides of the Irish Sea that: 'For every new job in Northern Ireland, one will be going elsewhere.'

Quinn was too busy playing the rival business development agencies against each other to worry about the competition. His glass plant would be built; so as far as he was concerned the opposition would have to simply deal with it. He initially estimated the plant was going to cost him £40m (though it would turn out that he'd grossly underestimated the cost, again). In the North, the IDB offered an attractive package of grants, which could ultimately come to 20 per cent of the cost. The Republic couldn't match the IDB's offer, but the officials at Forbairt emphasised the very attractive 10 per cent manufacture tax and the changes being introduced by Finance Minister Charlie McCreevy, which would see the corporate tax on profits drop from 32 per cent to 12.5 per cent. In contrast, corporation tax in Northern Ireland was 33 per cent in 1997.

The quarryman weighed up his options. Wherever he placed the plant, it was going to create more jobs for the people of south Fermanagh and west Cavan. In the end, he felt he'd no choice but to go north. After a rigorous, nine-month application process, the IDB offered him a grant of £12.5m for the plant. The offer, controversially announced by the Conservative government on Election Day 1997, marked a major turnaround in Quinn's relationships with the organisation that had previously reneged on their support for the cement factory. At that time, he'd alleged he was a victim of sectarianism. Now, with John B. McGuckian at the helm, he was getting every penny in support that the IDB could provide.

Bill Cook from the British Glass Confederation was livid, firing out another press statement: 'The IDB has resolutely ignored our advice all along that there is no room for the extra capacity.' The Labour MP for a constituency in Barnsley, in the north of England, went to the Parliamentary Ombudsman calling for an investigation into the grant. Eric Illsley, whose constituency just happened to be home to one of the major UK glassmakers, PLM Redfearn, said by pushing through the grant on an election day, the Tories may have breached guidelines restricting government to essential and vital business decisions only once a poll has been called.

Bill Cook employed a set of consultants whom he dispatched to Belfast to pore through every jot and tittle of Quinn's plans and the IDB support. They had only one mission goal: stop the Quinn factory. Cook said the government was shamefaced in announcing the decision to fund the project on the day of an election, which he said was against all parliamentary codes. He told the *Fermanagh Herald*: 'The problem is not that people shouldn't have jobs, it is simply the time and way this investment was taken. We have taken the matter to the government and how it will finally turn out I just don't know.'

Joining Cook was Robert Montgomery, the managing director of the Beatson Clarks glassworks in Barnsley, who predicted job losses in England and Ireland. 'People are going to lose jobs because the market is not growing, this is not scare tactics. If Mr. Quinn makes the progress he is claiming he can, the job losses will start to take effect within months,' he was quoted as saying in the *Fermanagh Herald*. He added that they had brought a complaint to the Department of Trade and Industry, arguing that Quinn was already on site and, according to its rules, the IDB could not provide funding to a plant that was already in the process of being built. When these criticisms were put to him, Quinn pointed to the fact that he was operating in a socially disadvantaged area. 'The plant will create vital jobs in an area with an extremely high unemployment rate,' he told the local paper.

Despite the complaints, Fermanagh District Council rushed through planning permission. As the plant began to rise out of the ground, Quinn was whistling his usual tune: 'We are going to have the most modern factory in Britain and Ireland. I think we can produce the cheapest glass and we will try to get the best price for it,' he was quoted as saying in *The Irish Times*. Quinn was going to install the most sophisticated production line money could buy. That alone would help keep his labour costs down and ensure that he could outstrip the opposition in price, and they knew it.

At one point, the *Sunday Tribune* reporter Tom McEnaney wrote that Quinn may have a partner, someone who had a vested interest in the manufacture of bottles for the pharmaceutical business. 'It is understood that another Northern Ireland entrepreneur, Eddie Haughey, has held discussions with Quinn about taking a small equity stake in the new glass company. Norbrook Laboratories, Haughey's Newry-based veterinary pharmaceutical firm uses about 800,000 glass bottles a week, currently bought in continental Europe.'

In reality, the approach from Haughey was considered but ultimately, and unsurprisingly, Quinn opted to go it alone.

***

Even those closest to him in the mid-1990s were never under the illusion that they knew everything Quinn was planning. He was moving at warp speed, beyond the ability of everyone around him. Decisions were being taken before his management team even knew the question or opportunity. So it was that with all the focus on the opening of new factories, pubs, plants and on the Slieve Russell, very little attention was paid to the new shop that appeared in the town of Cavan the first week of January 1996.

It was only the second day back at work after the Christmas holidays, not usually considered a savvy moment to launch a new venture and capture attention. But then Quinn was not looking for attention. It was the first time in ten years that Sean Quinn made any sort of move without fanfare. None. No press release, no photo of Quinn, arms crossed, looking steely and determined, no 'I'm taking on the big boys' or 'I'm going to break the monopoly.'

It was a simple office on the Dublin Road in Cavan with a 'Quinn Direct' sign above the door. Locals barely passed any notice on it, and any who did thought it had something to do with his existing business. They certainly didn't think that it was the first public signal that Quinn was moving in a completely new direction, one that would change the face of his company.

By the Friday of the first week in January, the story broke about what he was doing, though even then it was subdued. 'Quinn insurance firm opens doors', was the headline on the *Irish Times* story. Under it, journalist Mary Canniffe wrote: 'Mr. Sean Quinn's new insurance company, which has received its licence to write general insurance, has just opened for business. Quinn Direct Insurance, set up by the Fermanagh-based cement-to-hotels entrepreneur, opened its first outlet in Cavan town on Tuesday.'

Quinn had kept his plans tight to the chest. For twelve months he'd been secretly working on voluminous licensing applications with the Department of Enterprise and Employment in Dublin, seeking permission to write general insurance policies, such as car and house cover, as well as commercial policies. He'd received the go-ahead from the department just before Christmas and immediately set the wheels in motion to get the business up on its feet in the New Year. He entrusted David Mackey, the man closest to him, with the project and he was the one who was quoted in the *Irish Times* article, not Quinn. 'We are doing it in a quiet, controlled way and letting it develop slowly,' he said.

It was all very unlike Quinn. It wasn't his style to do anything in a 'quiet, controlled way'. He liked everyone to know what he was going to do, long before he did it. In contrast, he'd announced plans for the Slieve Russell five years before it opened. It was the same with the cement factory and the bottle plant. However, this was different. He recognised he was getting into a very different type of business, although, according to him, it was all down to instinct again. For some of his managers, it was a surprise, to say the least: 'I didn't see it as a natural extension. It was a totally different industry than he had been into before that.'

Regardless, Quinn says it was a very straightforward decision, based on his own understanding of the insurance industry. 'I saw the niche because, I suppose, of my knowledge of the industry before I went into it. We had 100 lorries, 200 lorries and plenty of dumpers and shovels. We may have had 300 or 400 vehicles all over the place and we were paying a very high insurance premium, millions of pounds a year in premiums. And we were never allowed to have any input into the settlement of those claims. In other words, the insurance company came along and they said, even though we could have somebody down in your block yard with a wee squeeze of a finger and we could have gone and sorted him out for two or three grand and moved on, but we couldn't do that. So that claim would be paid out maybe two or three years later at ten times what we could have settled the claim on day one. So, when I started in insurance we decided that there were only going to be two parties involved – the insurance company, which is Quinn Direct, and the client.'

Now Sean Quinn, a man who admitted that his only knowledge of the insurance industry was as a client who paid millions in premiums, was wading into a complex and sophisticated market of which he had very little understanding. As a result, he made sure to bring in some experts in the field, hiring Noel Corley as general manager and Ray Foley as his chief underwriter. Foley had been a production underwriter for over ten years, working with brokers Coyle Hamilton and later Cigna in Dublin before joining Quinn, while Corley was a highly respected consultant. After Quinn Insurance Limited had been incorporated as a company on 14 November 1995, Corley and David Mackey were both made directors, with Quinn in control as chairman and managing director.

In the *Irish Times* article, Mackey was at pains to stress that the insurance company was not a subsidiary of the Quinn Group. There had to be a 'church and state' separation as part of the licensing agreements

– a vital distinction with which Sean Quinn would never really come to terms.

Once again Quinn was heading into unchartered territory in an industry that was highly competitive. He'd no experience of being regulated by government and the responsibilities that came with it. Now, he had to make a series of commitments that he'd have to abide by or risk losing his licence, which would mean losing his business. A key commitment was proving they had the financial resources to meet the liabilities of the policies they were going to sell, resources they were going to have to put into what's called a 'minimum guarantee fund' – a reserve, or, basically, a large pot of money that Quinn would set aside to cover the risk he was taking on in selling the insurance policies. This money would have to be ring-fenced, untouchable, in order to protect the rights of his customers. This was a completely different kind of game to quarries or roof tiles or even expensive bottle plants. He had his license and could see the upside, but did Quinn really appreciate the risks attached to selling insurance?

Each year, insurance businesses produced an annual report, called the Blue Book. In 1994 it reported that over IR£1 billion of insurance premiums had been sold in Ireland over the previous year. But after sales expenses and claims of IR£850m, the industry recorded losses of IR£61m. Accident, health, fire and property insurance were profitable, according to the Blue Book, but motor, marine, aviation and liability insurance recorded losses. Meanwhile, motor insurance was worth IR£620m with two-thirds of sales coming from private car owners and the remaining third from commercial vehicles.

Despite this, Sean Quinn was not put off, believing his support network along the border counties would give him an edge on the established insurance companies. There were already around thirty companies selling insurance in Ireland, and in the year before he opened up shop in Cavan, there had been five new entrants into the market, all selling from call centres, which were fast becoming the most popular, and cheapest, way to communicate with consumers. The French-owned company Touchline was followed by First Call Direct, Guardian Direct and Celtic Direct. Bank of Ireland subsidiary Premier Direct had been the first company to offer customers the opportunity to buy insurance over the phone, which was the model Quinn intended to pursue with his base on the border.

On the day the Cavan office opened with fifteen staff, he already had plans to expand – namely, into a new 15,000-square-foot call centre close to his Kilmore Hotel in Cavan town. For the market in the North, a base would be established at the Quinn Group headquarters in Teemore. Quinn had already identified the former Cassidy Fabrics building on Dublin's Lower O'Connell Street for the company's base in the capital. While his mind raced ahead, it was now a case of seeing how this fledgling insurance company would compete.

***

In its first year in business, Quinn Direct sold premiums of IR£12m and increased that by over 50 per cent in year two, bringing in IR£19m. The people who know insurance believe that for a business to be viable in Ireland it has got to have at least 5 per cent market share. Quinn had started well, but he was a long way off that at the end of 1997, despite having 300,000 policyholders, an amount that equated to only 2 per cent of the market.

Still, despite the complexity of insurance and the inherent risks, there was no magic formula as far as Quinn was concerned. He had no doubt that they would soon reach a point of viability, driven by competent – and incentivised – staff: 'We had some brilliant people in Quinn Direct. They were settling 300 claims a year in the fast-track system. We had people in that system that were getting 100 per cent bonus. In other words, if their salary was €25,000, they were getting another €25,000 of bonus. Paying good people and doing good business, it's never that difficult, it's just common sense.' He elaborated, 'People are inclined to have this idea that insurance, and that various parts of business, is magic. There's no magic to business. Business is simple – get from A to B as handy as you can. Have the right people in place. Pay them properly. So as regards not understanding insurance, who could understand insurance better if they had dozens of pubs and hotels, hundreds of lorries and dumpers and shovels and they were paying reckless insurance for twenty or thirty years; who could understand it better than the guy who was paying out those cheques?'

With the business up on its feet, Quinn needed someone to drive it on. Enter Kevin Lunney.

Lunney was twenty-eight years old, the youngest of a family of ten, all born and bred on Molly Mountain. In 1987 he'd gone to Queen's University in Belfast and graduated with a degree in electrical and electronics engineering before taking up a position as a management consultant with Arthur Andersen in Dublin, which, at the time, was one of the big five accounting firms in the world. After six years of Dublin, mixed with a lot of travelling – he'd spent time in Seattle, working on the Microsoft account – he was ready for a change, preferably somewhere closer to home. His father wasn't well at the time and while the rest of the family were around to look after him, he was stuck in Dublin – or travelling abroad.

While Kevin wanted to be closer to home, others were working to make that happen. Kevin's brother Tony, the second youngest in the family, had been working for Sean Quinn for over twenty years and had risen through the ranks, becoming a very trusted manager. Unbeknownst to Kevin, Tony was whispering in the ear of his boss, telling him about the talented younger brother and his desire to come back home.

One afternoon in August 1996, Kevin was in Andersen's Dublin office when his desk phone rang. It was Sean Quinn. Kevin couldn't hide his surprise that Quinn, whom he had never met, would take the time to call personally. Quinn invited him to come up and meet with him and

David Mackey. 'The insurance business had taken off at the time. Sean had ploughed into it and now he needed someone to run it,' said one of those involved at the time.

He was offered the role of general manager of Quinn Insurance. It was a no-brainer.

He packed up and returned to his childhood home, living with his mother and father while he settled back in his homeplace. Not much time had passed in his new role, however, before Lunney realised that despite getting off to a great start in its first months of operation, Quinn Insurance was in chaos. There were no processes, no real procedures in place for managing staff, the premiums or the claims. 'It was crazy in those early days,' an executive at the time said. Soon, though, Lunney had proven himself to be the right man for the role, as, after only eight months in the job, he brought order to the business. Having introduced a new computerised system, the business was now fit for purpose.

Which was all well and good, as Quinn was hungry for growth.

Sean Quinn's personal wealth was certainly growing. The 1997 *Sunday Times* Rich List confirmed his status among the super wealthy, placing him as the 121st richest man in the United Kingdom, with a personal wealth of £130 million. His success in the 1990s has to be seen against the backdrop of a new economic phenomenon of the same decade, now being described as 'the Celtic Tiger', a name ripped from the East Asian Tiger economies. Ireland was enjoying its moment in the spotlight, with Quinn epitomising the country's newfound confidence.

As Fintan O'Toole already said, he was seen as a 'wild card' that was 'full of aces'. Wild card. Everyone who knew him knew that Sean Quinn revelled in risk. He wasn't known to back horses, to gamble. But, for many years, he'd invested in the stock market. Colm Tóibín noticed as much when he met him back in 1986. Speaking in 2019, the former journalist recalled a conversation he had in Quinn's office, concerning the newspaper the quarryman was reading: 'He had one item on his desk that was going to actually be his future and he didn't know that and I didn't know that. But I did ask him about it. Because on his desk was the *Financial Times*. And this was the middle of nowhere. I mean, this was really, you know, I said to him, how do you get that *Financial Times*, I mean, where would you buy that? I have it sent out every day from Enniskillen, he said. I'm starting to look at stocks and shares. And there was a sense he was talking, you know, that he had this extra money coming in and he was going to have to invest it somewhere. And it didn't occur to me to say to him, if you don't do that it'll be much better for everybody, if you just don't get that paper anymore and look at it ever. I mean, there was a moment where it could have been said.'

The moment passed, however, and Quinn continued to play the markets. By the time he was setting up Quinn Direct, he was following the rise of what was known as the dotcom boom, which appeared as a result of the huge growth around the world in the use of the Internet. Tech was where all the smart money was going, shares in the emerging industry rising over 400 per cent in the five years following 1995. Unknown to everyone other than his broker, Quinn was buying up dotcom shares. Just like Ireland at the time, Sean Quinn believed that he couldn't lose, the only way was up. He'd bought the hype. Which meant that, while publicly he could do no wrong, Sean Quinn was secretly laying everything on the line.

7

Failing to Compute

In the early months of 1998, the people of the North of Ireland had little patience left for talk of hope or expectation of a brighter future despite the on-again off-again ceasefires of the previous four years and a peace process which had initially promised much but had become bogged down in seemingly never-ending political negotiations.

One day in March provided evidence of the continued viciousness of the conflict. Damien Trainor and Philip Allen were lifelong friends who lived in the Co. Armagh village of Poyntzpass. On the evening of Tuesday 3 March, Philip, a Protestant, invited Damien, a Catholic, to meet him in the Railway Bar, a pub that drew customers from both sides of the religious divide. He'd something he wanted to ask him. Over two pints of orange juice, Philip asked Damien to be best man at his wedding. Philip's brother, David, joined the pair. He later told how when he first heard someone come into the bar and shout 'get down, you bastards' he thought it was a prank. He turned to see Philip and Damien getting off their stools and onto the floor and, realising his error, crawled into a corner while two masked gunmen opened fire. Philip and Damien were critically injured and died on their way to hospital. Two loyalists later convicted of the murders laughed and smirked when they were sentenced.

On the same evening, in another border county, Sean Quinn was also enjoying a celebratory pint. Earlier that day, he'd posed for photographs in front of his new £60 million bottle factory alongside the permanent secretary of the North's department of economic development, Gerry Loughran. Dressed in suits, hard hats and holding bottles of various shapes, colours and sizes, Quinn and Loughran were enjoying the moment as the cameras captured them in front of the huge factory. It was one of the largest ever built on the island, spanning ten acres and 643,000 square feet. The highly respected civil servant knew this was just the kind of good-news announcement that could be viewed as being part of the so-called 'peace-dividend' for the North, a real-life example of how an end to conflict and a stable political environment could help grow the private sector and attract further inward investment – even if, in reality, it was just Quinn doing nothing more than he'd been doing for almost twenty-five years by reinvesting his profits, building world-class factories and providing much-needed employment in his border backyard. All against a backdrop of continued conflict.

Quinn's plant opening would have been a headline story any other day of the week, but not in the aftermath of a day that will always be associated with the murder of a bridegroom-to-be and his best man. The following day saw front pages covered with pictures of the scene outside the Railway Bar, and not Quinn's bottle factory.

Still, a loss of headlines mattered little. In truth, the conflict had not held Quinn back in any way: if anything, he had risen above it, was untouched by it despite it overshadowing virtually every aspect of life in the North.

Despite the pessimism found throughout the North, the fact was that new hope and dramatic political change were just weeks away. The month after Quinn opened the bottle plant, the Good Friday Agreement was signed. It would be too late for Philip Allen and Damien Trainor – and the other 3,500-plus victims of the Troubles – but it would cement the peace process and end the conflict.

***

During this period Quinn did something that must have irked Gerry Loughran and his colleagues, particularly after they had just provided him with such a generous grant. He began the process of moving his cement business across the border.

Less than ten years since he had opened the cement factory, he was planning on replacing it with a new state-of-the-art IR£70m plant north of Ballyconnell, capable of doubling his output to one million tonnes per year. 'There were good margins in cement,' said Quinn. 'It might well be the only cement factory in the world that was ever closed after ten years. [No one would build a] whole new factory. In most cases, they would just do a reconstruction.'

Cavan County Council had already granted planning permission for the eighty-six-acre site, which was just half a mile south from the original factory. Quinn was making it clear to anyone who asked why he was making the move. 'We have a cement factory in Derrylin, Co. Fermanagh, but we are moving south to take advantage of the corporation tax,' he was quoted as saying in *The Sunday Business Post*.

When building the glass plant, he'd made the calculation that the IDB grant was more attractive than the corporation tax rate: this time, however, he decided that the other option was preferable. At the time, corporation tax had dropped to 10 per cent in the Republic compared with 31 per cent in the North.

The decision to build another cement factory while simultaneously overseeing a major investment in a new business, i.e. glass bottling, was typically instinctive. Similarly, making his plans public just as he opened the bottle plant was more than coincidental. Quinn was making a point. He was captain of his own ship and while he was genuinely thankful for the IDB support with the glass-bottling plant, the authorities should not take it for granted that he was going to continue building his manufacturing business inside the UK, even with a peace agreement in place.

Not that his intended move south was straightforward. After being granted planning permission by Cavan County Council, an appeal was lodged with An Bord Pleanála, the planning board, by a man called M. J. Brady, a local farmer, who had the support of the Northern Fisheries Board and environmental campaigners Earthwatch. He raised several objections on grounds of environmental, traffic and visual impact. It was an audacious move by a local to throw himself in front of Quinn's plans, one he had to know wouldn't go down well with the quarryman, or in his own community.

Despite the appeal, Quinn simply ignored, or indeed dismissed, any risk to his plans, and began work on the site. This refusal to accept the reality of the situation didn't last long, however, as six weeks after he opened the bottle factory he was ordered to stop work on the new site by Cavan County Council. The *Irish Independent* reported: 'Mr Quinn last night told the *Irish Independent* the work was merely to prepare the 86-acre site for construction. Work on site had now stopped.' Quinn also told the paper that the factory would produce a million tonnes of cement a year and would create 200 jobs by the end of 1999, if it got the green light from An Bord Pleanála. He said all this without pointing out, of course, that at least 130 of the jobs were not new, but were a result of him transferring the cement factory from the North.

Quinn was defiant, telling the paper that there was huge support in the area for the new factory. 'There are no houses within 500 metres of it. It will be a modern factory with very high standards and we have had extensive discussions with the Environmental Protection Agency,' he said, adding that the work already undertaken at the site 'was just earth moving, hedge cutting and drain repairs. It is very difficult not to do work when it is your own farm,' he pointed out, alluding to the fact that he already owned the land that was to be developed.

Quarrymen were well used to environmentalists objecting to their plans; it came with the territory. But during the course of 1998, while he faced local opposition to his new factory from his own backyard, Quinn was himself playing the role of an objector, albeit secretly and surreptitiously and without any motivational regard for the environment. Instead it was all due to his insatiable greed.

***

Kinnegad, Co. Westmeath, is 100 km south of Ballyconnell. It's a small commuter town, an hour from the centre of Dublin, with fewer than 3,000 inhabitants. But as Quinn was going through his own trying planning process, the Belfast businessman Kevin Lagan was having issues with his plans for a new cement factory at Killaskillen in the townland of Ballinabrackey, south of Kinnegad.

Lagan, perhaps encouraged by Quinn's success in breaking CRH's monopoly, had announced his intentions to spend IR£40m on the plant and create 200 jobs. But he faced some strong opposition from residents concerned about the impact on the environment, 'in particular on their water supplies, the quality of the local river water and the flora and fauna in the vicinity', according to *The Irish Times*. It was reported that there were also concerns about noise pollution and that the agricultural heritage of the area could be lost. Kevin Lagan disputed these claims, telling the newspaper they were 'totally inaccurate and exaggerated'.

The paper reported that Lagan had spent 'more than a year preparing the plans for the project with a wide range of independent experts to ensure it was developed with the highest environmental standards'. There had also been extensive consultation with local residents and their public representatives, it added, and this open-door policy would be maintained through the planning and subsequent construction phase. It said the company had also made various consultants available to local people, and it was disappointing that the Ballinabrackey Residents' Action Group – who were providing the 'strong opposition' – had not taken the opportunity to have its concerns discussed with those experts but chose instead to issue a 'very inaccurate' statement to the media. In its own statement, Lagan Cement Ltd said that more than 500 local residents had visited the site and had been 'impressed by the very high standards the company is committed to observing and also by the fact that the project will provide 300 jobs during the two-year construction phase and 200 jobs thereafter', reported *The Irish Times*.

Kevin Lagan may have wondered why, given all the outreach and engagement with the local community, there was still such continued and significant opposition to his factory. He may have found a clue in a somewhat obscure ruling by a very specialised court two years previously.

The Restrictive Practices Court is a UK court set up under the Restrictive Trade Practices Acts to judge whether restrictive trading agreements were in the public interest. By 1998 it had been abolished and replaced by the Competition Commission. The records of the cases it ruled on are held by the British National Archives. However, a search for the case referenced as J154/649 brings up a notice that the files relating to the action are closed until January 2081, eighty-five years after it was heard. The title of the case is the rather innocuous: 'Pre-stressed and reinforced concrete flooring in Northern Ireland'. Very little is known about the hearings, and the court was obviously intent on keeping it that way. A Freedom of Information request failed to get any further information. But what is known is that in the files is the evidence – and a subsequent guilty verdict – that Sean Quinn colluded with his once most vicious enemy, Cement Roadstone Holdings, to fix the price of cement in the North from 1985 to 1992.

Due to the nature of the proceedings, there was little reported about it in the press. However, *The Irish Times* was tipped off about the verdict and reported in March 1996 that 'The State's two biggest cement companies, the Sean Quinn Group and CRH, have been found to be among five companies [that] operated a price-fixing agreement in the Northern Ireland market between 1985 and 1992. An action in the British Restrictive Practices Court, which made orders against five concrete flooring companies in Northern Ireland, has shown that CRH subsidiary, Breton Precast, and the Sean Quinn Group were party to an agreement to fix product price. Other Northern companies involved in the price fixing cartel were, Foylespan Floors of Limavady, William A Lees (Concrete) of Magherafelt, and Spandeck of Portadown.'

The case had been taken by the Office of Fair Trading in the UK, which had conducted an investigation into the pre-stressed and reinforced-concrete flooring business. *The Irish Times* reported that an order was made against Quinn and CRH, along with the others, who had not appeared in court to offer their defence. Sean Quinn was found guilty of price fixing, being part of a cartel that was ripping off consumers.

At the time, the suspicions among his competitors had been rife that after his 'to the death' battle with CRH, Sean Quinn had come to a secret deal that ensured there wouldn't be a price war over the cost of a bag of cement, which, of course, suited both sides. *The Sunday Business Post*, in a profile of Quinn, in which he had given them an interview, speculated on what may have been the business case for the agreement: 'Quinn was only too aware that he could not beat a major multinational in a prolonged price war. His prices settled at a few percentage points below those of CRH. As a result, [they settled on] prices designed to give above-average margins to union-bound CRH, [and] gave super profits and a rapid pay-off of borrowings to Quinn's low-cost plant.'

No one was aware of the apparently cosy relationship he had developed with CRH. In public they were at war, while behind the scenes they were working together for their mutual financial benefit, to the detriment of their customers. Quinn was obviously prepared to go to any length to build his business.

In the same *Sunday Business Post* article, the reporter Des Crowley pointed out that 'CRH's prices have had to remain static since Quinn opened. This may have been to discourage new entrants. If that was the tactic, however, it failed.' The fact was that by 1998 new cement factories were being planned across the country, including Kevin Lagan's in Co. Westmeath.

Lagan was not just taking on CRH, but was now taking on Quinn too.

The border quarryman, about to build his own new factory, had already learned from the experts in subterfuge and industrial espionage and wasn't about to see Lagan open up 100 km down the road without a fight. Lagan may have thought that the opposition to his cement factory at Killaskillen was coming from the environmentalists. In fact, it was being fuelled by none other than Sean Quinn himself.

This was despite the fact that the two men had done business together. Lagan had supplied Quinn with cement he'd imported from Germany, before the quarryman had built his first factory. However, even then, there had been tension between them. At one point Lagan had increased his prices and Quinn initially refused to pay, but later backed down, sending a snide note to Lagan with a cheque stating 'I hope it does you good.' In 1984, when Lagan had bought a Co. Cavan brick factory, Quinn had asked him 'how did you find out about that business? Why did they not approach me, if they wanted to sell?' Lagan remembered Quinn's shock that a Belfast businessman could buy a border business from under his nose. He'd taken it personally.

Marie Goonery, who lived opposite the site for the new Lagan plant in Co. Westmeath, led the campaign against it. She placed advertisements in national newspapers stating her opposition to the plans and appealing for donations to help fund her campaign. She opposed the plans when they were first being considered by Meath County Council but when planning permission was granted, she led a case to the High Court in Dublin where the campaign was represented by the highly respected and expensive Senior Counsel, Michael Collins.

By going to court, however, Marie Goonery and her campaign had been opened up to the process of discovery, in which both sides provide documentation supporting their case. Critically, they also have to provide any documents that they may not normally wish to hand over but which may have information critical to the opposing team. So when the court sought evidence of how Marie Goonery was financing her expensive opposition, she was forced to provide documentation detailing how she had been sent almost €40,000 in cheques from three Dublin pubs in support of her cause.

They were all Sean Quinn's. Ms Goonery only realised this key fact when it was pointed out by lawyers for Kevin Lagan.

Quinn's backroom deal with CRH had already been discovered and now he was found to be using the kind of tactics that he'd once been the victim of himself. But if Kevin Lagan expected remorse, he wasn't going to get it from Quinn. Instead, Quinn opted for the tactic of attack as the best form of defence.

He upped the ante by saying that his own company would now enter the legal fray and take its own case against Lagan's new plant to the High Court. He told *The Irish Times* that he'd 'very good reasons' for objecting and promised these would be revealed in the weeks and months ahead. They never were.

Quinn Cement went to the High Court with an application for an injunction restraining An Bord Pleanála from deciding on an appeal against the Lagan plant. *The Irish Times* reported the judge, Mr Justice Quirke, stating that Quinn had not come to court with 'clean hands' and was involved in 'doubtful practices' in funding the protest group through the 'surreptitious' payments. Quinn appeared, said the judge, to be pursuing a financial and competitive interest rather than a planning one.

Lagan launched a counteraction against Quinn, applying to have his case dismissed on the grounds that it was vexatious and an abuse of process of the courts. The court agreed. In a ten-page ruling in October 2000, the judge said that Sean Quinn had mounted 'a cynical, calculated and unscrupulous' action against a business rival which it sees as 'formidable business competitor'. In a damning judgment for Quinn, it went on: 'I am quite satisfied that the sole purpose of the proceedings is to inflict damage upon its competitor [Lagan] and I am satisfied that that is an improper purpose for the commencement of proceedings and an improper use of the process of the courts.'

After the hearing, Quinn said he'd only decided to take the action after 'an issue was made of our funding the other party. We decided to do it ourselves,' as he told *The Irish Times*. He also claimed there had been a history of disputes between him and Kevin Lagan. 'We have never objected to planning permission before in our lives. Kevin Lagan has done lots of things to me he should not be proud of. This is the first thing I've done to him that I am not proud of.'

Kevin Lagan was bemused by this comment, telling *The Irish Times* it wasn't the first time Quinn alleged that his company had behaved badly. 'He has failed to substantiate these comments whatsoever. There is no basis to them. I think he is just trying to muddy the waters.' After the case was over, Quinn approached Lagan in an attempt to agree a deal on the costs of the legal action, but the Belfast businessman wasn't interested. Quinn, suffering from such a high-profile loss, was still trying to get something out of it, something to show for such a public humiliation.

Despite the objections and legal action, An Bord Pleanála would eventually grant Kevin Lagan the permission to build his factory, which, when it went live in 2002, began producing 450,000 tonnes of cement per annum, around the same quantity as Quinn's first plant.

In an interview with the author in November 2021, Quinn refused to accept he'd adopted the same tactics CRH had deployed against him: 'We had difficulties with CRH. [They] didn't want to see us building a cement factory and they made various moves to stop it. But look, at the end of the day, CRH are a brilliant company. I have nothing against CRH now. Hopefully CRH hasn't anything against me. It was all business at the time. We felt at the time it was a bit under the belt, but then I suppose Kevin Lagan felt that I was a bit under the belt objecting to him. I suppose I played a bit of football and you get a box on the mouth or you give one or get one and you have to get on with life, there is no point in crying about it, you just get on and move on. And I think in fairness to Kevin he was happy to do that as well.' Lagan did move on, building a hugely successful business, but this wasn't going to be his last, or worst, experience of dealing with Quinn's business.

The dispute highlighted the duality in Sean Quinn's personality. Up until then, the media had largely stuck to the depiction of him as being the unschooled, soft-spoken, border quarryman who had struck lucky and was revered in his local community. Now he was being seen for the first time as a ruthless industrialist, who was only interested in winning, whatever the cost.

Furthermore, could the decision to opt to build his old new cement factory south of the border now be seen in a new light? Was he really moving south just for the corporation tax, or was there another reason? After all, Quinn had already benefited from significant British grant support for his bottle factory. He was no longer persona non grata among the decision-making civil servants in Belfast. Now, with peace in the air, they wanted to support business along the border, no matter the politics of the businessmen. So why did he not take the Queen's shilling for the new cement plant?

Might it have had something to do with the fact that Fianna Fáil were in power with a new Taoiseach, Bertie Ahern, who, along with British Prime Minister Tony Blair had led the negotiations that brought about the Good Friday Agreement? Ahern hadn't adopted all of the bad habits of his predecessor, Charles Haughey, but he would prove to be very attuned to the needs of the businesses at the heart of the Celtic Tiger economy and the unheralded wealth they were bringing to the country. Quinn and Ahern even became friends during this period, so much so that during the 2002 election campaign Bertie Ahern hitched a ride in Quinn's helicopter to campaign in Donegal. And when Quinn opened new insurance offices in Blanchardstown, Dublin – an 11-storey glass-fronted office block – Ahern cut the ribbon.

In the pictures at the opening of the bottling plant, Quinn was almost dressing like Bertie Ahern: suited and booted in a smart pinstripe double-breasted suit, white shirt and tie. He was looking more and more like the businessman who spent his days in high-level boardroom meetings and offices studying spreadsheets than someone who would be shaking off the dust from a trip around a quarry. When Colm Tóibín met him in 1986, he'd described him as 'dark, good-looking, gruff man in his late thirties, wearing an old grey pullover'. By the late 1990s, however, Quinn realised that he had to dress to impress; an old grey pullover wasn't going to cut it in the circles in which he was mixing. Nor was it any longer the image he wished to project. He was dressing in the uniform of the male politician, banker or businessman, and he was now acting like one too.

***

Quinn Direct wasn't like any of the quarryman's other companies. He didn't need to get his hands dirty for a start. It was a smart-suit kind of business. By 1999 the turnover at Quinn Direct was IR£60m, up from IR£19m in 1997, with a profit of IR£8m and a market share of 1.4 per cent – still some way off the point where it would become viable.

However, those profits still had to be reinvested, as insurance companies do, as well as the money they take from their clients and their premiums. In setting up the company, Quinn had appointed himself as its fund manager, the person who would decide where these investments would be made. And perhaps it should come as no surprise that he decided to invest in a company that was connected to the quarry industry, as well as being Irish, rural and an international success.

Powerscreen International – or Ulster Plant, as it was first known – was founded in Co. Tyrone in 1966. Its niche was the production of mobile screening or, in simpler terms, it manufactured machinery that could allow for work at the quarry face at a time when businesses like Quinn's were having to first quarry stone and then move it to machines to be processed, which was time-consuming and costly.

Ulster Plant began exporting in 1969 and was renamed Powerscreen the following decade, producing machines for the quarry, mining and construction industries. By the mid-1990s, it was one of Northern Ireland's few blue-chip companies with a valuation of over £300m. It had been floated on the London and Dublin stock exchanges, and had been doing well before being engulfed in a storm that saw its share price plummet. In January 1998 its shares were trading at 550p sterling. Then a $50m hole was discovered in the accounts of one of its subsidiaries, Matbro. After the shock announcement that because of Matbro it would no longer be posting a £50m profit as previously forecast, but instead returning a pre-tax loss of £10m, the share price halved to 254p. *The Irish Times* reported that Powerscreen was now a ripe target. 'Analysts said that Powerscreen, once the star of the engineering industry could now become a takeover target. Possible bidders include Caterpillar and Ingersoll Rand, the giant US group.'

On the border, Quinn was watching the situation develop and, within months, had made his move, using Quinn Direct money to take a 6 per cent stake in the company, paying just 80p per share. Quinn knew Powerscreen and believed he understood their business well: so much so that he was willing to lay down £4.5m of Quinn Direct's money. Not for the last time in gambling on the markets, Quinn believed that the share price would come back up.

His instinct paid off in June 1999 when Powerscreen was bought out by the American Terex Corporation for almost $300m. Quinn Direct made a £6.5m profit on the investment in just eight months, although Sean Quinn may have seen it as a personal return, so blurred were the lines.

Not everything in Quinn's business was going so well, however. As he looked forward to the new millennium, Quinn suffered a significant loss when his chief executive officer, David Mackey, resigned. Mackey had been at Quinn's side for ten years but decided now was the time to set up his own property development company. The *Irish Independent* reported Mackey as saying 'there was no falling out and [he] stressed it was an amicable departure from his executive role. He added that he had been very well treated by Mr Quinn.'

Mackey would come back to support Quinn in his hour of need, but at the time his decision to leave was a major blow, only cushioned by the fact that two young executives had gained Quinn's faith and trust. Kevin Lunney was growing in confidence at Quinn Direct, and Liam McCaffrey, who had been appointed finance controller in 1996, was so respected that he was immediately appointed as successor to David Mackey. Lunney and McCaffrey were now Quinn's most trusted executives. Quinn had already been in business for a quarter of a century, but he was now entering a new phase with two young, hungry and ambitious lieutenants by his side. It wouldn't be long before their boss tested them as he once again followed his instincts in the markets.

***

With the return on his Powerscreen investment in his back pocket, Quinn began to focus more on technology and telecoms shares. At the end of the 1990s, the world was still coming to terms with the paradigm shift caused by the World Wide Web. New portal sites such as Yahoo were at the cutting edge of a global revolution, fuelling a new Wild West for investors. The rules of business were being torn up, according to the cheerleading experts. A perfect storm of low interest rates, availability of cheap finance and no shortage of ideas that were destined to go global caused investors to pile into the so-called 'dotcom boom'. As 1999 turned to 2000, and without the predicted millennial meltdown, investors dumped slower-growing stocks for dotcom stocks, which only fuelled the frenzy. The Nasdaq composite index of technology companies, a key market indicator, rose by a record-breaking 88 per cent in 1999 and peaked in March 2000.

But the following month it began to fall and, once it did, it couldn't stop. According to one analyst, in just fifty-one days in the spring of 2000, £1,700bn was wiped off technology stocks. Amazon founder Jeff Bezos saw his company lose £1bn in a single day. At the time, no one could really put their finger on what had caused the dotcom bubble to burst, although some pointed to a book by Yale professor Robert Shiller, called *Irrational Exuberance*, which was published as the market peaked. Shiller argued that the dotcom boom was 'a speculative bubble and was not grounded in sensible economic fundamentals'.

Sean Quinn obviously didn't read it. If he had, he wouldn't have reached the conclusion that he did. He bet Quinn Direct's money on a recovery. By the end of 2000, almost 37 per cent of Quinn Direct's investments were in tech at a time when the insurance industry was exposed at an average of 22 per cent. It was a very costly decision. The dotcom bubble *had* burst.

Quinn Direct drew back and counted its losses. And, as they might say in Cavan, they were brutal. The company had lost over IR£15m in the dotcom rollercoaster ride. Quinn had quietly taken the insurance company to the edge.

When the company did have to come clean about the extent of its losses, Quinn took the blame. In an interview with Simon Carswell, in *The Sunday Business Post*, he said the investments had been a bad decision. 'I myself would be the person who puts their hands up and says we got involved in some stocks we shouldn't have got involved in. We didn't have any technology stocks at the beginning of 2000. We decided three or four years ago that we should not get involved in technology stocks. But after the market corrected by about 30 per cent, I felt it was an opportunity to get into technology. But we paid a heavy price for that decision,' he said.

On top of the catastrophic losses in the market, Quinn Direct had an underwriting loss of almost IR£23m, bringing its losses to IR£38.5 for the first year of the new millennium. In one year, the company had wiped out all of its profits since it was first established, raising fundamental questions about its future.

'Quinn Direct is not in trouble,' Quinn told Simon Carswell, going on to make a statement that would come back to haunt him. 'The only time Quinn Direct will be in trouble is when Seán Quinn is in trouble.'

And Seán Quinn is in no trouble.' It was a sentiment that spoke to the quarryman's inability to see the boundaries between himself, the companies and a regulated insurance firm. They were all one, as far as he was concerned. It was all the same pot. It was a very dangerous mindset.

For his lieutenants, Kevin Lunney and Liam McCaffrey, the dotcom disaster was an eye-opener on Quinn's behaviour. 'Everything went great until the dotcom bubble in 2001,' said an executive from the time. 'Sean had ploughed everything into it.'

Quinn had to invest IR£55m into the insurance company just to keep it afloat, as well as putting IR£16m into its reserves. Over the first three years of business, Quinn Direct had not held enough capital in reserve – the amount of money an insurance company needs to have access to, so as to ensure it can meet all legitimate claims by its policyholders – and now Quinn had been forced to correct the imbalance.

At the time, the insurance industry in Ireland was regulated by the Department of Enterprise, Trade and Investment and the minister was Mary Harney of the Progressive Democrats, who were Fianna Fáil's junior coalition partners in government. At one point, Quinn and McCaffrey were called to a meeting with the regulator in Dublin. Quinn had no idea of what was being considered by the department, which was actively working behind the scenes to put Quinn Direct into administration and was so concerned about his actions that it had called in accounting firm Ernst & Young, who were already set up in the same building as the meeting and were ready to move once given the green light. When Quinn woke up to the seriousness of the situation, he made a phone call and left abruptly, he said, to meet with a very senior member of government. Within hours, the threat of administration was withdrawn and Quinn returned to the border licking his wounds yet still in control of his company.

But the dotcom fiasco had come at a cost. Quinn was forced by the regulator to fire himself as Quinn Direct's fund manager and, instead, appoint a fellow Fermanagh man and former secretary general of the Department of Finance in Dublin, Paddy Mullarkey, to take on the role, with the help of John O'Hanlon, a former chief executive of Allianz Insurance. The appointment of Mullarkey, who had left the Department of Finance in 1999, having been one of the top two civil servants in the Irish State, was a very public indication that Quinn had been left with no option but to resign. Quinn had little time for civil servants and a former secretary general would never have been his first choice for such an important position – indeed, one that Quinn thought he was best suited for. But it was a very Irish solution. Quinn suffered no real public humiliation, and the department now had a trusted hand moved into a position to help steady the ship and protect the policyholders. 'It was an important lesson for [Quinn] that he could not be involved in everything,' a company source was quoted as saying at the time.

But had Quinn actually learnt anything from the crisis? Rather, did he now travel in the firm belief that a Dublin government would never put his lights out, no matter how much trouble he got himself into?

***

While the turmoil inside Quinn Direct played out in the background, Quinn was doing what he did best: taking risks and building his business.

In the first days of 2000 he had launched Quinn Life, to sell personal-investment pensions and life-assurance products. Making the announcement in Dublin, it was the first time he was pictured with Kevin Lunney by his side. It was no surprise that Quinn was introducing a business model not seen in Ireland before. Quinn Life would have no branches and would not use brokers or salespeople. They would do all their business over the telephone, just as companies such as Virgin Direct were already doing in Britain.

Quinn allowed Kevin Lunney to sell the new venture. 'We examined the way business has been done in Ireland and have streamlined it to remove the jargon and simplify products, making them a lot cheaper for consumers and deliver them over the phone direct to our customers,'

Lunney said, who was quoted in *The Irish Times*, having been introduced at the press conference as the Director of Financial Services at the Quinn Group. They also made a point of talking up the success of Quinn Direct at the briefing, stating that it had more than 100,000 policyholders, was providing 10,000 quotations a week, and that over 200 people were now employed by the company.

For Fintan O'Toole, it was the insurance business that really made Quinn into a public figure south of the border. 'The idea that this guy sort of built his own empire, when he begins to come into public consciousness in the South, it's really through the insurance company. Oh, you know he's a really successful figure who's done all this great stuff. And actually if you want to move into insurance it's a great image to have, because, you know, what's insurance about but trust? So which kind of figure were you more likely to trust? Were you more likely to trust the nice man up on the border who makes things that you can understand, you know, makes concrete blocks and cement? He can do insurance, we trust him; he seems like a very nice, ordinary man. Or would you trust one of these kind of flamboyant, wheeler-dealer property developers? So I think, ironically, Quinn was probably a more trusted figure in terms of public image at that period than any of the other wealthy people in Ireland.'

This trust existed despite his mishandling of the shares. When the dust settled on the dotcom fiasco, Sean Quinn was in a different state of mind. Or so it appeared. Analysts and advisors told him that the business had now grown so big that he simply couldn't be involved in everyday decision-making. His instinct was to micromanage and he enjoyed having the element of surprise; of his managers not knowing when they would turn around to find him at their shoulder. It kept them on their toes, he thought. But now, in the aftermath of his misadventure in dotcom shares, those he trusted were, for the first time, advising him to seriously consider what he actually wanted to do with the business.

Retaining it in the control of the family wasn't his only option, they told him. And for a time, Quinn began to openly discuss his thoughts on the future shape of the Quinn Group. He also proved that he was prepared to sell, rather than following his usual strategy of holding and building, when he put three of the eleven pubs the company owned in Dublin up for sale – The Coal Porter and The Station in Rathmines and The Bird's Nest in Glasnevin, valued at over IR£8m – hoping to capitalise on the high prices bars were now demanding. But bars were one thing, and while IR£8m was, and is, a lot of money, it barely matched a day's turnover for the company. The question remained: could he, if required, adopt the same attitude with his prized assets: the cement or glass business or, indeed, the insurance company?

He was telling those around him that he was open-minded in the wake of the dotcom debacle. And soon he began to tell the media of a possible change in ownership structures at the Quinn Group. First, there were rumours that he was planning a public flotation. He explained his thinking to Simon Carswell in *The Sunday Business Post*: 'Quinn is turning his attention to reducing his family's interest in his group to less than fifty per cent over the next four to seven years,' reported Carswell, saying it wasn't because of Quinn Direct's difficulties. Instead, Quinn told him it was for more personal, family reasons. 'We have seen too many businesses where families have fallen out and have had problems from time to time. I am not going to mention names. But those companies have had huge success over 20, 30 or 40 years and all of a sudden a row started. With over 2000 employees it's important that we make the right decisions and get a good board of directors in place, so that the company is not dependent on family rows. The Quinns don't have a divine right to make decisions on the company over the next few years, because the Quinns wouldn't have the company if it wasn't for the support that we got from our staff. It's important that we make the right decisions, so that when Seán Quinn is dead and gone, the group survives and the 2000 jobs we created are sustained.'

Quinn also told Carswell that he was now seeking 'trade partners' for the business and that he'd been approached by a merchant bank, Dresdner, to ask if he would be interested in releasing equity in the group. 'He said that was the group's long-term aim,' wrote Carswell. Soon after, perhaps on the back of this interview, French construction group Lafarge, made an offer for the cement business, but it was rejected out of hand by Quinn.

What no one knew, apart from those closest to him, was that all the talk about flotations and selling was really about one thing: saving the insurance company. At the time, he believed that he might have to do something drastic to protect it. 'He was constructively trying to find a solution,' said one of his advisors. 'He was prepared to sell one part of the business to save another.'

Even talking about it in public had the benefit of reassuring new friends, such as the Taoiseach and the officials at the Department of Enterprise, Trade and Investment who, he may have felt, now had him on their radar, although he knew they were never going to revoke his licence. 'Did he understand insurance? Regulation? He didn't want to understand it,' said the advisor. 'He thought he was too big to fail. He got away with it that time.'

The fact that the authorities in Dublin had no appetite for taking on Quinn was what really saved his skin. But what was going to ensure he never had to contemplate any change in ownership had nothing to do with Taoisigh, regulators, or Quinn's own business strategies, and all to do with an attack on the United States being planned in the Safed Koh mountain range of eastern Afghanistan by a relatively unknown terrorist leader called Osama Bin Laden. It would cost the lives of hundreds of thousands of innocents and cause devastation in America, Afghanistan and Iraq.

But it would save Sean Quinn.

8

'Fuck It, Let's Get a Jet'

The people of south Fermanagh were used to helicopters in the skies above them and could tell the difference between a Wessex and a Lynx – both used by the British military to ferry troops and supplies around the various border bases – just by the sound of their engines. By the summer of 2001, however, a distinctly different type of aircraft appeared out of the clouds over the border area. Sean Quinn had bought himself an Agusta A109E helicopter.

He'd already had a helipad built years earlier at the Slieve Russell Hotel. At the time, he may have been thinking it would be for those staying at the hotel. Now, however, he'd joined the growing ranks of Irish businessmen whose travel mode of choice was a twin-engined helicopter. Quinn had paid over IR£2m for the Agusta, which he'd decked out in blue and added the serial number EI-SQG. With a range of over 550 miles, or 1,000 km, it could take him the length and breadth of Ireland and across the Irish Sea to England.

Sean Quinn was on the ground, in his office at the company head-quarters, however, when news of what was initially thought to be a major air crash filtered through in September of the same year. He huddled with his executive colleagues around a television in the boardroom as the true scale of 9/11 began to dawn on the world. Almost 3,000 people lost their lives on a day that changed the world.

Like the rest of the country, Quinn was stunned. In the days and weeks that followed, he began to consider the potential cost to his business, particularly Quinn Direct, as, in the immediate aftermath, airlines and insurance companies were the worst hit. However, much to Quinn's relief, within months the stock markets and economies around the world miraculously bounced back. Yet insurance costs remained high.

It was hard to explain to a Co. Leitrim householder why 9/11 caused their home insurance to go through the roof but, basically, if they took out a policy with Quinn Direct, the company offset the risk of a huge claim by purchasing a reinsurance policy, which covers every house insurance policy it sells. The reinsurance company then has billions of dollars of risk from around the world and so it too mitigates its risk by purchasing what's called 'retrocession cover', which is at the very top of the insurance tree. So, in reality, the policy bought through Quinn Direct is merely part of a global insurance chain, and when the claims for 9/11 mounted to over $70 billion, the retrocessionary companies, worried about further terrorist attacks and the potential for further claims in a new, destabilised world economy, set their prices high, which caused a waterfall effect through the system right down to Quinn's customers, who suddenly had to pay significantly more for their policies. And that not only saved Sean Quinn, it made him a fortune.

'9/11 saved Quinn,' said a very close colleague at the time, 'it's as simple as that.' On the day the planes hit the World Trade Center, 'Sean Quinn had already given HSBC bank a mandate to sell the company after the dotcom share debacle,' said the colleague. But when he realised that Quinn Direct was going to be an unexpected beneficiary of Osama Bin Laden's holy war on America, Quinn was able to ride out the crisis – and indeed ultimately thrive from it.

Despite this, he continued to talk about stepping back from the company in some shape or form. He was now in his mid-fifties, after all. But the question remained: could he really ever relinquish control?

***

With Ireland all but conquered, he set his sights more on the UK. The Irish punt disappeared in early 2002 when the country joined the single European currency, the euro. But Quinn's profits were looking good in any currency. In 2002–3, the Quinn Group made €150m profit on a turnover of €650m, doubling its profit levels from the previous year. Quinn Direct increased its profits by an incredible 40 per cent in the first six months of 2003, making a total underwriting profit of €72m for the year alongside over €50m in returns on the company's investments – a 180-degree turnaround from the losses of just a couple of years before. The dotcom crisis was now little more than a distant blip in the rear-view mirror.

Things were going well on the glass front, too, when his sole Irish competitor, Ardagh, threw in the towel by announcing it was closing its factory in Ringsend, with the loss of 375 jobs. Despite operating at the site since 1871, the entry of Quinn's new state-of-the-art glass plant into the domestic scene had resulted in Ardagh's profits plummeting from €8.9m in 2000 to €2.4m the following year. Despite reducing its prices, Ardagh had to ultimately admit that the factory was unsustainable. Quinn was now the sole domestic manufacturer of glass on the island of Ireland.

With Ireland all but conquered, he set his sights more on the UK during this decade. He met the news of Ardagh's demise with the audacious plan to build the biggest glass factory in Europe on the banks of the River Mersey in the north of England. Thirty years before, Quinn had revolutionised quarrying along the border by sinking wells, which meant he would not incur the expense of bringing gravel to water for it to be washed. On the 200-acre site of the former Ince Power Station in Cheshire, he was going to do something similar. Instead of supplying the bottles to the drinks industry to fill with whatever liquid they wanted, his clients would be able to fill their bottles at his plant. With British government grants of almost £5m, Quinn initially planned to invest £200m; however, after being granted permission for a factory that would have eight machine lines and three filling lines, he immediately sought to increase the size of the plant by 25 per cent. Once opened, the plant would have a capacity of 1.2 billion glass containers a year in a UK market with demand of around 7 billion per annum.

None of this would happen without a fight, of course, and in the opposite corner to Quinn was an old adversary, The Cooler. Paul Coulson may have had to withdraw from Ireland, but he was going to stand firm behind his Ardagh-owned Rockware company, which had an annual turnover of £180m, while adding the third-largest glass producer in the UK, Redfearn, to bolster his defences. And those defences certainly needed bolstering, given the external concern for the company. 'Naturally, the incumbent feels something of a threat,' reported *The Irish Times*, adding: 'And just in case it doesn't, there is no shortage of comment around to remind everybody of the changing face of the marketplace. In the last month alone, two international ratings agencies have raised the spectre of Quinn when voicing concerns about Ardagh's credit ratings. The most recent pronouncement – from Standard & Poor's – brought a reduction in the glass-maker's ratings and a warning about the possible loss of contracts to Quinn Glass in the short to medium term. The problem, said the analysts, is one of overcapacity at a time where costs are rising. Margins are getting squeezed, particularly because of higher gas prices. And in the background, customers are highly concentrated, with two-thirds of Ardagh's sales made to its top ten customers. It is, therefore, perhaps natural that Ardagh has not offered Quinn that traditional Irish welcome to England,' wrote reporter Una McCaffrey.

In a letter to shareholders, reported by *The Irish Times*, The Cooler warned of Quinn's impact on the UK market. 'It is believed that, at full production, the plant will be capable of producing the equivalent of circa 20 per cent of UK market demand. Clearly, the introduction of this new capacity will be very disruptive in the market and your board is examining strategies to minimise the impact of the threat posed.'

The battle intensified when Quinn made the somewhat impertinent offer to buy Ardagh's glass companies, but Coulson held firm, having secured backing from Anglo Irish Bank.

Eventually, Quinn got the Cheshire plant up on its feet, opening up twelve production lines and five filling lines capable of filling 1,000 bottles of beer every minute. Officially, he had no planning permission for a plant of that scale and so Coulson reverted to the courts in an attempt to have it torn down.

One online trade magazine, letsrecycle.com, reported on the battle of the glass giants. 'Neil King QC, for Quinn, told Judge David Mole QC that the benefits of the plant go beyond the boundaries of its locale, standing out as a success story in a period of economic gloom. The factory is good for the UK economy as a whole. It is the cleanest glass production factory in the UK in terms of air emissions,' he told the court, in response to Ardagh's plea that construction had also gone ahead without an Environmental Impact Assessment (EIA), as required by EU law. 'Ian Pearson MP, the Economic Secretary to the Treasury, is supportive of the development,' Mr King added, urging the judge to find that levelling the factory would be a 'disproportionate' step. The report added, 'Mr Robert McCracken QC, for Ardagh, argued that planners were now legally obliged to stop the factory from operating and issue an enforcement notice requiring its demolition. The court has heard that, when a four-year time limit expires later this year, the Quinn plant will effectively become a fait accompli and "immune" to enforcement action by the councils.'

Ultimately, the court sided with Quinn and threw out Ardagh's case. Quinn Glass director Adrian Curry was quoted by letsrecycle.com as saying the firm was delighted with the decision. 'It was an experienced and robust court and I'm glad they had no difficulty getting it right,' he said.

The Cooler and Quinn had fought it out and there was little doubt who had come out on top (even if Ardagh would go on to even greater success, owning dozens of glass and metal production facilities around the world). Sean Quinn had taken on their monopoly in Ireland and their market position in the UK and had changed the shape of the industry while he was at it.

Reflecting on the glass business in an interview in 2018, Sean Quinn was clear in where it stood in terms of the successful companies that he'd established. 'I suppose building the two best glass factories in the world, which I believe they are, I've got tremendous pride in that, because if you look at what's happening today, the plastic industry is in a wee bit of trouble. And it's not flavour of the week to be producing plastic, drinking from plastic or eating from plastic cups or whatever the case might be. But glass is getting more and more popular all the time. And we were making billions of bottles. The companies that I built are making billions and billions of profits, and hundreds of millions of profits for the new owners. I built them. I took great pride in building them. The use of the sand, which is used in making glass, is an inherent product. It can be reused. It's very comfortable for the environment. And I think in the long term over a twenty-, thirty-, fifty-year period, that has to be the greatest achievement I have had. It's the only factory in Ireland that's producing glass. And the one in England is the only one in England that's producing and filling glass. Some of the filling lines are filling at eleven hundred bottles per minute. Extraordinary stuff. And they're filling maybe 200 different products. So, I suppose, that might be my biggest achievement,' he repeats.

But Quinn wasn't resting on his laurels; in fact, it was the total opposite. In the spring of 2003 he opened a new call centre for Quinn Direct in Enniskillen, creating 600 jobs in a move again supported by British government grants – 'we chose to set up in Enniskillen because of the unrivalled telecommunications infrastructure, a well-educated workforce, the quality of which the group has already experienced, and the wide-ranging supported offered by Invest NI', he told the *Belfast News Letter*. He was also establishing a huge base for his insurance company in the South, buying an eleven-storey headquarters for the business at

Blanchardstown on the outskirts of north-west Dublin, costing €30m. He continued to invest in the hospitality sector, buying two English hotels, including a Holiday Inn in Nottingham. He opened a packaging plant on the southern side of the border outside Ballyconnell, expanded the roof-tile company and opened Quinn Therm to produce rigid foam board for cavity-wall insulation, a company which would create more jobs on the border.

Elsewhere, Quinn Financial Services, the company he established to make investments on behalf of the insurance company, took a 20 per cent stake in NCB Stockbrokers in a deal set up by investment banker Conor Killeen. He'd struck up a personal relationship with Quinn and described the company to the *Irish Independent* as 'free-thinkers and independent' who 'like challenging the establishment'. The NCB deal reflected Quinn's mindset at the time. Despite his dotcom debacle, he remained drawn to the markets and believed his instinctive understanding of business and how it worked provided him with an edge. While having no involvement in the day-to-day management of NCB, he did have access to its investment managers, who could provide him with vital market intelligence.

While the group he owned had now grown to include insurance, glass, cement, tiles, hotels and pubs, Quinn was still looking for more. His ambition was insatiable. With huge profits now pouring in, particularly from cement and insurance, and low-cost finance available to him from banks that was agreed after little more than a phonecall, Quinn had the ability and the resources to go much bigger, much further.

***

By the mid-2000s, Quinn had cornered 14 per cent of the insurance market in the Republic of Ireland and 6 per cent on the northern side of the border and had a total of 130,000 policyholders. He'd established a very strong base on the island of Ireland. Now, as with some of his other ventures, he was going to attempt the same on the other side of the Irish Sea.

It was a huge move. The UK insurance market was highly competitive, with the major companies having built their customer base over decades. There had also been significant change in the industry in recent times, with the advent of selling insurance over the phone, which had spawned new companies such as Direct Line. Direct Line cut out the middle man, i.e. the brokers. Regardless of all this, Quinn was determined to step into the market. 'Our head office is in Northern Ireland, which is part of the UK. So we were doing business there from day one, and I think it was very early on we made the decision to go into England,' he told *The Irish Times*.

Quinn Direct found a home for its sales support staff in the north of England, at Salford Quays in Manchester. Kevin Lunney was in charge of the roll-out and all went according to plan, Quinn believing the company's model meant it had a significant advantage over its rivals with cost savings passed on to its policyholders. 'Prices have reduced by more than 10 per cent on average in the period, in line with previous years, and similar reductions are expected in the current year,' he was quoted as saying in *The Irish Times*.

The company, which had first opened its doors in 1996, was now employing over 1,000 staff in at its offices in Cavan, Enniskillen, Manchester and Dublin.

This wasn't Quinn's only venture over the Irish Sea during this period, however. In March 2004 he took his helicopter to attend the annual Cheltenham horse-racing festival. The favourite to win the Gold Cup – the festival's biggest race – was Best Mate, the horse seeking to complete a hat-trick of victories. Every year, thousands of Irish horse-racing fans make a pilgrimage to the racecourse an hour north-east of Bristol, the festival usually coinciding with St Patrick's Day, which adds a distinct green colouring to the racing.

Quinn wasn't the only Irish businessman to arrive in style in his helicopter. Also there was one of the richest men in Ireland, Dermot

Desmond. He began his career in finance at Citibank before moving to PWC and, in 1981, at the age of thirty-one, founding NCB Stockholders, which became the largest independent brokerage in Ireland before he sold it to the Ulster Bank in 1994 for IR£39m. (At the very time of the festival, Quinn was taking a 20 per cent share in NCB, supporting a management buyout in the deal set up by Conor Killeen.) Desmond was raised in Dublin and was very well connected. He'd been one of the businessmen who'd financially supported Taoiseach Charles Haughey, as revealed in the Moriarty Tribunal and reported in the *Irish Independent*, even going as far as paying for the refurbishment of his yacht, *Celtic Mist*. Like Quinn, he was self-made, but the two men were polar opposites. Quinn was the outsider who revelled in his status as a border chieftain, while Desmond was a smooth, shrewd operator who had amassed his fortune through diverse investments.

At the festival the two very different businessmen got to know each other over their shared love of racing. But, of course, they were soon talking business and, in particular, about a radiator-and-plastics manufacturing company in which they both had a stake.

Barlo was established in the mid-1960s by Aiden Barlow and was floated on the Irish Stock Exchange, but in the early 2000s its share price was becalmed, valued at less than €50m. The company's chief executive, Tony Mullins, went on an acquisition spree, buying a plastics firm in Slovakia and Athlone Extrusions, which manufactured polystyrene sheet and film. But his strategy failed to impress the markets and, by 2004, the company become the subject of intense speculation. Tony Mullins put together a management buyout (MBO), which priced the company at €70m, or forty cents a share. For a bid to be accepted, it required the support of 80 per cent of the company's shareholders. And Mullins didn't have it.

During the early months of 2004, Desmond had been quietly buying up shares in Barlo and by the time of the races, he'd built up a 19 per cent stake, primarily through convincing investment house Gartmore to sell its entire holding in Barlo to him. Desmond's stake had cost him €7m. Through Quinn Direct, Quinn had also bought into Barlo, holding 2.4 per cent of the shares while continuing to buy more every day. So when Desmond and Quinn arrived at Cheltenham, they were enjoying the craic and laying down bets on the horses, but their minds were on Barlo.

Quinn wanted to mount a takeover of Barlo, but he needed Desmond's shares. The two men jousted throughout the festival until the final evening. After Best Mate romped home in the Gold Cup, it was now or never for Quinn.

In a box in the stands, he met with Desmond, who was holding out for as much as he could get on the shares which he'd bought for forty-two cents each. They couldn't agree on how much Quinn would pay him so the two businessmen decided that the only way to settle the final price was to toss a coin. Quinn won and agreed to pay Desmond forty-eight cent a share, a 15 per cent return, or a tidy €1m profit on his €7m investment. At the end of Cheltenham, Quinn flew home high on adrenaline. He now controlled 30 per cent of the company.

Within weeks, he had full control, blowing the MBO out of the water by paying shareholders eight cents more than Tony Mullins had offered. In the end, he took over Barlo for €85m. One of Quinn's senior executives says the Barlo deal marked the moment Sean Quinn ceased to be a border businessman.

The following Monday morning, back in Cavan, Quinn told his colleagues a helicopter was no longer going to be enough. 'Fuck it,' he exclaimed, 'let's get a jet!' The company staff had flown commercial airlines when travelling abroad for business, but now Quinn wanted to have his own plane. A Dassault Falcon 2000EX private jet costing over €16m was duly ordered up. Dermot Desmond just happened to have the same plane.

Clearly Barlo wasn't the only thing Quinn had come back with from the races; hanging around Desmond for just a few days had given the quarryman a taste of how wealthy businessmen operated.

Considering Sean Quinn's mindset at the time, one of his former colleagues said: 'The problem with Sean was that he [began to] believe his own myth. He liked to be the man who plays cards for 50p but, in reality, he liked to be in those [high-flying] circles. He would have always been impressed by it whilst maintaining he wasn't.'

He wanted the trappings of success. For those around him, nothing would be the same again after Cheltenham 2004. His head had been turned, as the people of Fermanagh might be heard to say.

***

The Barlo deal was the most significant yet for Quinn in terms of pure scale. Given that he was already producing many of the elements required for the building of a family home, adding a radiator manufacturer made a lot of sense. However, it did take his executive team, led by Liam McCaffrey, some time to get their heads around the impact that Barlo would have on how the business operated. 'We hadn't appreciated the size of the operation,' said one executive.

Through that one deal, the manufacturing business went international. While they had a packaging plant in Athlone and others in Clonmel and Wicklow, its factories now stretched from Belgium to Spain and France. There were another two plants in Germany and another in the Czech Republic, and of course they also had to manage the plastics company Mullins had purchased in Slovakia.

Also out of the Barlo deal came the plans for a plant producing MMA monomer, which is used in the production of acrylic glass, in the town of Leuna, just outside Leipzig. Around the same time, MMA was starting to be used in Germany in the production of LED televisions, causing its price to triple. Kevin Lunney's brother Tony would work alongside the Danish project manager for what would become one of the world's most advanced plastics factory. The technology would be Japanese, while the design came from a German company, Udhe.

Dermot Carey was hired as purchasing manager for the vast project. 'The decision to build an MMA plant in Leuna was like an earthquake in the industry,' he said. 'Change traditionally in the chemical industry is very slow. All of a sudden this seeming cowboy comes along but he has the infrastructure, the money and the site.' Carey recalls that the first time he met Quinn himself was when he took his boss on a tour of the site. 'Next thing,' he said, 'you are having a beer [together] and you say that you have an idea that could save five million. Then the next morning they come back and say that's a good idea, now make it happen.' Carey wasn't used to having access to the man at the very top of the organisation and can remember his shock when he was contacted directly by Quinn. 'The phone rang and I picked it up and it was Sean Quinn. It was such a shock. He can be very direct but it was always important to have your homework done in advance.' Another rule seemed to be, 'if you make a wrong decision that's okay, just don't make the same mistake twice'.

At the start of the project, Sean Quinn shrugged off the huge costs associated with the build – estimated to be over €350m at the outset. 'He may not have fully understood,' said a colleague, 'but once he agreed, he was fully behind it.' The build would continue throughout the rest of the 2000s – at double the original cost estimation. At one point a bridge was built over an autobahn so that a furnace could be delivered.

There were those within the company who were concerned about the Barlo deal, never mind the Leipzig plant. The fact was that Barlo had struggled in the years preceding Quinn's purchase. With the benefit of hindsight, some questioned whether Dermot Desmond's strategy to put himself between Barlo and Quinn was by design, knowing the quarryman couldn't then resist the lure of the radiator business.

Undeterred, Quinn would later consolidate his position by announcing that he was going to build a €133m plant in Newport, South Wales. The one-million-square-foot state-of-the-art plant would create 460 jobs. Quinn Radiators was projected to turn over £300m per annum and the new plant, which came with Welsh government grants, would make compact radiators, 'the product of the future' for the domestic heating industry.

The Quinn Group – particularly its executive team – were being stretched physically and mentally. But they believed in Quinn, and his voracious appetite for success was infectious.

One executive described the environment in Derrylin at the time: 'Quinn was so highly driven and looked at things in an uncomplicated way. He was of the mindset: if you build it they will come. He always started with the answer and worked backwards.' The executive then added the interesting tag: 'But, on the other hand, Sean thought he owned you.'

Still, while the company was growing, succeeding and profitable, the executive team around Quinn threw everything behind him, working around the clock to support him and ensure his every wish became a reality. He was the rainmaker, the guy out front who knew more than them, whose instinct had made him the success he was, and while the sun shone on Sean Quinn there was no reason to doubt his abilities.

This period, after all, had seen a blizzard of expansion, which was manifested on the bottom line when Quinn announced the accounts for 2004. *The Irish Times* reported that 'increased income from premiums despite falling rates helped Quinn Direct Insurance make a pre-tax profit of €153 million in 2004, a 19 per cent increase over the previous year. Further premium cuts are expected in 2005. Written premiums increased by 33 per cent to €473 million last year, while underwriting profits increased 36 per cent to €98 million,' reported the paper, adding that 'Quinn Direct said underwriting margins had been maintained despite reductions in the average premiums charged to consumers and that this had been achieved through ongoing operational efficiencies, proactive claims management and strong underwriting. The Quinn Direct performance helped to boost profits at the overall Quinn Group, which rose by nearly 40 per cent to €221 million last year. The group is also believed to have met its target of raising turnover by almost 70 per cent to €1 billion, although it has not yet released figures.' Quinn couldn't have hoped for more. Right across the group, profits were up.

Sean Quinn was now being seen as one of Ireland's leading businessmen – in 2004, his fortune was estimated to be in the region of €850 million. He'd amassed property valued at over €230m, having added the 788-room, five-star Prague Hilton at the start of the year, paying €145m in a deal that also included the 226-room Ibis Karlin Hotel. Just like the pubs in Dublin, Quinn would own the hotels, but Hilton would continue to manage them. The estate agent who put the deal together, Robert Seabrook, told the *Irish Independent*: 'Prague is probably the most attractive hotel market in central and eastern Europe with hotel values in the city expected to show significant improvement following the Czech Republic's accession to the EU.' Back home, Quinn had also taken a stake in the wind energy company Airtricity. In what was another deal brokered by NCB, he paid €40m for a 16 per cent shareholding, describing the business in a press release published by *The Irish Times* as 'one of the leading players in Europe'.

Quinn also found time for matters domestic, deciding to build a home that matched his newfound status among Ireland's wealthy elite. A month after the Cheltenham races, Quinn filed a planning application to demolish the family's modest two-storey home at Greaghrahan outside Ballyconnell, where he and Patricia had raised their family, and replace it with a 15,000-feet, seven-bedroom, four-storey house with a swimming pool and leisure area. When completed, the house would overlook Lough Aghavoher and the Slieve Russell golf course.

The 'leisure area' alone was twice the size of the average family home and there was parking for nine cars. But rather than criticise, locals were impressed and proud. After all, many of them had been able to purchase their own homes because of the wealth and employment he'd brought to the area.

Quinn himself knew that he could build a supersize house without causing any embarrassment.

***

While locally the focus was on the construction of the new home, in the boardroom Quinn was putting the foundations in place for his legacy.

There had been continued speculation about the structure of the business ever since Sean Quinn himself raised it in the aftermath of the dotcom shares disaster. He'd talked about taking the company public, of releasing some of his shareholding, and even of selling the business. But he'd done none of these things. His inner circle at the company, Liam McCaffrey and Kevin Lunney in particular, were aware that he'd considered all his options. He'd even talked about offering them an opportunity to buy into the business, but, as with the other options, he had never followed through.

Post-Barlo, some of the Dublin media returned to the topic. In the *Sunday Tribune*, Business Editor Brian Carey asked: 'Has Barlo pushed Sean Quinn closer or farther from a flotation? The audacious Barlo bid puts Quinn very close to the top of the pile of Irish family-owned companies. The transaction has also refreshed speculation that the company is bulking up for a future stock market flotation. The difficulty in estimating the value of the empire is compounded, however, by the entrepreneur's decision some years ago to place his insurance company, Quinn Direct, at the centre of the group's operations.'

The journalist also raised the issue of the complex financial infra-structure of the company. 'About €100m of Quinn's property assets, for instance, form part of the reserves of the Quinn Direct company. These property assets include the Slieve Russell Hotel. A loan to the cement company for €12m is also listed as an asset of the insurer in its last company accounts. In the past, Quinn has dipped into his other businesses to help boost the reserves of the insurer, investing some €30m in 2001. If Quinn did float, it might require two separate offerings to get it away – the insurance company and industrial holdings. The days of the diversi-fied conglomerate are long gone.'

The *Tribune* business editor was making the point that Quinn had made his businesses inter-dependent, when he should really be making his companies stand-alone entities. Quinn Direct, for example, really shouldn't be reliant on the properties Quinn had bought for its reserves. In an article which really cut through a lot of the misunderstandings and misrepresentations of Quinn and his business, Carey signed off with another clear-sighted observation: 'Be it the acquisition of a 20% stake in NCB or indeed the venture in radiators with Barlo, or his massive property foray into Prague, the Fermanagh entrepreneur cannot help himself. If he sees an opportunity, in no matter what sector, he will go for it. And right now, the place for such opportunism is not on the stock market.'

What wasn't publicly know at the time was that, during 2004, Sean Quinn had in fact quietly but fundamentally restructured his company. He'd created Quinn Investments, which would control all of his business interests, from insurance to the hotels and pubs to the cement and glass factories. All of it. And, for the first time, neither he nor Patricia would be shareholders. Instead, the Quinn Investment shareholders were his children. Colette and Aoife had 38 per cent each while Ciara had 20 per cent. Shares would be held in trust for the youngest two, Sean Junior and Brenda.

Despite his own previous suggestions that he was interested in offering shares to staff, he had decided to keep the business in the family's ownership. 'That was about control. He always needed that,' said one of his former colleagues.

Quinn was fast approaching his sixtieth birthday and it was clear he had no intentions of divesting himself – or his family – of his core assets. If anything, he remained determined to add to them.

His focus fell on golf clubs and the famous Wentworth course, close to Windsor, in Surrey, England. It was on the market for sale at an asking price of £95m and, having made a success of the Slieve Russell Hotel and course, Quinn thought it would fit right in to the group. There was some competition, however, when an initial bid was tabled by Richard Caring, a former promising golfer-turned-entrepreneur who had made his money selling Hong Kong fashions into the British market. 'As a sporting facility in the UK there is nothing similar. Wentworth is to golf what Wimbledon is to tennis. It's priceless,' Caring was quoted as saying in the *London Evening Standard*. 'There's only one Wentworth in the world.'

Businessman Surinder Arora, who was already a shareholder in the course, was also preparing an offer, while Quinn made a number of bids, rising from £87m to £102, which Caring trumped with an offer of £110m. Quinn was told by the agents handling the sale that he would have to offer at least 10 per cent over the last bid, so he slapped down £122m. He thought that he'd gotten his hands on one of the world's greatest golf courses, but Caring outmanoeuvred him, persuading Wentworth's shareholders to delay closing the deal with the quarryman until he and Arora could put together a winning joint offer of £130m. According to *Sunday Business Post* journalist Gavin Daly, Quinn then wrote to the shareholders to complain about the way in which he was treated: 'I am minded to write this letter because I believe there has been a lack of clarity and order surrounding the conduct of the sales process to date and the treatment of our approaches.' It made no difference, however, as Caring won, and Quinn would quickly move on.

In an article published at the time of the Wentworth sale, in September 2004, Gavin Daly, who would write *Citizen Quinn* with Ian Kehoe, commented on the contradictions between what the quarryman said and what he was doing when it came to the future of the business. 'While Quinn has proved most of his critics wrong, those who remain say he lacks an exit strategy for what is effectively a conglomerate. A flotation of some divisions is a possibility, but the bid for Wentworth seems to indicate he is still focusing on growth rather than an exit. With his new house plans and luxury purchases, however, he seems to have abandoned his plan in 2001 to "live poor and die rich", as he told this newspaper,' Daly wrote in *The Sunday Business Post*.

Within months of the Daly report, Quinn bought his golf course, paying £186m for the De Vere Belfry near Birmingham – another of

Britain's major sporting venues and the spiritual home of the prestigious Ryder Cup tournament, which it had hosted several times. He offered 50 per cent more than the net book value for the course, which, in the year before being sold, had made £12.2m profit on a turnover of £33.9m. It was going to be some time before Quinn would get his investment back.

Quinn was acting media shy at the time, with Liam McCaffrey sent out to explain the strategy behind the latest acquisition. The CEO, quoted in *The Irish Times*, said the deal for the golf course, the 324-bedroom hotel and leisure complex was part of plans for an 'extensive expansion' in Britain. 'In addition to providing a satisfactory return on a stand-alone basis, this asset will provide the group with an excellent base for meeting customers and business associates in high-quality surroundings,' he explained.

It was a costly exercise for 'satisfactory' returns, but, at this time, what Quinn wanted, Quinn got.

All this expansion meant that, in 2005, the Quinn Group was officially the most successful family-owned business in Ireland. It was over thirty years since he'd started the company, but now Sean Quinn had created the most profitable private business on the island. His achievements were as staggering as the numbers that were making headlines on a very regular basis. All this had been achieved through following his instincts.

But he'd also reached this point through failing to listen to his advisors: to those who warned that he couldn't maintain the growth and the diversity strategy that he'd adopted; those who said he should dilute the family's shareholding; and those who were still worried that rather than learning lessons out of the dotcom failure, it had provided him with the belief that he could do whatever he wanted, without fear of the consequences. Rather than sell off parts of the business, Sean Quinn was determined to hold onto everything he'd built.

And that was about to take him down a rabbit hole from which he would never escape.

9

215,619,414

Sean Quinn stepped up his plans to secure a legacy for his children to a whole new level during the mid-2000s. He bought the Belfry Golf Course with borrowings from Bank of Ireland and Anglo Irish Bank, but the new registered owner was his son, Sean Junior. His sister Colette now owned the Hilton and Ibis hotels in Prague, while Brenda Quinn's name was over the door of the Slieve Russell Hotel, which was growing in scale with more bedrooms and a day spa added in an expansion.

The company was also becoming more of a family affair on a nine-to-five basis. Sean Junior was working in Quinn Direct. Colette was in the hotel division, while her sisters, Ciara and Aoife, were also working in Quinn Direct. Only Brenda, the baby of the family, was yet to take up a role within the company, as her immediate plans were to study marketing and human resources at the Galway–Mayo Institute of Technology. But a move into the Quinn Group could well follow after graduating.

Also in the company was Peter Quinn's son, Peter Darragh, who was known to all as 'Petey'. After attending St Michael's School in Enniskillen, he had followed his father to Queen's University in Belfast where he studied accountancy. He'd been born in Dublin, where his father was based at the time, and returned there after Queen's before heading to Australia for a couple of years. Once he'd dealt with his itchy feet, he returned home to join Uncle Sean, who put him to work as an investment analyst in Quinn Insurance. All the family were very fond of Petey, who had played for the Fermanagh minor and senior football teams and had become the manager of Teemore Shamrocks. His father had now joined the company's board, which also included Patricia Quinn, Liam McCaffrey and the former senior civil servant Paddy Mullarkey, who had come in to steady the insurance company after the dotcom bubble burst. Conor Killeen, who'd become one of Quinn's key advisors, had also become a board member, as had Dara O'Reilly, a Belturbet native who had started in the hotel division before becoming an assistant to McCaffrey in the company's headquarters, later rising to the position of Quinn Group financial controller.

All the pieces felt in place for Sean Quinn. The group was making money 'hand over fist'. He was building his dream home and his family were coming through the ranks, learning the ropes the hard way. In his own mind, he'd abandoned the idea of a flotation or even bringing in partners for the business: he and his family would retain full control.

Still, the board wanted to know what his plans were, moving forward. 'And I said, well, I'm a bit concerned about growing the manufacturing business too much because we could lose control if we open too many more factories, so we want to be careful there. And I said, property is one we would like to be involved in. So what I said was, we would spend a third of our surplus cash on manufacturing, a third of it on property outside of Ireland and a third of it on blue-chip companies in the stock market. Now, in fairness, what those directors would have said, well, the last one's a no-brainer, that's the one, we're all happy with that, buying into blue-chip companies, we're all happy with that. And we're all happy with the manufacturing because you're good at it, and you've proven it over thirty-odd years that you are good at it. [But they were] a wee bit worried about spending money in Ukraine and Russia and Prague,' he admitted.

Sean Quinn never really believed that he needed the agreement of anyone to do as he pleased, never mind his board. They just had to be managed, like everyone else, and they wouldn't have been there in the first place if they were concerned about Quinn's management of the company.

This control also prevailed when it came to the company's debt and borrowings. During the autumn of 2005 the company restructured its debt, putting all the €700m it owed into one facility provided by a group of lenders led by Barclays. By the spring of the following year, he'd borrowed another €700m from international bondholders. He now owed his lenders €1.2 billion, but with the company firing on all cylinders, the debt could be paid down over ten years at relatively low interest rates.

Against the backdrop of such phenomenal business activity, the Quinn family came together to mourn the loss of their mother, grandmother and matriarch, Mary Josephine Quinn, who died at her home in Gortmullan in May 2005, aged ninety-two. The dignitaries who attended the funeral at St Mary's Church in Teemore spoke to the status of both Sean and Peter Quinn. *The Anglo-Celt* reported that the president of Ireland, Dr Mary McAleese, sent her aide-de-camp and that several Irish government ministers made the trip to Teemore. 'The attendance of politicians and public representatives included Mary Coughlin TD, Minister for Agriculture and Food; Noel Treacy TD, Minster of State at the Department of Taoiseach and Foreign Affairs; Pat the Cope Gallagher TD, Minister of State at the Department of Communications, Marine and Natural Resources; Brendan Smith TD, Minister of State for the Department of Agriculture and Food and Ceann Comhairle, Dr Rory O'Hanlon TD. The Taoiseach Bertie Ahern TD was represented by Commandant Michael Murray.' Along with the politicians, the current president of the GAA, Seán Kelly, and three former GAA presidents were also there.

After she died, Quinn knocked down his mother's home and built a new two-storey office block on the site, expanding the adjacent headquarters. He needed the space, as, after the restructuring of the debt, Quinn had also decided to make changes within the company.

The main change was that Kevin Lunney became head of the International Property Group (IPG), the vehicle Quinn would use to build a global property portfolio for his family. Before the new office was built – which would house the IPG – Lunney had been forced to run the show from a portacabin out the back of the main office. Alan Hynes, who had been head of the hotels division, became a senior member of Lunney's team. 'Sean wanted an exotic property portfolio for the family,' said a colleague at the time. The refinancing opened up a line of credit that was going to give Lunney and his team the deep resources required to build such an ambitious property portfolio.

'Some people go for a safe return, we go for a bigger return' was Quinn's mantra. To get bigger returns, Lunney and his team had to go east. They'd already bought the two hotels in Prague; now Quinn wanted them to go further, faster and find him the kind of returns he was seeking.

It was in Russia that they made their biggest purchases, paying a reported €140m for a twenty-storey tower block and a business centre in Moscow, which had an annual rental income of over €16m from tenants that included Coca-Cola and Dunlop. In Kazan, a ninety-minute flight east of the capital, they struck a €50m deal for a logistics centre and then went further east to the city of Ufa, where they picked up a retail, leisure and logistics development. In the Ukranian capital of Kiev, Quinn bought the Univermag shopping mall for €60m. Kevin Lunney and his team would take a trip every couple of months. 'I went to places I never thought I'd see,' said one of those involved. 'It was an innovative time. We bought a site in Hyderabad, India, and built a tower block, which was ten times the size of our building at Blanchardstown. We built it from scratch and it was one of the best in the world,' he added.

By the end of a two-year spending spree, Quinn had secretly amassed a property portfolio worth over €500m. With the company accounts never published, no one but a handful of those around him, his family, and his lenders knew what he'd been doing.

Quinn would go with the property team on many of their trips. He enjoyed Lunney's company and knew that he would be taken care of while Kevin was there. He knew he had his total loyalty and that he was discreet.

They'd fly out on a Monday morning, with Quinn insisting that they be back in Derrylin before close of play on Friday. Inevitably, that Friday evening Quinn would be at the bar in a pub in Ballyconnell with his close group of friends, behaving like he'd just come off a shift at the cement factory.

Quinn enjoyed the mystery around what he was doing, where he had been. He knew there were rumours on top of rumours about what his next move was going to be. But, unknown even to his children, Quinn had already made the move that would change everything.

***

Around the time of his mother's funeral, Sean Quinn had established another new company with a rather bizarre name: Bazzely V Consultadoria Economica E Participacoes Sociedade Unipessoal LDA. This was going to be the secret vehicle for Quinn to gamble on the stock market. They weren't going to be small bets either; he was going to pour hundreds of millions of euros into the company in order to purchase shares.

Quinn says that it was the business advisory services provider, Price Waterhouse Coopers (PWC), who advised him on how to set up the company, but that the idea originally came from his financial planning director, Shane Morrison, who'd joined the company as financial controller at Quinn Direct in 2001, having spent two years previously working as an accountant at Ernst & Young. By 2003, Quinn was so impressed with Morrison that he'd moved him into the aforementioned new, key role.

After seeking advice from a range of specialists, including PWC, they decided that the investment vehicle should be based on the Portuguese island of Madeira, off Africa's north-west coast. Known for its volcanic ruggedness and its wine, Madeira was chosen because of its tax regulations, which were particularly attractive to businessmen such as Quinn.

The company came to be known simply as 'Bazzely' but it was unlike any of Quinn's other businesses. It didn't have a bank account, for example; it had no directors, or even staff. In fact, it was just another investment vehicle the likes of which is used by the wealthy around the world, based in a free-trade zone (like Madeira), in order to exempt its owners from capital gain or income taxes. (Companies such as Bazzely tended to pay just 3 per cent corporation tax.) Given the scale of Quinn's investment intentions, and the potential financial benefits that would follow, he looked to be doing all he could to avoid paying either the British or Irish taxman, all while Madeira's banking legislation allowed him maximum secrecy to make his moves on the share market.

While Bazzely was set up for the benefit of Sean Quinn, he wasn't even a shareholder. Instead, he put the business in the names of his five children, although they would later claim that they knew nothing of the company at the time and only found out they were legally responsible much later. However, Liam McCaffrey and Kevin Lunney were both aware of Quinn's plans, as was the group financial controller, Dara O'Reilly. He was the point person for anyone seeking to contact Bazzely.

Once the company was set up, Quinn knew that he had the money to make a series of big plays, and that's exactly what he did. And contracts for difference, or CFDs, were a key component of these plays.

Originating in futures and options (stock derivatives traded in the share market), CFDs were originally developed in the early 1990s by Smith New Court, a London-based brokerage trading firm. The innovation is accredited to Brian Keelan and Jon Wood of UBS Warburg. CFDs first emerged in the over-the-counter (OTC) or equity SWAP markets, where they were used by institutions to cost-effectively hedge their equity exposure by utilising certain risk-reducing and market-neutral trading strategies.

Initially, CFD trading represented a cost-effective way for Smith New Court's hedge-fund clients to easily sell short in the market (i.e. invest in such a way that the investor will profit if the value of the particular asset falls) with the benefit of leverage, and to benefit from stamp-duty exemptions that were not available to outright share transactions. In particular, by using CFDs, institutional traders and hedge funds no longer needed to physically settle their equity/share transactions, which in practice meant that such contracts didn't require delivery or acceptance of the underlying instrument. In this way, these large clients were also able to avoid the cumbersome and sometimes costly process of borrowing stock when they wanted to sell short. At first, CFDs were a very specialised tool used only in the London markets, but by the early 2000s they was being used by traders around the world (except in the US, where CFDs were banned by the Securities and Exchange Commission because of their high risk).

Quinn outlined his understanding of CFDs as such: 'If you go to buy a house or a farm you pay 20, 25 per cent deposit and the bank pays the rest. Well, a CFD is no different. The CFD provider, who is one of the major international banks, they will put up the 70, 80 per cent and we would put up the 20 to 30 per cent. And that's what we did. So it was no different than paying a deposit on a house or a farm.'

Their attraction to people like Sean Quinn was twofold. Any gains were not taxed and they allowed you to buy shares in a company without the company knowing you held them. But there were also major potential pitfalls. If you go into a pub and put €50 in a poker machine, your maximum loss is €50. But, with CFDs, you lose the €50 and a whole lot more.

CFDs were a high-risk, high-reward gamble. CMC Markets, a London-based financial institution, explains the risks attached to using the financial instrument on its website: 'If you place a CFD trade worth £1,000 and the margin rate is 5%, you only need to fund 5% of the total value of the position, known as position margin. In this case, you only need to allocate £50 to open the trade. If, however, the price moves against you by 10%, you would lose £100 – double your initial stake in the CFD trade. This is because your exposure to the market (or your risk) is the same as if you had purchased £1,000 worth of physical shares. This means that any move in the market will have a greater effect on your capital than if you had purchased the same value of shares.'

Somewhat worryingly, those closest to Sean Quinn think he never really understood CFDs, one saying: 'He wasn't keen on reading the small print,' while another added, 'He loved banks, how they made their money. But Sean could only see the multiples, the wins. He didn't compute the risk.'

At the start he did at least spread his bets, first buying options in, amongst others, Ryanair, Paddy Power and Tullow Oil. And Anglo Irish Bank. By the end of the year, Quinn had built a heavily diversified portfolio with, according to Gavin Daly and Ian Kehoe's book, *Citizen Quinn*, his CFD 'units' in Ryanair being worth around €60m and Anglo Irish Bank €100m.

The expert advice is that anyone entering the CFD market should create a trading plan so that their motivation, goals and attitude to risk are clear and understood by all. But, according to *Citizen Quinn*, there were no independent directors or advisors working with Sean Quinn specifically on CFDs.

In an interview in the spring of 2019, Quinn explained his thinking: 'In fairness not that many people knew [about the CFD purchases]. You know, we kept this as quiet as possible, or we didn't say too much about it, because over the previous thirty-five, thirty-six years, you'd always get wee bits of shocks for a month or two, and you don't go to the pub and say, Jesus, I bought shares yesterday and I bought CFDs yesterday, they are down 10 per cent today. You don't go broadcasting that. So it wasn't in the public domain.'

However, if more people had known what he was doing, and were able to advise him, perhaps he wouldn't have made the ruinous errors that came next.

***

Being diversified allowed him to spread his risk. In 2006, however, Quinn changed the CFD strategy, going in the opposite direction, as he cashed in all his Ryanair and other CFDs and ploughed everything into Anglo Irish Bank. According to Daly and Kehoe, his CFDs in the bank were worth more than €650m at this point, roughly 5 per cent of the bank's market valuation.

Quinn has since tried to explain his attraction to the bank. 'Anglo [compared to other Irish banks] would be much the same as Ryanair and Aer Lingus. Their growth pattern, Ryanair's growth pattern is much higher, of course. It would be the same with Anglo versus Bank of Ireland and AIB – the growth pattern was much higher [for Anglo]. And I suppose we could include ourselves in that as well: the Quinn Group's growth was much higher than CRH, just as examples, you know. So obviously seeing those I would always have a preference for the high-growth companies.'

One of his executive colleagues at the time said there was a pretty straightforward explanation for Quinn's love of Anglo: 'What attracted SQ to Anglo? He liked the model. He saw a lot of his own entrepreneurial traits in it. They had a short chain of command and, of course, the whole "taking on the establishment" thing.'

Seán FitzPatrick, its CEO, had built what was described as 'the best bank in the world'. Under the headline 'Anglo Irish Bank is world's top performer', the *Irish Independent* declared in January 2006 that: 'Anglo Irish Bank has emerged as the world's top performing bank over the past five years. The Irish business lender just shaded United Health Group, a $70bn capitalised American health company, at the head of the global rankings for the period 2001–05.' It had ridden the economic miracle known as the Celtic Tiger the whole way to the top. Anglo was hungry and was taking on the big boys at home and abroad, and winning.

To Quinn, it seemed like a reliable, even safe, bet. 'At the time we were major shareholders in a broker [NCB] in Dublin and I used to get the Davy's monthly book and it would say clearly there that AIB and Bank of Ireland, the two dominant banks, their cost-to-income ratio was in the fifties, 55 per cent of an income went on costs; 22, 25 per cent of the Anglo income went on costs. And the margins were pretty much the same. And, of course, Anglo, I thought, were closer to their customer base because they would only have, they had mostly big customers. The majority of them would be in the million-pound bracket. I thought that they were, had thirty-three successive years' increase in profits, so I just thought they were a great bank. I thought they were doing all the right things. So, we had total confidence in them [and] all of the records were there, going back five, ten, fifteen years. And we had no doubt but the company was going to be successful.' Quinn's CEO, Liam McCaffrey, also had little doubt about Anglo – he too invested heavily in the bank.

And little wonder. In 2006 alone, Anglo Irish Bank recorded record profits of €850m, up 38 per cent from the previous year. It had total assets of €73 billion and its customer lending had increased by 45 per cent to over €15 billion. In its annual report, Anglo reported that '2006 was another year of outstanding growth and investment. The Bank continues to leverage and strengthen its franchise in all target markets through the execution of its focused strategy. We are confident that by consistently delivering for our customers, the Group will create and sustain superior returns for shareholders into the future.'

Quinn had total faith in the bank and its accounts, which he devoured year after year. He read FitzPatrick's statement in its accounts, heralding 2006 as 'another year of excellent growth'. He added, 'Our group has generated excellent returns for the shareholders by maintaining the balanced, client-centric strategy that has served it so well through the past two decades. The bank's focused offering of tailored and responsive secured business lending is highly distinctive – if not unique – in the marketplace. Our consistent approach is to deliver strong returns by capitalising on the competitive edge with clients, while ensuring rigorous and effective control of risk and our cost base.'

It was all bullshit, of course, and Seán FitzPatrick and David Drumm – the young executive who became CEO at the bank in 2005 – knew it.

But Quinn didn't. The fact was that by lending vast sums of money to developers with little due diligence, FitzPatrick and Drumm had strapped booster rockets under the Irish property market, which gave the false impression that Ireland was still enjoying all the success that came with a Tiger economy. But, in 2006, everyone was still buying FitzPatrick's hype.

Anglo's share price was now at €12.90 and would rise to a high of €15.71 by the end of the year. Daly and Kehoe reported that Quinn had first bought into the bank when the share price was around €11.30, so he was up, well up. The following year, 'Fitzy' announced the bank's twenty-second year of 'uninterrupted earnings growth, with underlying profits increasing to €1,221 million'. He said the performance was all due to the bank's prudent risk appetite. It was a work of fiction worthy of a decent prize, but sitting up in Cavan, Quinn continued to swallow it whole, putting everything on the line based on what he was reading.

On top of his €650m-worth of CFDs, he bought €800m more in the first three months of 2007, according to Daly and Kehoe, and went back again for €655m later in the spring. What he didn't realise was that it was his position that was actually driving the Anglo share price north, reaching its zenith of €17.56 in May 2007.

The markets didn't realise that it was only one man who was buying so many CFD positions in Anglo, as Quinn was able to keep his position in the bank secret – in part, thanks to one of the aforementioned perks of CFDs. Quinn lost his anonymity, however, when it was reported in *The Sunday Times* in January 2007 that he'd amassed a 5 per cent stake in the bank. When the markets opened the following morning, the revelation did nothing for the share price. This slipped back 1 per cent on the back of the story, which erroneously reported that Quinn had bought thirty-six million shares in the bank. Quinn refused to comment but it was reported that sources close to the company said the 'stake' was an 'investment'.

Later, the *Sunday Tribune* posed the question the story understandably provoked: 'what are we to make of Sean Quinn's €500m investment in Anglo Irish Bank? As ever with such investments, the only indications from the purchaser are that he sees value in the shares. Still, if you were just about pure investment, would you not spread the cash around a little to hedge your bets, notwithstanding whatever confidence you had in Anglo Irish and its international expansion plans?'

The reports did not say who their source for uncovering his stake in the bank was, but Quinn wasn't worried; in fact, he appeared to enjoy the fuss it created. The leak could even have come from Quinn himself in an attempt to be seen as a master of the markets, someone who had correctly read Anglo's rise and had bought in at the right time and now stood to make a huge amount of money from its record profits and rising share price. Nobody around Quinn would put it past him to have been the source.

If he'd cashed out his position at the time, he would have made a profit of over €200m. But just as he never truly considered selling any of his own companies, he refused to depart Anglo, instead telling his brokers and anyone who would listen that the share price was going to go higher. He'd no insider knowledge, it was just pure instinct, which, to be fair, had mostly served him well to date.

'The misjudgement was that I trusted Anglo Irish Bank: that they were giving me the true facts, and the figures were genuine. I was impressed with David Drumm and I was impressed with FitzPatrick; I thought they were two good operators. I suppose there was a lot in common with myself as well, you know. They were ambitious and they were growing fast and maybe that's the mistake that both of us made, is that we were growing too fast and maybe taking too many risks, as it turned out, and we didn't have this wide board maybe of ten or twelve people sitting around to make decisions,' said Quinn in 2018 in an attempt to retrospectively analyse the attraction and the risk.

Following the disclosure of Quinn's investment in Anglo, questions began to be asked. Irish *Sunday Independent* business editor Shane Ross, who was known to campaign for small shareholders, wondered: 'Has Anglo grown too big for its boots?' In an article, he directed several questions to Seán FitzPatrick about Sean Quinn's 'mysterious' share purchase. 'Is the purchase welcome? Does he see Quinn as an investor or a predator? And if he suggests this is a vote of confidence, ask if he is going to invite the Fermanagh tycoon or one of his representatives on earth to join the Anglo board.' Ross was reflecting the concern that Sean Quinn's real intention was to take over the bank. 'We did approach the authorities in Dublin for a banking licence,' said one of his former colleagues, 'but it never went any further and I don't believe he wanted to take over Anglo.'

Quinn admits that his attraction was simply in the way banks made their money. As a quarryman used to physical work and getting his hands dirty, banks, like insurance companies, made their money easily. It was that simple. In his head, the grass was greener in finance. And given that he was in the business of building a billionaire legacy for his family, it seemed like a rational – if risky – investment. In 2007 he could have sold the insurance company instead, but as a colleague said, 'he could never sell. The insurance business was worth two or three billion alone, but he never seriously considered a sale.'

Quinn saw himself as a creator, a person who'd been given a gift to create wealth and employment. He wasn't someone who could build, sell and move on. He was going to hold tight. 'I've a very simple philosophy in life,' he said, 'and that is that you have creators, people who try to achieve something, and I'd like to think that I was one of those. I always liked to be creative, money was never my God. But I got tremendous enjoyment in creating the thousands of jobs in the local area and building hotels and having jobs for male and female, I enjoyed all of that.'

His colleagues certainly supported this statement – at least in part. 'Money wasn't his motivator – it was power, and the control that comes with that. He had a very domineering personality,' one said, adding that while Quinn appeared at times to be collaborative and that he wanted staff to share in his success, in reality 'it was clear to everyone, this was his train set'.

And Quinn was still acquiring new trains for his set.

***

Quinn wasn't just focused on the CFDs, he was still in the business of acquisitions and made more headlines in February 2007 when he took control of health insurance company Bupa Ireland in a deal valued at €150m.

He'd spotted an opportunity and moved fast to grab it. The previous December, Bupa had announced it was pulling out of Ireland. The announcement came after the company was told by the courts that it was liable for annual 'risk equalisation' or compensation payments of €52m to the Dublin government's health insurance provider VHI, which were due because Bupa's customer base was much younger than the older, more expensive subscribers VHI managed. The Quinn deal saved the day for Bupa's 475,000 customers and 300 employees, although the quarryman would also refuse to pay VHI the compensation it said it was owed, claiming as a 'new health insurer' he should benefit from a three-year exemption from the compensation payments.

The government moved to protect VHI by enacting emergency legislation, a move that infuriated Quinn. 'It's War Declares Furious Quinn', roared the *Daily Mail* headline over a story by reporter John Breslin. 'In a furious and uncompromising statement, Mr. Quinn said he intended to fight the "draconian" laws brought in retrospectively on Wednesday night. Breslin said it was an "extraordinary attack" by the "usually reticent" Mr. Quinn, who had insisted that he "had both the money and the determination to fight the government by whatever means necessary to bring fairness to the healthcare market".'

It was fighting talk by Quinn, unknown up to then to talk about taking a war to the government, which was still led by his friend, Taoiseach Bertie Ahern.

The Bupa deal, perhaps even more than the reported move on Anglo, threw Quinn back into the public spotlight. He was clearly seen as being the white knight who was protecting the Bupa customers, with the *Sunday Independent* declaring him its March 2007 'Person of the Month' because 'Quinn will undoubtedly bring his common sense and customer-friendly approach to bear on the health insurance market, nurse the ailing insurance company back to health and confirm his place as the most outstanding entrepreneur of his generation,' said the glowing tribute.

Quinn may not have liked the press attention, but the press clearly appreciated him. His approval rating was through the roof, with each of the main daily papers praising him for the move, one even depicting him as an actual knight slaying the VHI dragon.

Quinn Healthcare was quickly established and it was announced that on top of retaining the 300 Bupa jobs, the company intended to create another 500 jobs in a massive expansion plan. 'We are in the health insurance market for the long-term and will build on all the elements of Bupa Ireland's success, particularly the extensive range of benefits and high standards of customer care,' Quinn told the *Irish Examiner* on completion of the deal in April 2007.

Just a month before, Quinn had announced a pre-tax profit for the Quinn Group of €632m for 2006. The insurance business had made more than half of the final figure, €332m, which was up 39 per cent on 2005. Manufacturing, including the cement and glass factories, added another €100m, and the family businesses 'which are not part of the Quinn Group', as one newspaper reported, 'principally property interests in Europe, Russia and India' made another €200m.

Speaking at an 'Innovation and Competitiveness' conference organised by the County Cavan Enterprise Board at his own hotel, The Slieve Russell, he told delegates that while the group had grown by 30 per cent a year, it would slow over the next five years, but his 'non group' international property portfolio would 'accelerate'. It also became clear from a rare speech full of typically bashful *'I may be rich but I'm just the same as you'* shtick – claiming he'd never done a feasibility study in his life and didn't own a mobile phone – that he still had no intention of slowing down. The *Irish Independent*'s Tom McEnaney reported him telling the conference: 'I have never been more enthusiastic about the business than I am now. Other people look at their business and think: "If I could get ten times or forty times as much business, I'd be successful." I look at my business and think: what other business should I be in? I look at business areas and if there's a Seán FitzPatrick or a Michael O'Leary [Ryanair Chief Executive] there we might avoid it, but otherwise we might think it's a healthy idea. We are always looking for the next opportunity.'

It wasn't long before that 'next opportunity' presented itself. After Bupa, he announced that he intended to invest €1 billion in the Irish electricity market by building two natural gas-fired power stations in Co. Louth and Co. Galway, as well as building two wind farms. The two power plants would be able to satisfy '35% of current consumer demand', according to a company press release. Quinn said his reasoning was that 'Quinn Group is a big user of electricity and wants to bring competition to that market', citing the same rationale for moving into insurance – his company needed a lot of it, had been at the consumer end of the experience so was best placed to shake things up.

The print media ate up the story, splashing it across front pages. Quinn was now taking on the electricity suppliers, another highly regulated industry, and was planning to be the guy with the finger over the switch of the power supply to a third of the nation. However, this time there wasn't as much as an eyebrow raised, let alone moves made to oppose him. He'd join the ranks of the undeclared untouchables. He did, after all, have the wealth to do whatever he wanted. In the *Sunday Times* Rich List, Quinn's wealth was estimated to be €4.6 billion. *Forbes* magazine placed him as the 177th richest person in the world and he now topped the rich league in Ireland, with more money than Dermot Desmond. 'There was always forward momentum,' said a colleague, 'he didn't ever want to pause and look back. Sean Quinn thought he was too big to fail. He was used to succeeding.'

He was at the height of his powers, but, unknown to everyone, he was at that precise moment gambling not only with his own future, but with that of his wife and family, and the thousands of people who worked in his companies.

And those gambles were about to fail, spectacularly.

***

When New Century Financial declared bankruptcy in April 2007, it didn't exactly make front-page news. A few months later, American Home Mortgage Investment Corporation also filed for bankruptcy. Both were heavily involved in what was known as America's 'subprime' mortgage market (i.e. mortgages given to those who may have trouble meeting repayments). They were the canaries in the mine for the economic death-spiral that would start in the States and soon sweep across the world.

Both New Century and American Home Mortgage had noted loan applications dropping off in late 2006. It wasn't long before their lenders got wind and pulled their credit, which led to their ultimate collapse. When the world woke up to what was going on, it was too late to stop the impending crash. The American housing bubble burst and its implosion was starting to threaten much bigger names than New Century Financial. For example, Bear Stearns, a New York investment bank, revealed it was exposed to the subprime market and had to bail out two of its hedge funds at a cost of billions.

Back in Ireland, the newspapers started to note the decline in the property market. During the 'boom' its pages had been full of advertise-ments for homes for sale at exorbitant prices. Then, all of a sudden, they began to see fewer and fewer advertisements. The concern in the advertisement departments of the papers soon spread to editorial, where journalists began to pick up on a downturn in the housing market.

Just as New Century Financial went under, housing prices in Ireland began to drop, although slowly at first. There was also a decline in sales of the new builds that were going up all over the country. Many were left vacant, creating what would become known as 'ghost estates'. By May 2007,

Teemore Shamrocks crowned Fermanagh Senior Champions, 1969. Sean Quinn scored the winning point.

Sean Quinn outside his new £30 million cement plant at Derrylin, Co. Fermanagh, 1986.

Kevin Lagan being interviewed on RTÉ's *Today Tonight*, 1988.

An arson attack destroys Quinn machinery and damages a building at Sean Quinn's tarmac plant in Ballyconnell, Co. Cavan, in July 2011.

Posters in support of Sean Quinn, Ballyconnell, 2012.

Sean's daughter Ciara addresses the crowd at a support rally in Ballyconnell, 2012.

Sean and Patricia Quinn walk through the streets of Ballyconnell, 2012.

A section of the crowd gathered in support of Sean Quinn, Ballyconnell, 2012.

An oil tanker bearing the logo 'Cassidy Oils' is driven into the front door of QIH headquarters, 11 December 2013.

Liam McCaffrey (left), Sean Quinn Jnr (centre) and Kevin Lunney (right) at a protest meeting in Ballyconnell.

December 2014: 'The Second Coming.' Sean Quinn greets John McCartin with a tray of drinks to celebrate the QBRC deal and his return to the business.

The Quinn family home at Ballyconnell.

One of Quinn's quarries on Doon Mountain, home to the Molly Maguire gang.

The Slieve Russell Hotel, the jewel in the family crown.

Cyril McGuinness, aka 'Dublin Jimmy', leaving Dublin District Court on 10 July 2014.

The three men who were Quinn's most trusted lieutenants and now run Mannok: Liam McCaffrey, Dara O'Reilly and Kevin Lunney.

Posters that appeared in the Ballyconnell/Derrylin area after Sean Quinn had left the business in 2016.

A police cordon close to the home of Kevin Lunney in the aftermath of his abduction and torture in September 2019.

Liam McCaffrey, CEO of Mannok holdings.

Tony Lunney (right) removes a lone Quinn supporter who appeared at the rally held after the attack on Kevin Lunney.

'I now believe there has been a Mafia-style group with its own godfather operating in our region.' Ballyconnell Parish Priest, Oliver O'Reilly's homily in the aftermath of the Kevin Lunney attack.

Sean Quinn looks out over his former empire, 2019.

construction was slowing but, despite some warnings from respected economists, there was denial at the top of government that anything was wrong, with Taoiseach Bertie Ahern, who'd just been re-elected for a third time, widely reported as telling an audience in Donegal on 4 July that 'sitting on the sidelines, cribbing and moaning, is a lost opportunity. I don't know how people who engage in that don't commit suicide because frankly the only thing that motivates me is being able to actively change something.' In government and the construction industry, he was severely criticised for the remark, but he was reflecting a general anger at those columnists and journalists who were reporting on the early signs of the downturn.

Quinn was also taking note of the developing situation. His manufacturing business had helped build the 75–90,000 homes a year that went up in Ireland during the first years of the new millennium. He'd supplied the cement, the concrete blocks, the radiators, the roof and floor tiles, the lot. Any downturn would hit that side of the business hardest, if it wasn't for the secret CFDs.

If he didn't understand CFDs fully – 'Sean Quinn never read the small print,' as one advisor close to him said – then he likely didn't appreciate that while he was speculating that Anglo's share price would go up, somewhere out there in the markets, someone else was betting that it would go down. Sure enough, brokers soon began to sell Anglo shares. They were shorting Anglo's stock. Now, much too late, Quinn began to fully realise the downside to CFDs.

As Anglo's share price began to fall, a series of 'margin calls' had to be made on the CFD units that Quinn held. (Margin calls are demands for additional capital or securities to bring an account up to the minimum maintenance margin.) This alone cost him hundreds of millions of euros. However, rather than unwinding his position, Quinn decided to double down on his bet, buying over €340m more Anglo CFDs. 'Once the shares in Anglo started going down in value,' explained Quinn, 'I thought they were very cheap, because the figures were still extraordinarily strong and even when the thing was in real trouble, it was showing a 40-odd per cent increase in profits from 2007, and the shares were going down to half of what they were. So I said, this thing has been overdone and we took money out of good companies – me foolishly, I'm blaming nobody else – I took money out of good companies and put the money into Anglo because we thought that they were being over-penalised for what was being done. And it just accelerated from there. And I was wrong, I was wrong on that.'

What Quinn had done with CFDs in just two short years was to bring himself, his family and his company to the brink. When the margin calls started coming in, Quinn took the money to pay them from his own companies. When that ran out, he looked to the cash-rich Quinn Direct. He knew it was a regulated business and it wasn't as simple, nor as legal, as withdrawing millions from the accounts of his bottle business or the cement or the hotels, but he nonetheless ordered Dara O'Reilly and Kevin Lunney to make what they described as a 'treasury agreement' between Quinn Direct and Quinn Group, allowing them to transfer hundreds of millions of euros that were supposed to secure the car- and home-insurance policies of their customers in the event of a claim. It was wrong, and Quinn knew it at the time. 'He had a relaxed attitude to corporate governance, let us say,' commented a former close colleague. 'Sean Quinn's mindset was "I'm right, I'm always right."'

There was understandable concern among his executive team at the financial manoeuvrings and a meeting was called with Quinn, which was also attended by his children Colette and Sean Junior. 'CFDs were the elephant in the room,' said one of those present. 'It went around the table and everyone said "cut the losses, sell the CFDs" – it got to Sean and he said "well, we can't agree then!"'

Quinn was convinced that he would be proved right. 'I would have known that I shouldn't have been doing it. Other people in the office would have known we shouldn't have been doing it. I suppose it just sort of happened. Maybe our system was a bit weak and maybe we didn't have enough people just looking over this thing and maybe I was too dominant a factor in this. And I suppose when I asked it to be done it was done. So I'm blaming nobody for it. I mean, did other people know it was wrong? Did I know it was wrong? Yeah, I did. Did I think it would be over maybe two, three, four weeks, maybe all passed over? That's the way it was. But there was no … it was no excuse. I shouldn't have, I shouldn't have touched a penny in a regulated entity, I shouldn't have done that,' said Quinn, admitting now that he was wrong.

At the time, however, he clearly wasn't worried or concerned about the danger of messing around with money he should have been holding to protect his customers' policies.

***

Anglo Irish Bank's board of directors had become aware of the rumours circling Dublin's financial sector of the scale of Quinn's CFDs, so Seán FitzPatrick and David Drumm decided on a showdown with the quarryman. They arranged to meet with him and Liam McCaffrey, who had personal concerns about his own investment in the bank, at the Ardboyne Hotel in Co. Meath on 11 September 2007.

Seán FitzPatrick described Quinn to journalist Tom Lyons for a book he wrote with Brian Carey, *The FitzPatrick Tapes: The Rise and Fall of One Man, One Bank, and One Country*, 'as a real 1960s Irishman. He was one of those hail-fellow-well-met, ah sure I will go down there and play the old cards, five or six lads for ten bob, or whatever it was.' He added, 'He was very human, but I didn't easily like him.' FitzPatrick said David Drumm wanted him at the meeting 'because he always felt that Quinn regarded me as a superhuman, as a superhero. He wanted Quinn to see how disappointed I would be [at the scale of his CFDs].'

Quinn told his version of the meeting in a spring 2019 interview. 'We welcomed the meeting. Because at the time Anglo shares had started to fall, and we had mopped up a bit of our spare cash by supporting the share. And I wanted to meet the two men that counted, the chairman and chief executive to say, look, we are big shareholders here, we want to know what the story is, because this share price is falling very fast, and we want to know where we are. Do we sell the shares or is the company going to be profitable, or what's the story? And they said, Sean, the company has never been better, the company is actually flying, we are showing 30, 40 per cent increase in profits. And I went home happy. Now, they did say in fairness, they did say, look, Sean, we are disappointed at the level of your CFDs, we are disappointed with that, and could we get some agreement that you might dispose of those? And I said, surely, if you want me to dispose of those whenever the share recovers I'll be more than happy to do that. And they seemed happy with that. And at the time, at the time they seemed genuine in the fact that they felt the company would grow again and that the share price would recover. I don't think they were telling me lies. I think they did believe it,' he said.

In FitzPatrick's version of the meeting, there was only ever one item on the agenda. 'There wasn't a lot to say. The main question was: how big was Quinn's CFD position in the bank.' When Quinn told them it was 25 per cent, 'we were shocked', said FitzPatrick. '[There was no] banging on the table or anything like that. [But there were] voices raised. I mean: "Jesus that is terrible, dangerous." I was physically shocked. David said afterwards to me that he looked at [Quinn] and he just saw the surprise in Quinn's eyes at my reaction. How negative I was.'

FitzPatrick did admit to Lyons, however, that when Quinn asked, they painted a very bright picture of the bank. 'I think he also felt listening to David, and possibly me as well, that things were going well within the bank. Therefore the rest of the world had got it wrong. Sean [Quinn] had got it right and time would show that he had got it right and the share price would come back again.'

In other words, Quinn heard what he wanted to hear, i.e. the bank was in good shape and was still making huge profits. He was so convinced that the share price would bounce back that he went out and bought more CFDs after the meeting, taking his stake on the bank up to 28 per cent. 'We did,' admitted Quinn. 'We bought on weak days, just to try to support the share price. It was stupid to increase it at all, I accept that. We shouldn't have bought any more shares. But we bought some more shares, but not very many.'

Now Quinn's problems were Seán FitzPatrick's problems too. The bank wanted Quinn not to buy more CFDs but to sell those he had. Quinn stubbornly refused. He was trusting his instincts and wasn't prepared to listen to anyone around him. But he'd burned through every shilling his companies had in their accounts and had taken money he shouldn't have from the insurance business. Now, he had no choice but to borrow to pay the margin calls – from the very bank that he was betting on, the bank with a share value that was tanking: Anglo.

And they had no other choice but to meet his requests. After the September meeting, Dara O'Reilly, and Elma Kilrane for Anglo, would discuss the margin calls, the CFDS held and how much Quinn needed to pay up. Over ten days in September alone, Anglo loaned €100m to Quinn. Bazzerly had bought the CFDs, but it didn't even have a bank account. Therefore, it was decided that the loans should be put in the name of the five children, Aoife, Ciara, Colette, Sean Junior and Brenda. This allowed the bank to mask its huge loans as being for the property development portfolio Sean Quinn had been building in the names of his children.

As the family prepared for Christmas that year, all the Quinn children were called to the headquarters to sign more loan documents, this time for €500m. Later, the Quinns would argue in court documents that when they gathered together on 17 December 2007 to sign the back page of the loan agreements they had no financial or legal advice.

Soon they would be needing lots of advice of the legal variety.

***

This trend continued into the early months of 2008. Dara O'Reilly intended to spend St Patrick's Day 2008, like he did every other, at home with his young family. This year, his in-laws were coming to join the party.

But by lunchtime he was distracted by phone calls and email messages. Finally, he explained to his wife that he'd have to go to the office, leaving her alone to look after their two young children and prepare the dinner for her family. It wasn't going to be a day of celebration for the O'Reillys, instead it was becoming a very worrying day for the Quinn business.

Six months earlier England had witnessed its first run on a bank in 150 years when long queues formed outside Northern Rock building society branches. 'The run on the rock', as it was described, came amid a credit crunch in the UK, which had the most personal debt of any Western economy after sixteen years that had seen an explosion of borrowing. In February 2008 the Bank of England had stepped in and nationalised Northern Rock. The markets around the world had become increasingly nervous since then and on St Patrick's Day the attention of traders turned, as might be expected, to Ireland, and, in particular, to Anglo Irish Bank – 'the best little bank in the world'.

In just a few hours, €3.5 billion was wiped off the price of Irish shares. Anglo's share price was down 15 per cent, sparking the appeals to Dara O'Reilly to come back to the office, as Sean Quinn would have to make a margin call on his Anglo CFDs.

It was a bank holiday on both sides of the border so O'Reilly had to scramble to get one of the company's English banks to meet the cash call, or payment, which had to be transferred to the broker. With so few people aware of the CFD purchases, Dara had to go to the group headquarters to oversee the transaction himself. He was struck by the deadline – the payment had to be made before 2 p.m. He met with Quinn, who himself was preparing to go into Ballyconnell for the annual parade, so that he could sign the required paperwork.

To pay the margin call, Dara had first to get the money from Anglo. He spoke to Elma Kilrane, explained that Quinn needed to borrow another €220m to make that day's margin call alone. He'd already drawn down €20m earlier in March and would need another €60m before the month was out. In just four weeks, Quinn would borrow €300m in new loans.

Anglo recorded them as being for property development projects in Russia and India but, this time, the money went to accounts held by Barlo Financial Services, one of Quinn's companies, which then paid the CFD providers. Dara O'Reilly had used the English company Barlo on St Patrick's Day due to the banks being closed in Ireland.

The Quinns' total borrowing from Anglo was now close to €1.6 billion. 'The business never really suffered in previous financial crises – in the 1980s, for example,' said one executive, 'So Sean Quinn got a degree of confidence from this, for good or bad. But 2007 and 2008 was a different kettle of fish.'

Quinn Cement was seeing demand dropping by around 20 to 30 per cent of where it had been in previous years, putting that part of the company under pressure for the first time. But it was nothing compared to the CFD situation. The press was already reporting that Quinn could have lost as much as €500 million and there was speculation it could be closer to €1 billion.

Something had to be done, and Anglo had a cunning plan.

Quinn didn't have anything close to a strong hand to play when he met FitzPatrick and Drumm again on 25 March 2008. This time the four men met in Quinn's Dublin Hotel, Buswells, known as 'the third house of the Oireachtas', located just across the street from Dáil Éireann. It was a week after the so-called St Patrick's Day Massacre. In their book, *Citizen Quinn*, Gavin Daly and Ian Kehoe revealed that Quinn was close to tears in the meeting as he began to face up to the reality of his position.

To save themselves and the bank, David Drumm and Seán FitzPatrick proposed to turn Quinn's CFDs into actual shares in the bank in the hope that it would stabilise their position on the stock markets. David Drumm put the proposal to Quinn, but with a caveat. The bank simply couldn't have him holding what would amount to a 25 per cent stake in the bank, as they believed – wrongly, as it would turn out – that even the rumours of such a substantial investment would destabilise their share price, which, Drumm argued, wouldn't be good for Quinn or the bank. So Quinn would have to take a 10 per cent reduction down to 15 per cent.

Quinn wasn't at all pleased with the plan, his tears turning to anger. However, there was more. The second part to Drumm's plan would be to put together a group of ten investors, i.e. wealthy individuals who Anglo were already in business with (and who would become infamously known as 'the Maple Ten'). They would buy 1 per cent of the bank's shares for €45m each – an amount which the bank would, very kindly, lend them to make the share purchase, thereby taking on the stake that Quinn had been forced to relinquish.

It was the kind of arrangement only Anglo could come up with, en-abled as they were by an environment of soft-touch financial regulation. Experience told them they could get away with it. No other bank in the world would have attempted it, but in Dublin, at this time, it was a case of doing whatever it took, no matter the law or regulation.

Quinn was sore about the losses. However, despite his prostrations, he found he'd no choice but to agree to go along with the proposal. The quarryman, who had held CFDs equivalent to 215,619,414 shares in Anglo Irish Bank, was beginning to realise what he'd done.

It took a few months, but while Northern Ireland was closed up for the Twelfth of July Orange Order celebrations in 2008, David Drumm got the plan over the line. The following Monday morning, Liam McCaffrey emailed the bank to say that Quinn was on board. The Quinn Group then announced that it was getting rid of its CFDs and buying a shareholding in the bank of 15 per cent (although in fact it was the family who had held most of the shareholding and the 15 per cent was now in the names of the five children).

The Irish Times led with the headline 'Quinn and family confirm Anglo stake of almost 15%'. The paper reported in August that the family had confirmed they had completed the purchase of the shareholding. 'The spokesman [for the Quinns] said no formal notification would be made to the stock exchange as no family member had taken a stake of 3 per cent or more, the threshold at which a shareholder must declare an interest in a listed company.' The paper also reported that the family's 15 per cent share was worth almost €715m based on the closing price of €6.28 of Anglo shares.

In an article Quinn wrote for the paper he admitted that 'not unexpectedly given the significant stock market downturn since mid-2007, the Quinn Group and my family have suffered equity losses. While this is not pleasant it is not the most important thing to me.'

What he failed to admit was that he'd lost €2 billion in his bet on the bank.

The crisis was taking its toll. That autumn, Quinn took a trip to view progress at the plastics plant outside Leipzig in Germany. 'From the moment we took off to when we landed he never said a word. I was concerned he was going to top himself. He even talked about writing a letter saying that it was all his fault,' said one of his colleagues who travelled with him.

Sean Junior was approached by one of the executive team and told there were serious concerns for his father's health. In September 2008, the month after the Anglo share deal had been announced, Sean Quinn vanished. He wasn't seen for a week. Some of those who were close to him at the time believe he may have suffered a breakdown. 'That's the moment where you saw change. I'm convinced Sean Quinn was never the same after that,' he added.

Up to this point, the general feeling across Ireland was that Sean Quinn was too big to fail. He'd believed that too. But now, for the first time in his life, Quinn knew that he was in real trouble.

10

'More than a Billion, Yes'

Sean Quinn was playing it down, but he knew he was in trouble and the situation just kept getting worse. The shock created by the collapse of one of the world's largest investment banks, Lehman Brothers, only drew more attention to the perilous state of the Irish banking institutions. On the last day of September 2008, Brian Cowen – who had become Taoiseach after Bertie Ahern was forced to resign when he'd been found to have illegally taken money from supporters – controversially stepped in to guarantee the assets and liabilities of five banks, including Anglo Irish. It would take some time to sink in, but the fact was that Quinn no longer owed billions to the bank; he was now in debt to the State and its taxpayers.

And the bad news just kept coming.

Irish Financial Regulator Patrick Neary had been told by Quinn's auditors, PWC, of the inter-company loans from Quinn Insurance to Quinn himself. As a result, the month after the banking guarantee, Quinn Insurance was hit with a record €3.2-million fine and Quinn personally was fined €200,000. He also had no option but to step down as chairman at the insurance company.

Announcing the fines on the annual October bank holiday in a vain attempt to bury the bad news, Patrick Neary wasn't even specific as to what the offences were. However, the truth soon made it onto the front pages, so it was now public knowledge that Quinn had taken €288m out of his insurance companies to cover the margins on the Anglo Irish CFDs.

At the time, he was furious at being publicly humiliated, failing to come to terms with the enormity of what he'd done. He issued a statement accepting that mistakes had been made but that there had been no risk to policyholders or taxpayers. 'I took loans from Quinn Direct that I shouldn't have taken,' he now says. 'I was wrong to take them. It wasn't illegal to take them, but I should have got permission off the regulator. So I was wrong in that,' he added, citing the fact that the same regulator had signed off on the huge dividends he'd taken from Quinn Direct in the previous years. 'I mean, one of the things that really annoys me, and I can't understand for the life of me how nobody has got their head round this – we took a billion pounds out of Quinn Direct from 2001 to 2007, agreed by the regulator and signed off by the regulator, in dividends.'

But taking dividends with the agreement of a compliant regulator is one thing; secretly removing hundreds of millions of euros to pay personal debts was a flagrant breach of his responsibilities. Things were already dire, but they were about to get worse – for the nation, and for Quinn.

***

By the end of 2008 Ireland was in economic freefall. Anglo, Seán FitzPatrick and Sean Quinn were fast becoming the focus of the media's attention as the inevitable crash approached. FitzPatrick resigned after it was alleged that he and his family had secretly borrowed over €100m from Anglo Irish Bank. The bank's share price had now tanked completely, dropping from sixty-seven cents to seventeen cents through the month of December 2008.

When the Quinn family gathered together for Christmas at the mansion, the atmosphere was one of crisis. The Quinn shares in Anglo, which had cost him over two billion euro, were now worth less than €20m.

In the new year, Finance Minister Brian Lenihan had no choice but to nationalise Anglo. David Drumm resigned as Anglo's CEO, and next out the door was the financial regulator, Patrick Neary, who was accused of being asleep on the job. Economist David McWilliams told RTÉ radio in 2015 that Neary was 'the worst financial regulator the world has ever seen'.

A man who was used to nothing but positive press, Quinn was now making headlines for all the wrong reasons. 'The gamble that went wrong', 'Quinn got what was coming' and 'Loans, fines and losses leave Quinn reeling' read some of the headlines.

Quinn decided that he needed to try to get ahead of the story by telling his version of events. An interview with RTÉ's Northern Editor, Tommie Gorman, for current affairs programme *Prime Time* in the last week of January 2009, was designed to address 'inaccurate innuendo'. Quinn, said Gorman, was fed up with the speculation but admitted that 'we all got a bit carried away and a bit greedy'. Gorman reminded viewers that Quinn was Ireland's richest man, 'who'd done it his way' and never gives interviews.

Now, he was in front of a camera in his own office, his red leather chesterfield chair in the background, somewhat glassy-eyed and clearly uncomfortable with the scrutiny. 'We can survive. We've written it off,' Quinn stuttered and then attempted to shut down any further questions about the Anglo dealings. In doing so, however, he only raised more queries about what had gone wrong.

At another point he looked to deflect any personal involvement in Anglo. 'It's the five kids and the wife that owns the shares in Anglo Irish Bank and I'm not discussing what their losses are but they are substantial.' However, Gorman pressed Quinn as 'the key figure in the most important family-owned group of businesses in the country' to put a figure on what Anglo Irish has cost them. 'It's more than a billion, yes,' Quinn admitted, laughing nervously, before again looking to downplay the extent of their troubles, 'it's substantial money but our company makes four or five hundred million profits per year and we'd probably be making six or seven hundred million but we're in the middle of a recession right now.'

Quinn assured Gorman that the 8,000 jobs in the Quinn Group were safe, including the 5,500 people who were employed in Ireland. 'We never put our company in doubt,' he repeated. 'Any money we put in shares was money we could afford to do without. That may seem a bit cheeky to say, but that's the reality of it. There's very few companies in Ireland as successful as we are. But, with hindsight, we were too greedy in being so much involved in stocks and shares.'

He was using the plural but there was only one person responsible for bringing the business to its knees. His family had simply facilitated his gamble, but he was, awkwardly and unconvincingly, putting them out there as if they'd decided to put a €2.8 billion bet on Anglo Irish Bank.

If Quinn thought the interview would steady the ship, he was wrong. His performance only drew the ire of those people who were appalled at the likes of 'the self-confessed greedy billionaire' who had helped create the economic crisis. 'I think at the time the media hung Sean Quinn out to dry, you know, he was crucified in the media,' said a former colleague.

This charged attitude in the media would only increase in the months ahead.

***

The group's accounts for the year told the tale, revealing €829m in write-offs, turning a €400 pre-tax profit into a €425m loss. For the moment, however, it did appear that Quinn would be able to dig himself out of the hole he'd made for himself. With so much money around, surely he had the means and the wherewithal to swallow the debt over a period of years and move on? Quinn Insurance had made over €200m in profits in 2007. The international properties were valued at €500m. If he sold the property portfolio and Quinn Insurance, he'd put a serious dent in what he owed to Anglo.

What many were unaware of was that Quinn still owed the €1.2 billion he'd borrowed from Barclays and the banking syndicate in 2005 and 2006. So his total exposure was in fact €4 billion. Quinn, indeed no company in Ireland, could handle that scale of debt, particularly in the midst of a global recession.

Quinn, Liam McCaffrey, Kevin Lunney and Dara O'Reilly were bunkered down in meeting after meeting at the group headquarters dedicated to finding a workable way out. They believed that it was possible, if Quinn was flexible. Critical to their plans was the insurance company. It was the cash cow and, without it, Quinn would find it impossible to repay his debts. But it was possible that he would have to consider selling off part of the business, and because of its value – which some suggest could have been up to €2 billion at one time – Quinn Direct was the obvious number-one choice. The next option was the cement business, although all the manufacturing companies were now of less value due to the economic collapse. Plans were worked and reworked with nothing agreed.

Meanwhile in Dublin, Patrick Neary was succeeded as financial regulator by a tough young Englishman, Matthew Elderfield. At Anglo, Brian Lenihan brought in former Fine Gael leader and finance minister Alan Dukes, to be a director at the bank. In an interview in 2019, Dukes admitted that, once at the helm, he was shocked to learn of the scale of the problem at the bank. 'We had an intensive set of board meetings from November through December into January 2009, when it rapidly became apparent that the situation was far worse than had been expected, even by the government, when the bank guarantee was put in place,' he said.

Highest on the list of the bank's problems was Sean Quinn. Dukes explained what he initially thought were the specific difficulties with Quinn's debts. 'Number one, the fact that somebody was, you know, taking punts, losing punts on bank shares, and that he kept getting bigger and bigger and bigger in a poorer and poorer and poorer bet. Then the efforts the bank made to deal with it in order to try and regain control of those shares and the things that had to be done – the whole Maple Ten ploy, so to speak – and what that meant and how that was being presented and how it was being looked at by the regulatory authorities and subsequently in other contexts. So that was obviously one of the big issues we had to deal with.'

At the time, Quinn was just one of Anglo's clients that owed billions. Property developers had also borrowed billions from the bank. Even among them, though, Quinn stood out. He was not only one of the biggest Irish losers of the economic collapse of 2008, he was the world's biggest single loser. A huge amount of Duke's time would be taken up dealing with Quinn alone.

One of his first tasks, however, was to hire a new executive team to manage the now-nationalised bank. Mike Aynsley was put in charge. From Sydney, Australia, he was a highly experienced banker. Having agreed to take on the roll, he brought in a former colleague at the National Australia Bank, Richard Woodhouse, an Englishman with a cut-glass accent. Alan Dukes immediately took to both Aynsley and Woodhouse. '[Mike] is pretty direct. If he doesn't agree with you he doesn't beat around the bush. If he agrees with you he doesn't spend forever telling you why he agrees with you. So, you know, it was a good relationship. He, looking at what was facing us in the bank, just thought about people he knew that he had worked with before who might be able to help, but he identified Richard Woodhouse and Richard came, talked to various members of the board, and we decided that he was a person we could use,' he said.

They were attempting to breathe new life into a zombie bank and once they got their heads around the scale of the problems, they set up a meeting with Quinn. 'I remember saying to them, look, selling Quinn Insurance is not going to get your money back very quickly,' said Quinn of the first meeting. 'Because you're not going to get the value of Quinn Insurance. They were talking at the time they might get two billion and

I was saying that that company is worth a lot more than two billion. I said, look, we will pay you back this money reasonably quickly. We will have it all paid back in less than ten years, 100 per cent of it paid back in less than ten years.'

It is clear from this that while Quinn may have been showing pragmatism to Liam McCaffrey and his colleagues regarding the potential selling of some parts of the company, he wasn't budging with the bankers. Quinn wasn't going to sell and he wasn't going to give up his total control of the group. His gut feeling, his instinct, was that the Dublin politicians would not see the jobs of thousands of voters on the border put at risk. They'd call off the dogs, i.e. Elderfield and Dukes, and reach an amicable agreement.

Quinn felt that no one else could run the businesses as profitably, so therefore he wouldn't get the sale value the bankers were looking for. 'I wrote to them the following week and I said, look, selling the business, selling any part of the business would be a mistake. It's very closely managed, it's micromanaged, it's running very well. It's a major part of our business [Quinn Insurance] and if we lost that our ability to repay the rest of the loans would become more difficult. And I said, what we can do between now and the end of 2012 is reduce your debt by 400 million, with the profits we were achieving. And Aynsley wrote back and said, that sounds not too bad, we will just keep in touch.'

Throughout 2009, with the country still coming to terms with the bill that was now owed for the extravagance of the past decade, Aynsley and Woodhouse briefed Alan Dukes on their discussions and communications with Sean Quinn, whom Dukes had no relationship with previously. 'I mean, one read occasionally about, you know, the Quinn companies and what they were doing, but they were quite prominent in the kind of business literature. And people admired, rightly, what had been done. When I got closer to it and was dealing [with] it from the bank's point of view, it seemed to me that this was really something, really quite remarkable – starting with sand and gravel, going onto cement, blocks, building materials and then moving into glass, into radiators and insurance. It seemed to me that this was a wholly admirable thing to do. And to this day I feel that what was done was absolutely remarkable, a terrific piece of business imagination and drive and purpose. And it was ruined because the person who led it all turned out to be a gambler and took a gamble at a very bad time on a very bad bet. And the more it went against him the deeper he got into it. And I felt it was an awful pity that such a good complex of businesses was put at so much risk so unnecessarily by this desire to gamble.'

Dukes explained that there wasn't just a concern in getting back what the bank was owed; there was also a genuine fear for the border community. 'We were very concerned, as a bank, both in terms of getting back what the bank was owed and also in terms of what we were dealing with on the ground, to make sure that if we could find a way of doing it, [so that] we preserved the maximum of what we could preserve of what the businesses were doing in the economic life of the area. And given where it was, and given what I had seen already about the border, I could see it was really important for that whole area. Not so much maybe the insurance company, although that I think was an important piece of the picture.'

Given Quinn's desire to hold on to every part of the business, conflict inevitably ensued between him and the bankers. 'It would have been hard to convince me to agree to sell assets. I accept that. It would have been hard to convince me, because I'd never seen any need for that. I didn't see that we were any way close to that, particularly when I wasn't looking for a write-off. If I was looking for a write-off of bad debt, that would be a different story. I was looking for no write off, I didn't want one. I certainly wasn't overly impressed with their attitude. So we didn't gel that well together.'

Another point of conflict was that he wanted to remain at the centre of it all. Talking about himself in the third person, something that has become a habit, Quinn said: 'They seemed to think that Sean Quinn felt that if it wasn't him was doing this it couldn't be done right. And they give that impression that he felt that he was invincible, he was the only man who could run any of this show.' He paused, then continued: 'If anybody came along and said, look, we want to take you out, I suppose I wouldn't have been happy with that. I'd have been asking why do you want to take me out? Is there anybody in the country [who] has been more successful in the last thirty years than I have been? Is there anybody [who's] grown their profits more than I have? Is there anybody you walk into their office and you get a cheque within thirty seconds every day, there is no issues with money?'

Dukes wasn't impressed by Quinn's plan, nor by his referring to himself in the third person. 'I know a few people who do that, and they're all a bit odd. And I find, most of the people I know who speak of themselves in the third person, have huge egos, and this is a way of kind of promoting themselves. The ego is so big that I have to admire myself, you know? They probably don't see it that way, but I think that's the psychology of it. They are seriously sick people in that way. It's because they have a huge ego.'

Chances of agreement soon faded. Quinn can admit now, more than a decade later, that he badly misread the situation. 'I have to take some of the criticism myself for that, maybe my attitude or maybe the fact that I wasn't as negotiable as I should have been [caused the negotiations to collapse]. I would maybe accept that, that I should have been – you see, we felt we were so strong, we genuinely felt we were so strong, it didn't occur to us, this is before administration, and this was, we were just making armfuls of money. Well, we had been. During that recession for a year or two, things were a bit tighter for everybody, profits generally halved, but that was a temporary thing. But our profit base was always there, you know, the whole factories and the whole insurance and the whole, everything was in place. And it never occurred to us that anybody … was going to take this draconian action to try to break up the Quinn Group, take it away and destroy it and take it out of my control.'

The wheels of such 'draconian' actions were already beginning to turn, however.

***

While the team at Anglo considered their next move, over at the financial regulator's office within the Central Bank on Dublin's Dame Street, they were poring over the finances of Quinn Insurance. They weren't happy with what they found.

Quinn had given assurances to Patrick Neary that he would put back the €288m he'd taken from the company, but now Neary's successor, Matthew Elderfield, saw that he had yet to do it. Colin Morgan, chief executive at Quinn Insurance, and Jim Quigley, who'd replaced Quinn as chairman after the regulator's fines in the autumn of 2008, worked up a repayment plan but throughout 2009 they failed to impress Elderfield or his team.

Then in March 2010 came a discovery that would change the dynamic, for the worse as far as Quinn was concerned. It was revealed that Quinn's borrowings from the Barclay syndicate and American bondholders, the €1.2 billion, was essentially secured against his €450m property portfolio. However, the property portfolio was owned by Quinn Insurance. So if Sean Quinn failed to repay his debts to his lenders, they could take ownership of the property. And that, in turn, would blow a massive hole in the insurance company's reserves.

How the property owned by a regulated insurance company came to be put up as collateral guarantees remains highly contentious. Quinn blames his executive team, while they say he was the one in charge and knew exactly what he was doing. According to Quinn, it came to a head in a boardroom meeting. 'We were saying, look, there are no guarantees given, guarantees are not given. Then Liam McCaffrey or somebody [said] there are guarantees given. Who gave them? Quinn claims to have asked a series of follow-up questions: 'How did that happen? Mistake. Did you read the documentation? No. And you did sign that there was a lien on some of this property? Yeah. But I said, but sure, we know that it was illegal, a guarantee can't be given on a regulated identity. Yeah, we will have to check that out, check that out. Up to Goodbody's [they went], who were the solicitors at the time.'

Contracts were pulled up and gone over, but it was clear – the lenders did have a guarantee on the property. There was nothing the quarryman could do to change that fact. He – or his executives, or both – had failed to read the small print and, as a result, the regulator was closing in.

Kevin Lunney would later tell an inquiry that he was 'as shocked and surprised as everybody' to discover that the guarantees had been given. According to an *Irish Times* report, although Lunney 'accepted his signature was at the bottom of the enabling documents, he said he believes that these were signed as part of a volume of paperwork that passed through his desk'. Lunney also told the inquiry: 'What I can say is that if it had been considered for a moment by me that the documents I was being asked to sign could have put additional risk on QIL or its subsidiaries, that would have been a red flag.'

Liam McCaffrey told the same inquiry that the Quinn Group had relied upon their lawyers, A&L Goodbody, to complete the documents for the loans. The lawyers had been advised that the financing couldn't effect Quinn Insurance. McCaffrey said: 'Unfortunately, the wording only carried "Quinn Insurance". It should have had "Quinn Insurance and its subsidiaries",' he said, adding that it was 'an omission that did not come to light until 2010'. According to the *Irish Times* report, McCaffrey also said: 'I have asked myself whether I should have spotted this issue. Whereas I wish I had … it didn't occur to me. The facts are that we took and followed appropriate legal and financial advice.'

A&L Goodbody denied that they'd ever been told by anyone at Quinn Group that the insurance company and the properties were not to be put up as guarantees. And while the insurer's auditor, PWC, did admit that it was aware of the guarantees, *The Irish Times* reported that the inquiry was told they just hadn't 'joined the dots'.

In March 2010, when the regulator began circling, the board members at the insurance company were told of the guarantees. Until then, they had been kept in the dark.

When Jim Quigley found out about the guarantees, he had to tell Elderfield. Quinn recalls the ultimatum that was subsequently given to him by Elderfield's team: 'On a Wednesday or Thursday of that week, they said we want it sorted out between now and Friday evening. By Friday they gave us until Tuesday.'

Even with the extra time, they couldn't walk the guarantees back and they couldn't deny that they were given. The die was cast. Quinn had stalled them on the repayments and had failed to put the business on the right footing. The days of light-touch regulation were gone. As a result, Quinn Insurance was about to go into administration.

***

On Tuesday, 30 March 2010, Matthew Elderfield's team went into court and in an *ex-parte* hearing (i.e. a secret hearing where they presented their case without Quinn being represented) lasting no more than thirty minutes, Quinn Insurance was taken out of the control of the Quinn family.

When he learned of the court hearing, Quinn was apoplectic. He believed he was in a negotiation, that the bankers and the regulator would come to an arrangement with him. 'I thought I had huge experience in business generally, but I had no experience as regards administration or the law or anything like that,' he said, adding, 'We didn't like the idea of a Quinn company going into administration, you know, that was making half a billion a year profit. We didn't like that idea, so there was sleepless nights. But we thought it would be sorted out.'

A senior manager was with Kevin Lunney at a meeting in the Quinn Insurance headquarters in Cavan when news filtered through of the administration. 'We all just huddled round, talking about it. We just couldn't believe it. It was absolutely, totally out of the blue.' He added, 'I suppose a lot of confidence was knocked out of a lot of people after that.'

Because it was *ex-parte*, there would be another hearing at which the Quinns could seek to have the initial decision overturned. Quinn called in the lawyers to fight back and urged all around him to put pressure on political representatives on both sides of the border. Despite Quinn's finger-pointing on the guarantees, the executive team also exhausted every possible opportunity to push back on the administration.

A week later, the first protest in support of Quinn was held in Cavan, where 1,000 protestors took part in a march. Two days later, 300 workers with 'Hands off Quinn Insurance' and 'Save our Jobs' placards marched to Dáil Éireann. The following week over 3,000 people took part in another Dublin march, this time to Matthew Elderfield's office, while back in Cavan, another 1,500 took to the streets. Thousands more marched in Enniskillen, while within days, over 17,000 people had signed a 'Save Quinn Insurance' online petition. The anger at these marches was primarily directed at Matthew Elderfield, 'The Financial Wreckulator' as one placard described him.

Quinn was talking to anyone who'd listen, including the Taoiseach. He was convinced the administration was temporary and would be reversed. Even the administrators still believed that Quinn could simply write a cheque that would allow him to come to an agreement with Elderfield. A court date was set for 15 April, and with both sides lawyered up, a showdown was expected. However Quinn failed to raise an objection to the administration being confirmed. Outside the court, Liam McCaffrey explained to the waiting journalists why, as detailed in the following day's *Irish Times*: 'We had to allow the administrators get on with finding a solution rather than fighting this in court, because nobody wins there. In order to resolve this, we need constructive dialogue with the regulator. The court is not the best place to do that. We have to accept the cold reality that we are in administration.'

The Quinn team had decided that, as they had the public onside, certainly on the border, a court hearing might only cause uncomfortable facts they didn't want their workers to discover to come into the public domain.

Quinn was going to try to get his company back through political pressure. It had worked at the time of the dotcom shambles and, he believed, it would work again. But these were different times and the wind was blowing in a very different direction now in the halls of the financial regulator. This Taoiseach didn't have any room to manoeuvre, given the state of the country's finances. Still, Quinn positioned the campaign to restore control of the company to him as being first and foremost about saving thousands of jobs in Ireland's rural communities. Given the deepening recession, did the out-of-touch politicians in Dublin want to economically devastate the border community that was so overwhelmingly reliant on Quinn for employment?

Quinn was gambling that he'd win in the boardroom – with the support of the people on the streets – rather than in the courtroom.

***

Over the course of the summer of 2010, Quinn sought to pull together a plan that would reverse the administration. But while he did this, the administrators had to deal with the reality at the insurer.

Initially, Matthew Elderfield decided that the company shouldn't be in the British market, that it was losing too much money there. But the administrators pushed back, hoping that there would be something that could be salvaged out of the UK business. However, after a review which, according to the *Irish Independent*, found that Quinn Insurance 'has insufficient capital to support its UK book', Elderfield said that the company would need to obtain sufficient new capital that could return it to the 'required solvency levels' before he would reconsider allowing it to trade in the British market.

Clearly, even the regulator at this point still believed that Quinn had the money to save the company.

During this period, the administrators also announced that 900 of the insurance company's 2,450 staff would go through voluntary redundancy and natural wastage. Over 230 jobs would be lost in Cavan and another 190 in Enniskillen. A decision still had to be taken about the long-term future of the business, but by making the job cuts and redundancies, it was clear that the administrators were preparing for one thing: a potential sale.

Behind the scenes, attempts continued to get the insurance company out of administration. But time was running out. Quinn knew the maths and he didn't need the help of a calculator to tell him that if the insurance company was sold he could never repay the bank, and worse, his whole business empire could collapse.

Throughout the summer, intense discussions took place with the management at Anglo Irish Bank, who, at the time, would have preferred to keep the Quinn Group intact, rather than selling off parts of it, as long as Quinn could pay off what was owed. Quinn said 'at the time we felt that it [the administration] would be reversed, that they'd find out that the company was very profitable; they'd find out, they would look through the figures and see that we were after increasing cash by half a billion. They would see that we had the highest reserves of any company in the country, any insurance company in the country. So we thought it would be reversed and that our management team would get together and sort this, meet the regulator and say, look, this is all a bad dream, there's no problem with this company. I suppose that's sort of where we were. I suppose we were very naive.'

Quinn and his executive team put together a new thirty-two-page proposal that would see him pay down his debts. However, for the plan to work, he needed another €650m in loans from the bank to stabilise the company. The money, Quinn proposed, would be used to meet the insurance company's solvency requirements. With this proposal, it was now clear to all involved that he didn't have billions squirrelled away that he could use to meet the regulator's demands.

Alan Duke recalls his reaction to the plan: 'He was in a different world as far as I could see. You know, there were issues about the effect of his actions on the companies, and he didn't seem to realise that he was a big part of the problem. And he kept insisting that he was the only person who could run these companies. And we were sitting there on the other side of the table, seeing the effects of his actions on the companies and the difficulties they had caused, and he still felt he was the only person who could do this. He produced plans that were financially just not feasible, that were all designed to keep him in control. Because the plans were just not feasible, we couldn't go along with them and we couldn't have him in control, obviously,' Duke added. 'To my mind it was pure fiction, fantasy. And the same view was taken by senior management in the bank. It was just a non-runner.'

If Quinn had no money, then it became even more likely that he was going to lose the insurance company. It looked certain now that it would have to be sold to help pay off his debt.

***

Whatever about the opinions held by those in the bank, those along the border felt that what was happening to Sean Quinn was an injustice. Tony Doonan – a border native and business owner, who often played cards with Quinn – was horrified by the administration. He believed, like thousands of others on the border, that it wouldn't have happened to a Dublin company. Quinn was being singled out because he'd had the audacity to take on the establishment.

A supporters' movement began to gather momentum. Doonan, along with two friends, worked the phones and called radio stations to put the case for Quinn. They helped form Concerned Irish Business (CIB) to lobby government. Doonan remembers how, 'A lot of people put a lot of time and effort into that. And there was a fantastic effort put into that to try and get them to turn it [the administration] around and to try and get the government to see, you know, that there wasn't, there was no need to do what they did.'

At one point, there was a plan to drive hundreds of trucks into Dublin city centre in a protest. 'There were 400 trucks assembled at Tucker's service station in Naas, outside Dublin. And they were from all over every county in Ireland. And the idea was to shut Dublin down. And that was our intention.'

They assembled on the outskirts of the city from early in the morning. 'Some people had left at three o'clock that morning, four o'clock that morning, to be there. But everybody was there with the one single intention, you know, that that's what was going to happen.'

Soon, however, the gardaí became involved. 'When they saw the huge convoy and then when you see all the trucks parked and think, these were heading for the city centre, they obviously knew what was going to happen. So they started to negotiate, and tempers were starting to get frayed and people were starting to get annoyed that, you know, they had come from all parts of Ireland and they had made sure they got their permits and they were going one place and one place only. So after a phone call to Sean Quinn, he conceded that [only] forty trucks would demonstrate. He had nothing against the people of Dublin, but unfortunately it's where everybody goes to make their protest most effective. And it almost led to fisticuffs,' said Doonan, expressing the fear and frustration felt by many on the border at the time.

CIB were independent of the company, but, as with the trucking protest, it was Sean Quinn who was the ultimate decision-maker. Nothing happened with which he didn't agree. The proposal to Alan Dukes and Anglo hadn't worked, but they kept piling on the pressure on the streets, believing that the politicians would ultimately see the sense in the Quinn plan.

In the meantime, plans for the sale of the company continued. As part of the due diligence ahead of any sale, the administrators had called in a British actuarial firm, EMB, to look under the bonnet of the insurance company and find anything that a prospective buyer would want to know, good or bad. The findings shocked Dukes and the administrators.

The report found fault in almost every aspect of the business. For the first time, the administrators realised that Quinn Insurance wasn't profitable. It wasn't worth €2 billion or anywhere near it; in fact, it was close to worthless. Alan Dukes, looking back, said it was, 'an insurance company that was badly run, that had business practices that were not going to be profitable. And none of the plans that we were ever presented by Sean Quinn for the development of the insurance company recognised the weaknesses that were there.'

Quinn and his team never accepted the findings, Quinn seeing it as part of the conspiracy designed to bury him and his business.

It was certainly a difficult finding to understand for the people employed at the company and their families living on the border. This was, after all, a company making hundreds of millions of profit, one that was hailed for its ingenuity and positive disruptive impact on the insurance industry in Ireland and the UK.

Still, despite the negative findings, the administrators decided to push ahead with the sale of the company. They soon opened talks with one of the biggest insurance firms in the world, Liberty Mutual, which had shown an interest in the company. Two weeks before Christmas 2010, Sean Quinn was told that Anglo and Liberty were putting together a bid.

Yet another festive season at the Quinn home was taken up by crisis talks, although this time the mood set by the patriarch was one of defiance. The New Year would see them put all the troubles behind them, he proclaimed. He was still confident that, despite everything, the regulator and the banks would back down and he'd get the insurance company out of administration and back under his control.

Quinn had brought his brother Peter in to advise him by this stage, and had David Mackey working alongside him once again. Outside of Liam McCaffrey, Kevin Lunney and Dara O'Reilly, Peter and David Mackey were his two closest advisors, and all were trying to find solutions.

It didn't help that other problems continued to appear. In parallel to the attempts to solve the insurance company's problems, the syndicate led by Barclays and made of up American bondholders that had lent the Quinn Group €1.2 billion had appointed a Scotsman, Murdoch McKillop, to represent its interest and come up with a plan for getting its debts repaid. McKillop proposed that the bankers take a short-term share in the group until the debt was repaid, albeit at a higher rate of interest than Quinn originally agreed. Quinn rejected it outright, seeing McKillop as another 'outsider' determined to break up his company.

Quinn was blind to it, but it was the last deal to save his company he would ever be offered.

***

On the afternoon of 13 April 2011 Alan Duke's office contacted Quinn and asked him, Kevin Lunney and Dara O'Reilly to come to a meeting in Dublin at 9.30 a.m. the following morning. The meeting would be on the same day that Quinn's supporters were holding another protest rally in Dublin. They were going to hand over a petition to the financial regulator, calling for the insurance company to be put back in Sean Quinn's hands. It had over 93,000 signatures.

The timing bode well, in Quinn's mind. He drove his colleagues down to the capital in his Range Rover, sure this was going to be the breakthrough. Finally, they'd all come to their senses and realised he was their best bet. They were going to do the deal. As the three headed south, he told them of his confidence that they'd be celebrating back at the Slieve Russell that night.

'Sean was convinced that he would be presented with a solution during the meeting,' said O'Reilly later.

Dukes said he'd a clear plan for the meeting. 'Ostensibly the reason for the meeting was to talk to Sean Quinn about, on a kind of a last-chance basis, is there an agreement we can make?' He added, 'We knew, we expected, pretty much with certainty, that he wasn't going to accept any kind of plan that we would put to him.'

Mike Aynsley and Richard Woodhouse were on Duke's side of the table, which was only to be expected, but the Quinn team were surprised to see a note-taker in the room. Very quickly they realised this wasn't going to go as planned. 'I tried to make pleasantries, but I knew the mood was cool,' said Quinn.

What the quarryman didn't know was that, for the previous four months, KPMG's Kieran Wallace, on behalf of Alan Dukes and IBRC, had been putting together a sophisticated plan for this very moment. And Quinn played right into their hands.

It is unusual for two sets of lenders – in this case Anglo (now IBRC) and the bondholders – to come together to agree a plan for liquidating the assets of a company. But because Quinn wasn't playing ball with either party, IBRC and the bondholders had gone into an intensive set of negotiations about how best to retrieve the €4 billion owed to them, once the company was put into liquidation, which was looking more and more inevitable in early 2011. A deal was eventually struck that would put the Quinn group into receivership. IBRC agreed that they would seek to recoup the €2.4 billion owed to the Irish taxpayer out of the property assets that Quinn had amassed in Ireland, the UK, Eastern Europe and Asia. As for Quinn's border businesses, the bondholders would take a 75 per cent ownership with IBRC taking 25 per cent, but with the proviso that they would see none of their money until the bondholders recouped all of theirs plus interest. It was an agreement that would have long-term ramifications for both parties and, most importantly, the Irish taxpayer. But it was a unique situation, which called for a unique, workable solution. With an agreement on the assets in place, Alan Dukes invited Quinn to Dublin for one final meeting. One final chance.

When Quinn again rejected out of hand any compromise, Dukes cut to the chase. In a 2019 interview, Quinn vividly remembered the moment it dawned on him that this wasn't the meeting he was expecting to have. 'Dukes said they were taking over the company and there was people gone to Derrylin this morning as we speak, there was people taking over The Slieve Russell and the Quinn Group. Sean's gone and you two boys are gone as well, you're sacked. Everybody's gone.'

Dukes recalls Quinn's reaction. 'He's not a very demonstrative man, but he was obviously shocked and he didn't say a whole lot very quickly, but he then asked what the implications of this were. Were we going to take all of the businesses, or were we going to take all of the units, all of the property assets? To which the answer was, yes. And he said at the end, I can't agree to that, I don't agree to that, there's no point in going any further. And he got up and left. And when he left, the phone calls were made to say the meeting had not succeeded in obviating the operation, so the operation was to commence, and it did.'

Quinn said he warned Dukes that his actions weren't going to go down well. 'I said, look, if you are taking over the company, I can't see where that's coming from, because there's going to be big fights here. Because the assets, a lot of the assets, India, Russia, Ukraine, you never financed those. Those were, we financed those out of our own cash flows. And how can you take those? And we are going to fight those.'

Quinn became 'incredibly angry', according to one of those in the room. Amid all the revelations, Dukes also dropped a final bombshell: he told them that the insurance company was going to be sold to Liberty Mutual. (Though in the end this deal did not transpire.)

As they left the meeting, Lunney and O'Reilly were given brown envelopes with letters terminating their contracts with immediate effect. The three men staggered out of the bank's headquarters and onto Burlington Road, where they hurriedly called Liam McCaffrey back in Derrylin. However, he was already dealing with the arrival of dozens of men in dark clothing and high-visibility jackets who'd just arrived unannounced at the company headquarters.

The three men set off for the offices of their solicitors, Eversheds, where Quinn would make a decision that would come to haunt him for the rest of his life. 'When we left Anglo's office,' he recalls, 'we were in complete shock. And we arrived at Eversheds, I suppose, some of the kids were there as well, and we started to gather up a little bit and what's going on, what's happening. Everybody was just looking at each other in amazement ... why has it come to this?'

They all gathered in a meeting room. There was nothing they could do to stop Dukes putting the company into receivership, but a plan was put forward to protect the family property portfolio, which, it was argued, hadn't been financed by the bank, so they had no lien over it. 'Well, it wasn't my idea – it wasn't that I wouldn't do it, I would do it – but I hadn't thought of moving the assets that they hadn't financed. Other people who were smarter than I, they thought of it. And I said, that's a good idea. I supported it, so I'm not trying to blame anybody, and if I thought of it myself I'd probably have proposed it, you know. It was a Quinn decision. And that was it. People were on airplanes that evening.'

He'd just lost his manufacturing business, the hotels and the insurance company were being sold, but Quinn was determined to hold on to the €500m of offices, hotels and tower blocks he'd bought for his family across Europe, Russia and India. It was a bold plan, indeed an illegal one, and in that moment, in a fit of rage, he agreed to a proposal that would eventually cost him his freedom.

Having taken the decision, Quinn, Dara O'Reilly and Kevin Lunney set off for home, stopping, as was usual, for a steak in the Ardboyne Hotel in Navan. Later, as they crossed the border, Dara, who was selling his home at the time, got a call from the estate agent asking if he was prepared to sell his sofa with the house. 'You've got me on the wrong day,' he told him with a degree of understatement.

With military planning and preparation, IBRC and the bondholders had appointed KPMG to take over the running of Quinn Group (ROI), the ultimate parent company owned by the five children that controlled everything outside of Quinn Insurance, which was already in the control of administrators. As Quinn and his two executives had been driving south, dozens of accountants and officials, backed up by an ex-military security company, Risk Management International, passed them heading north. The bankers were not just taking over, they were sending a clear message to Sean Quinn and the border community: they were now in charge.

But their decision to send in a heavy security team to an area which had lived under the control of the British Army for a generation was provocative and established a tone to the events that would have a long-lasting, disastrous effect. 'It was hard to believe that a team of people could come from southern Ireland, cross the border, go into Northern Ireland, take over head office, take over the whole company. Obviously [it] showed there was a lot of cooperation between the northern and southern authorities to allow that to happen. But the local people were in shock over it to be honest,' said one senior manager.

The bankers had spent months planning this pincer-like movement on the group headquarter buildings, as well as the insurance offices in Cavan and Enniskillen, and by 11 a.m. were in full control of Quinn's businesses.

One of the senior managers was in Dublin at the time, helping to hand over the petition calling for Quinn Insurance to be handed back to the quarryman. Afterwards, they'd gone to another of Quinn's hotels, Buswells, which is a short walk from Dáil Éireann, when word filtered through. 'It was disbelief,' he said, 'because it was not something that we saw coming. We rang back to a few people in Derrylin and they gave us some details of what had happened, how they had come in and took over head office.'

A former finance director at Ulster Television in Belfast and IWP International in Dublin, Paul O'Brien would be the new chief executive officer. Just a few months before he had been appointed as a non-executive director in Quinn Group (NI). Now he was the guy in the firing line, who was going to have to deal with the changeover from Quinn's team to his own team appointed by the bankers.

O'Brien was given round-the-clock security. He was going to need it.

11

The Molly Maguires

For years, Sean Quinn and his executive team had been in the trenches, waging a war of attrition. Now it was over and they had lost. But that's not to say that there wasn't a sense of relief, at least for some of them.

In the weeks after Thursday, 14 April 2011, Liam McCaffrey, who left the company after a severance package was agreed that included a write-off of €500,000 in director's loans that he'd taken to pay off his own Anglo CFD margin calls, was told that he looked ten years younger. The stress he'd been living under had fallen away. One of his executive colleagues said that for the first time in many years he could ask himself: what do I want to do with my life? Since the wheels came off when Anglo shares began to go south, there had been a sense of helplessness in the offices of the headquarters. They'd been through four years of intensity that never let up. 'Now it was all someone else's problem,' said one of the team.

Liam McCaffrey, Dara O'Reilly and Kevin Lunney had stood behind Quinn. After all, he had provided them with opportunities they could only have dreamt of; in return, they'd given him every second of every working day – and more. Their lives had become dominated by their jobs. They lobbied for him, they put their integrity on the line for him, and despite all that he'd been guilty of, they remained loyal. They could walk away knowing that they owed the quarryman nothing.

There would be time to answer the question 'What now?' but over the weekend after the takeover, emotions were raw on the border. Quinn was out. Liam, Dara and Kevin had given the best years of their careers to Quinn. Who was next? How many jobs would survive by the time this was all over? While there were concerns over individual jobs, worries also started to grow regarding Quinn's empire. Over the weekend it dawned on those who knew the process of administration that, just like the insurance company, Quinn's entire organisation could now be broken up and sold off. Selling the company off to recover what was owed to the bank was unlikely to benefit the thousands employed in the cement factory, the bottling plant, the roof-tile and radiator businesses, and the hotels.

With that realisation came fear and anger. A senior manager, who'd worked for Quinn for thirty years, summed up the mood at the time. 'Sean Quinn never played golf with High Court judges and politicians in Dublin. He had no connections in Dublin. And the media, as I say, just spun the one line, that he was totally to blame. And I would take a different view on that. Obviously, he could have done things better. He took a huge punt on Anglo. It went sour. But he has built a tremendous operation.'

However, it wasn't just the fact that Quinn had lost the businesses, it was the way in which it had been done that created a resentment felt by those living along the border, even those who weren't directly impacted. The bankers in Dublin had not just taken Quinn out, they had humiliated him and his team. They'd tricked him into thinking he was going to come home with a deal, invited him to a spurious meeting, while they were preparing to take him out by the roots.

The government, of course, was eager to cast a positive light on the takeover. Speaking in the Dáil, Fine Gael Finance Minister Michael Noonan, who'd sought cabinet sign-off for the receivership forty-eight hours before the takeover, claimed that the move was 'a good news story' for the workers and the border region. 'The fact that all the jobs are protected [means] the same spend will be going on through the community up there,' he said. Noonan's comments only added fuel to the fire for those on the border who saw the politicians in Dublin as conspiring to make Quinn the poster boy for all that had gone wrong in the Irish economy, and to help absolve the political classes of their role in the meltdown. Many years later, they are still remembered by Quinn and his supporters as evidence of the ruthless intent of the Fine Gael minister.

Quinn has said that the day of the takeover was the worst of his life. 'I suppose the lowest point for me was when Anglo Irish bank sent a hundred people down to Cavan and Fermanagh to take over the companies that I had built over a thirty-seven-, thirty-eight-year period. And when I heard the Minister for Finance coming out that night and saying, this is a good day for the border area, I just couldn't believe it. I just couldn't believe it. After getting no support from the Irish government over a forty-year period, no grants, no nothing, paid them hundreds of millions of tax, directly and indirectly, created 7,500 jobs in one of the poorest regions in Europe, and the day they put Sean Quinn out, the man that created it all, the Minister for Finance of the Irish government to come out that night and say, "This is a good day for the border region." I just said to myself, where in the name of God do we go from here? This is what we're dealing with. That was my low day,' said Quinn, still feeling the cut of the wounding comments almost ten years on.

Until the takeover, the dominant mood in the community had been one of worry and concern mixed with a belief that, in the end, the Mighty Quinn would survive. Now they'd lost their chieftain, the man who had given them not only jobs but careers, helped them build families and homes in an area where generations had to leave to earn the kind of money Quinn's companies were paying.

To add insult to injury, there was a growing feeling that they were being laughed at for believing in a man like Sean Quinn. 'There was only one story that was ever spun in the media, and to be honest, if they got their way they would have blamed him for the financial crash that happened,' said one company manager. 'He was blamed practically for everything else, you know. But the local people had tremendous loyalty to Sean, and I suppose rightly so at the time, when you look back at what he created and what he put into the area. And bear in mind, as I said previously, the governments both sides of the border invested practically nothing in the border regions. And that's, I suppose, where the loyalty came from.'

When Sean Quinn was in charge, there had never been a single redundancy in any of the companies. Now, hundred of jobs had already gone in insurance. 'Everyone feared for their jobs, and that a liquidator, well, their job is to first and foremost secure their own salary first and see that there's enough to sell off to pay them, and then sell off to the highest bidder,' said Tony Doonan.

Sean Quinn still retained some of his fight, however. He went to Sunday Mass as usual, where he shook hands and accepted the support and condolences of everyone there. But he assured them, this wasn't over. He hadn't given up.

By the Monday morning, Kevin Lunney had lined up a series of meetings with politicians, anyone they thought would give them a fair hearing. But while the executives were plotting their moves, one worker decided it was time for more direct action.

Just before lunchtime, he commandeered a dump truck from the quarry and hared down the main Derrylin to Ballyconnell road to the group headquarters, where he drove it directly towards the offices where Paul O'Brien and his team were based, only to be stopped by the concrete bollards in front of the building. It wasn't a spur-of-the-moment action by a crazy loyal employee. The man driving the truck was known as a very significant figure at the company. The workers knew who he was. It sent a clear signal that senior staff were on Quinn's side.

As the Quinn employees gathered in the company canteen at lunchtime, the atmosphere was tense, conversations laced with rumour and counter-rumour of what had happened and what was being planned.

Tony Doonan's group, Concerned Irish Business, condemned the attack, but he says it was understandable. 'There was trouble in the area because [of] the way the company was taken over initially,' he explained.

Quinn's supporters were already mobilising.

Padraig Donohoe owned grocery stores in Ballyconnell, Belturbet and Ballinamore. He'd first managed his father's pub in Ballyconnell before going out on his own. Donohoe helped form a new group that emerged after the takeover: The Cavan, Fermanagh, Leitrim Community Action Group. 'We were all devastated when Quinn was dethroned. He had transferred this pothole-ridden countryside into a beautiful industrial oasis. What was once one of the poorest parts of Ireland had become one of the wealthiest. And like a great fallen animal we saw the vultures flying overhead: the liquidators, the regulators, the financiers, the accountants, the lawmen, the bondholders and the bankers. All ready to tear off the flesh of this very tasty carcass,' he said.

What was already clear was that Quinn was not the only one with fight still in him; many along the borderlands were determined that Quinn be restored to what they saw as his rightful position.

***

The morning after the dumper-truck attack, a dawn meeting was called at the Teemore GAA Club to prepare for a protest rally at the headquarters. Tony Doonan was there. 'We had a letter prepared to hand in to Paul O'Brien.'

When they arrived at the headquarters – a large crowd, by now – things quickly escalated. 'When we went to the door, we got in and then everyone sort of followed, upstairs and downstairs in [to the] headquarters. All the protesters were in and we were looking out windows. And we had the building taken over.'

Having somewhat unexpectedly stormed to the headquarters, they began a sit-in. Padraig Donohoe was among them. 'There was a hardcore of about 200 protesters, but at one stage there were up to 1,000 people in the building,' he said. 'The doors were not locked when we arrived. We were not obstructed.'

Donohoe told RTÉ radio that, 'We are here today to look after the property of the rightful owner until he returns. I believe it is customary in this area for people to stand by their neighbour when they are being evicted,' he said to loud cheers.

The protestors, some with placards stating 'Anglo Bailed Out, Quinn Sold Out' and 'Quinn Gone, Jobs Gone', took over Sean Quinn's office, holding a black-and-white photocopied picture of him with a simple message, 'Bring Back Quinn'. Many of them in hi-vis jackets and workmen's boots walked the corridors they'd never seen before, the very inner sanctum of the Quinn empire. Padraig Donohoe made a short speech, demanding that Quinn be reinstated to loud and noisy cheers from the quarryman's hardcore supporters. Soon camera crews arrived and got pictures of them. Their message was clear. This wasn't going to be a normal business administration. Quinn Country wasn't going to take the actions of the Dubliners, the regulator nor the politicians lightly.

Tony Doonan said it was Quinn himself who ordered the ending of the sit-in. 'I think there was only two or three police officers present, at no time did they feel threatened. Someone went down and rang Sean and Sean said, look, you have made your protest, you have done your bit, vacate the building. There's people there that have jobs, they need to get paid. You're going to be interfering with stuff. You've made your point, thank you very much, vacate the building. And again, in my view, and in a lot of other people's views, that was another mistake we made. But sure, I suppose, we never envisaged getting into the building.'

As the protestors withdrew, Kevin Lunney and Dara O'Reilly arranged to meet with Paul O'Brien to agree the terms of their departures. It wasn't a negotiation, so the process was completed within the week. The new CEO also had to deal with Quinn's son, Sean Junior, and his nephew, Peter Darragh Quinn. 'Petey', as he was known to all, had been a key player in building Quinn's international property portfolio with particular responsibility for the Russian and European buildings they owned, while

Sean Junior had worked in the insurance business. Both Petey and Sean Junior were offered severance packages, which they refused.

There were even discussions on a package for Sean Quinn himself, but these came to nothing when he refused to give up his right to sue the bankers. Sure enough, within weeks, he'd served notice in the Dublin courts that he was going to launch an action in the names of his children, the shareholders.

Amid the protests and lawsuits, Petey and Sean Junior criss-crossed Europe and India, trying to secure the property that Quinn had bought before the bankers could take ownership of them. Quinn says that he believed, wrongly, that because Anglo Irish Bank hadn't financed the properties, they belonged to the family. 'If we lost the manufacturing business or we lost the insurance, fine, but at least we would have these properties. And they were very comprehensive. We had a lot of properties. We had India, Russia and Ukraine, we would have had twenty companies, twenty properties that they had never put a penny of finance into. So we thought that at least it's a back door and something we would have.'

Petey and Sean Junior's job was to move all the properties out of the names of the family and into companies and individuals that were unconnected to the Quinns. That way, it could be argued, they were no longer under the ownership of the family and therefore weren't covered by the receivership. It was a complex task, riddled with risk, but with a value of over €500m, and throwing off €70m of profit each year, it was felt that it was one worth taking.

***

In an email to staff, the new chairman of the Quinn Group, Pat O'Neill, a businessman who'd joined the board in 2009, tried to reassure them that there would be no immediate redundancies (outside of the insurance company) and it was business as usual. But the general workforce remained sceptical, if not downright hostile.

Paul O'Brien, who quickly became the face of the bankers in Derrylin, could understand their distrust. 'When you see your colleagues who've been in business with you for a long time move on, it makes you fearful,' he told reporter Rodney Edwards of *The Impartial Reporter*. 'For the first couple of weeks you were living and breathing it, but I had to say to myself, "Hang on a minute, I can't be concerning myself with things that are outside of my control." The best thing I can do is to look after the business.' Apart from the protests, O'Brien was aware that some big customers were also displaying loyalty to Quinn. 'We've a couple of customers who have suspended their activity until they see how Sean is dealt with but we'll be fighting very hard to get them to come back to us,' O'Brien told Edwards. 'I can't say we won't lose any customers – we've got to fight like hell so we don't.'

If he was going to return value to the bankers, he had to placate the protestors, keep the management on board, retain his customer base, and find buyers for the business. Not only had he businesses in Derrylin and Ballyconnell to consider, there was the huge radiator plant in North Wales, the Barlo businesses that stretched across Europe and the plastics plant outside Leipzig, which was still only half-built.

But with Quinn loyalists still within the ranks of management, O'Brien found it impossible to maintain any secrecy as to what he was trying to do. 'They tried to outsource the transport and logistics to a third party. They were trying to sell Quinn Glass,' said one such loyalist. 'I suppose they went in with the remit to get maximum return to the bondholders, and to do that they had to sell the most profitable companies. I suppose [one of] the crown jewels at that time was Quinn Glass, and they certainly made attempts to sell that, but that created a lot of, I suppose, anger in the area. I sent an email – I think to Paul O'Brien at that time – just outlining some of my concerns, and he summoned me down to head office. I sat across the table from him and he was quite irate, banging the table, telling me why was I doing this, why was I doing that. When I left I suppose I knew I wasn't in line for any promotions.'

Other loyalists were determined to keep Quinn in the loop. While Kevin Lunney had left the business, his brother Tony remained in position. It was reported by *Bloomberg Businessweek* magazine that he got the nickname 'Tony Two Phones' due to the suspicion that he had one for the business and another to keep in touch with Sean Quinn. Tony Lunney told the magazine that the second phone was a BlackBerry he used for emails. One of those who worked with him at the time told of an incident in which he dropped the second phone in Sean Quinn's old office, only for it to be discovered by one of Paul O'Brien's colleagues. Before Tony Lunney realised that he'd misplaced it, the phone was found to have Sean Quinn and a number of other former colleagues' contact details on it. Eventually, Tony Lunney too left the business, though not before having been promoted by Paul O'Brien, who was likely following the 'keep your friends close but your enemies closer' strategy.

Despite these distractions, top of O'Brien's to-do list was to get to the bottom line of the company: what shape was it in and what was it worth. Based on the figures of the previous management, the bondholders believed the company profitability was projected to be between €120m and €150 in the 2011/12 financial year. Having arrived at that figure, a calculation could be made on its overall value. Using EBITDA (Earnings before interest, taxes, depreciation and amortisation), the bondholders believed it would be around €675m, which would go some way to repaying what they were owed. The rest of their debt – €800m of it – would likely have to be traded on the junk bond market, with the bondholders unlikely to ever see a cent of it. However, as O'Brien pored over the figures, he came to believe that the previous management had massively overstated their profitability, which was somewhat understandable given their plight and their hopes to borrow their way out of trouble. He believed the company's profits were going to be closer to €70–80m, seriously below the original valuation made before the liquidation.

It wasn't what the bondholders wanted to hear and caused a number of acrimonious meetings. However, once they came to agree on O'Brien's figures, they realised that the debt would have to be restructured, causing the company value to be seriously written down. The bondholders might be lucky to get €500 million back if it was all successfully sold off. It wasn't the best position to be in. But the bondholders believed in O'Brien and threw all their support behind him as he struggled to get on top of the task he'd taken on.

While this was going on the Quinn family threw its first punch of the fightback that had been signed off on by Sean Quinn in his solicitor's office following the meeting with Alan Dukes. Some of the international property was managed through Swedish companies and the family instructed lawyers in Stockholm to go into court, *ex-parte*, and ring-fence their assets so that they couldn't be claimed by Anglo, thereby protecting the huge 'rent rolls', i.e. the money paid by those who leased the properties, as well as ensuring that the ownership of the property remained with them. By the time Anglo found out, it was too late to do much about it.

Word soon hit the border that the Quinns were not taking the take-over lying down and were at work across Europe, trying to secure what was theirs. Petey knew he was up against the clock. Anglo would soon discover what he was up to and would be on his tail. He flew to Russia and, with the help of other members of the family, pulled the same move with the Kutuzoff Tower, essentially creating new companies and debts to allow the buildings to be transferred into new ownership, and, on paper, away from the family. It would also ensure that the €22m in annual rent the tower brought in would flow into Quinn-controlled bank accounts.

Back in Dublin, Alan Dukes and those working with him on the Quinn property portfolio recovery plan, Richard Woodhouse and Mike Aynsley, were beginning to realise just what a tangled web Quinn had woven. 'The bank, and this was one part of Richard Woodhouse's genius, looked to acquire security over all the assets in the group, because of the level of debt that there was arising in the activities in Ireland,' said the former Anglo chairman. 'And the bank had got itself into a position where it had a security over the shares of all the companies that owned all of these investments. Now, that looked neat on the surface, [but] in practice it turned out to be much more difficult to deal with than one might have expected, because there were so many companies, there were so many different relationships.' He added, 'We knew we were in for the beginning of something new, but we didn't realise at that stage quite how difficult it was going to be.'

Throughout 2011 Alan Dukes, Richard Woodhouse and Mike Aynsley would employ teams of lawyers across the continent to take on the Quinns in a costly cat-and-mouse game while, in parallel, working with Paul O'Brien to restructure the company. At the end of this process, a blueprint had been drawn up of the viable and non-viable companies within the group.

Meanwhile, other groups were planning to stop the bankers through whatever means necessary.

***

The Molly Maguires were a violent secret society that grew up out of the border 'badlands' of western Cavan, Leitrim and Fermanagh. They took their name from a widow, who, in the 1840s, had protested against the English landlords occupying Irish land. She led the 'Anti-landlord Agitators', who were known to take on the landlords in bare-knuckle fights. Molly herself was reported to have worn pistols strapped to her thighs, although very little else is known about her or her death. According to local historians, 'take that from a son of Molly Maguire' was often the cry after a landlord had taken a beating.

In the latter half of the nineteenth century 'the Mollies', as they were known, inspired tenants in England and in the US to take on their landlords. On the border, they were known to dress in women's clothing in order to hide their true identity. '[The Mollies] were primarily about using violence to undermine the landlords and strike out at anything that affected the ordinary workers in the hope of improving things for them,' explained *The Impartial Reporter*.

There were no English landlords on the border in 2011. But in the days and weeks after the bankers came into Quinn Country, men began to meet to discuss how best to react. In a family barn on Molly Mountain, one group of men got together. They were neighbours, had been for generations. There was distrust among them too, due to some dispute between their antecedents that was still an open wound. But what bound them together was their support for Sean Quinn and their distaste for what Anglo had done to him. Anglo was now the modern-day version of the English landlords who had not only evicted their chieftain, but were threatening the future of the workers who'd helped to build his empire.

A new iteration of the Molly Maguires was established in that barn on the mountain above the Quinn headquarters. Among their membership were republicans who had experience of conflict. Those putting the Mollies together knew who to turn to, who had the knowledge and ability to help execute the plans they were already forming.

It wasn't long before the attacks began. On 15 May, in darkness, members of the Mollies set out across the fields they knew well. Their target was an isolated electrical substation. Working from information gained by members who had knowledge of the electrical grid in the area, and from the staff inside Quinn's companies, they knew exactly which substation served the wind farms. Using quads, the Mollies crossed the fields to the substation where, armed with the keys to get inside the fencing, they proceeded to pour petrol into the circuit breaker and power transformer and set it alight.

No one was ever arrested or questioned about the attack.

The glass plant was seen as the one part of the business that had to be protected above all the others. The Mollies were briefed by figures still within the Quinn structure that if it could be destabilised, without damaging the plant itself in any way, it would put off any prospective buyers. Following the substation attack, the Mollies sourced heavy chains – not difficult in a farming community – which they carried to particular sections of overhead cables. They were told that if the chains were thrown over the lines, it would cut the power to the factory. On a Friday night in July 2011, power lines supplying Quinn Glass were targeted. The saboteurs had been given directions by someone with clear knowledge of the electrical supply; someone who knew the grid and how it could be cut. The following day, two vans and a lorry were burnt out at Quinn Tarmac.

The vans and lorries could be replaced, of course, but for Paul O'Brien, three months into the administration, the trouble was of growing concern, particularly as it appeared that the PSNI and gardaí were clearly unable to apprehend those responsible.

The Mollies then began to cut down the electrical telegraph poles. They targeted the 'corner pole' on a particular section of the grid so that it messed up a supply to the plants and factories below. At the time, Northern Ireland Electricity said the vandals who cut down four poles supporting the 110,000-volt cables were 'lucky to be alive'. Not that this apparent close call stopped them: if anything, their activities intensified.

There were over a dozen such attacks across the summer of 2011. The Mollies would use chainsaws to cut two-thirds of the way through the pole, leaving it still standing, knowing that a slight gust of wind would blow it over once they were long gone.

Not all the attacks went as planned. One of those involved was seriously injured when he was electrocuted by one of the power lines. Fellow members of the gang got him across the border and secretly treated by an off-duty doctor.

Buoyed by their general success, the Molly Maguires increased the frequency of the attacks. Fibre-optic cables leading to the Quinn Group headquarters and the wind farm were also targeted. In July two vans – a loading-shovel vehicle and a tarmac-spreader – were destroyed in a fire at the Quinn tarmac plant. Damage was estimated at over €300,000.

Diesel pumps were destroyed to prevent delivery trucks refuelling and sugar put into their tanks. The attacks kept coming, with more power lines cut down and steel spikes thrown across the main route out of the cement factory to stop Quinn lorries from going about their business.

In Dublin, Anglo believed Sean Quinn was stoking the fire of the weekly attacks across the summer of 2011, inciting hatred of the bank and against those involved in the administration of his former businesses.

Those in Dublin would be shocked by the next attack.

Shortly before 11 p.m. on Monday, 8 August, a lone figure carrying two jerrycans of petrol walked through the cul-de-sac of homes known as Fox Lodge, in the village of Ratoath, ninety minutes south-east of the Quinn headquarters in Derrylin. Given the late hour, no one noticed the man as he approached one particular home and jumped the wall. In an attack which took a full twenty minutes to execute, he coolly opened up the cans and poured the fuel over the BMW X5 and Ford S-Max parked in the drive. Using a lighter, he set the two vehicles on fire before jumping back over the wall, pausing only to ensure they were ablaze. Unsatisfied, he coolly jumped back over the wall and used a stick to fan the flames. He made his escape only when certain that the flames had taken hold.

Within ten minutes the neighbours had called Ashbourne Fire Station but by the time they got to the scene, the BMW was completely gutted, while the Ford as well as guttering and window frames on the house were also damaged.

Paul O'Brien was on holiday in Portugal when he got the call. His home had been attacked. The violence was taking on a new dimension.

The following morning, the Quinn Group described it as a 'terrorist attack' while O'Brien said: 'When you go down the route of a personal attack, it's a much different matter. It's crossing the line. It is unprecedented that it is a personal attack. The previous attacks have been on the property of the business. It is escalating to a very dangerous level where somebody has the potential to be killed.' The acting CEO told RTÉ Radio: 'You'd be fairly hard-nosed to say you wouldn't be scared.

But I'd be a strong character. I don't think you can let people face you down.'

Quinn condemned the attack in a statement he released to the press: 'When I was contacted by the chairman of the Quinn Group in May to condemn reported acts of sabotage and intimidation, I replied that this was a clear inference that I was interfering in the business. In my response I also stated that I found such an inference "deeply offensive". I wish to state in the most categoric [sic] terms that I have no knowledge whatsoever of any unlawful acts in relation to individuals or property associated with the Quinn Group other than what I have read in the media.'

But O'Brien wasn't comforted. 'Either he fails to recognise it [his impact on the situation] or he's choosing not to,' he told *The Irish Times*.

Under the headline, 'Quinn in bitter clash with new group boss O'Brien after attacks', the *Irish Examiner* reported that the quarryman had himself spoken to an inspector in the Police Service of Northern Ireland (PSNI) several weeks before about the attacks on his former business. 'I stated, in clear and unequivocal terms, that persons carrying out such acts were not acting in my name and requested them to cease,' Quinn told the paper.

Violence on the Fermanagh–Cavan border was nothing new, of course, even to a generation that had lived in peace for over a decade. If you take something away, be it their land or, in more modern times, the Aghalane Bridge in the Troubles, you have to expect a response of some sort. It is deep in the soil.

They had lived in peace for over a decade. In that time, Quinn had built his empire. Now, locals feared it was being dismantled. Being suspicious of Dublin, London and Belfast was in the soil on the borderlands. A dozen IRA volunteers may have sustained the campaign on the Cavan–Fermanagh border, but they had widespread support in a community that feared the heavy military presence and political indifference. The communities here have learned to expect little from governments and to be suspicious of outsiders making promises.

Quinn had motivated the championship-winning Teemore Shamrock team through raw emotional appeal – 'the first man to cross the forty-yard line gets his leg broke' – and had built an empire on his ability to inspire and motivate. Over 95 per cent of the thousands of people who worked for him never met him personally, nor spent any time in his presence, but they were prepared to go the extra mile for what he stood for; for what his company stood for. There was no doubt he was going to do all that he could to get the company back. He knew that, in his community, he was a leader, a champion, a chieftain. And while there was a line, for him, that he may not have been prepared to cross, for others who were very close to him that line didn't exist.

***

The attack on Paul O'Brien's house saw him increase his security. He travelled to England and bought an armoured jeep to replace the burnt-out BMW. His friends took the piss out of him for having to have a security team drive him everywhere, even to the pub for a pint, but he wasn't prepared to take any chances. His family home was known to his enemies. He had to protect them no matter the cost.

While he attempted to run the company, the former Quinn team were still together, meeting on a daily basis. They had set up a new headquarters in offices owned by Tony Lunney, Kevin's brother, in Belturbet. They were akin to a shadow cabinet, planning how to overturn the administration while constantly lobbying in Dublin for the viability of their plans for bringing the company back under the control of Sean Quinn.

But by late summer, tensions began to emerge. Liam McCaffrey, Dara O'Reilly and Kevin Lunney had to answer the 'what next' question. Of course, they wanted to see Paul O'Brien and the bankers sent packing but, as time went on, a quick fix became less and less likely. But Quinn didn't have any plan B. He simply had a myopic focus on getting his business back. At times, it was clear that he didn't fully appreciate that his executives still had to pay their mortgages. They were getting used to the fact they'd been sacked, and had to consider what the future held for them and their families. But, for now, they were working in a tiny office, which was also not what they were used to. Neither had they a team supporting them, but they kept crunching the figures, putting plans together and preparing for the day they could get the company back. They were not doing it for themselves, they were very aware that thousands of employees were looking to them to make it happen.

By the time summer turned to autumn, however, tensions had begun to boil over. In one meeting Sean Quinn accused Dara O'Reilly of being disloyal. Not once but several times. Dara, who'd worked as hard as Liam and Kevin to keep the hope alive, snapped. He lost it. He got up and walked out. 'It was a defining moment for Dara. Sean Quinn felt that he owned you. Even after losing the business, he still thought it,' said one of Quinn's former colleagues. Kevin and Liam would continue to keep Dara in the loop as they both knew how vital he was to the business, but it was a definite turning point in the relationship between Sean Quinn and his former group financial officer.

The slow fracturing of his inner circle wasn't the only difficulty for Quinn. In November he suffered yet another public humiliation. The takeover had, as he admitted, left him penniless. He had left nothing in the tank for a rainy day, because, for Sean Quinn, that day was never going to dawn. For billionaires, it generally doesn't. In a Belfast court on a dark, wet Friday morning, Sean Quinn was declared bankrupt. Dressed in a smart overcoat, shirt and tie, he faced the media outside having just told the court that he had a total of €11,169 in three bank accounts, a Mercedes car worth €4,670, interests in a forestry worth £35,000 and two pension funds valued at €200,000. He didn't own his 15,000-square-foot home – that was in the name of his five children. His total outgoings, he told the Master in Bankruptcy, Fiona Kelly, were just under £2,400 per month. The hearing lasted less than ten minutes. In four short years, he'd gone from Ireland's richest man, to appearing in the publication in which no one ever wants to read about themselves, *Stubbs Gazette*.

Afterwards, he issued a statement to the press. 'I was born, reared, and worked all of my life in County Fermanagh. It is for this reason that my bankruptcy was made today in Northern Ireland. I have done everything in my power to avoid taking this drastic decision. The vast majority of debt that Anglo maintains is owed is strenuously disputed. I cannot, however, now pay those loans which are due,' he said outside the High Court. 'I am certainly not without blame. I am not in the business of pointing fingers or making excuses. However, recent history has shown that I, like thousands of others in Ireland, incorrectly relied upon the persons who guided Anglo and wrongfully sought to portray a "blue-chip" Irish banking stock.

'My family and I have been subjected to relentless negative media coverage over the past three years. I have been portrayed as a reckless gambler who bet on a bank. I have never sought publicity, nor have I courted the media. On the contrary, I have developed a reputation for avoiding the media glare. Sadly this now seems to have worked very much to my disadvantage, especially when compared with the sophisticated and massively expensive publicity campaign operated for and on behalf of Anglo,' he said, adding that the bankers, and the Irish government, were now intent on making him and his family scapegoats. He finished by saying that he must look to the future with hope for the opportunities that lie ahead.

The bankruptcy didn't go down well in Dublin, where it was perceived as Quinn attempting to pull a stroke. Just the month before, Anglo Irish Bank had been erased from the banking landscape when the government merged it with the Nationwide Building Society to create the Irish Bank Resolution Corporation (IBRC). The State had pumped over €34 billion into the failed banks to cover their debts and would now run them down over a ten-year period. 'I strongly believe that, in addition to meeting practical requirements for the merged organisation, this name change is of symbolic importance to all of us as we move on from the past,' said

Mike Aynsley, who was now chief executive of IBRC, in a press statement. 'The cost to the Irish taxpayer caused by disastrous lending practices and poor stewardship of Anglo Irish Bank and INBS will not be forgotten or forgiven.'

But Quinn wasn't going to be allowed to move on from his past. It can take up to twelve years to be discharged from bankruptcy in the Republic. In the North, however, Quinn could escape from it after twelve months. Quinn still contests that declaring himself bankrupt in the UK was appropriate. 'I was born and reared in Northern Ireland, and when I got married I lived in Northern Ireland for the first few years and my two eldest daughters were born in Enniskillen. I never worked a day outside of Northern Ireland. It doesn't mean that I wouldn't have been in an office in Dublin or London or Cavan or whatever it might be, but every morning for the guts of forty years, I got into my car and I drove straight to Derrylin. So I worked all my life in Derrylin.'

When IBRC discovered that Quinn had gone North to be declared bankrupt, the bankers immediately moved to have it declared null and void so that they could have him declared bankrupt in the Republic. After a lengthy process – involving a hearing back in the High Court in Belfast in which the bankruptcy was overturned – Quinn was, in January 2012, eventually declared bankrupt for the second time, on this occasion in the Dublin High Court.

Quinn said the fact that he paid 80 per cent of his taxes in the UK, that the Good Friday Agreement allowed all NI residents to choose between holding an Irish or British passport (his was Irish), was ignored. The bankers were being simply vindictive. 'I suppose it should have been a lesson to us about what we were up against,' he said in 2019. 'I don't know of anybody else, and I mean this sincerely, I don't know of anybody else in the Irish State that's better entitled to a UK bankruptcy than I was. We should have known we were going nowhere with this, that this couldn't be won. Because that was the most blatant breach of justice that I have, that you could possibly think of,' he claimed.

The Quinns would fail to learn the lesson of the bankruptcy; their days in court were only starting.

**

The IBRC team working on the Quinns had discovered Petey Quinn's plan by this point but found it impossible to get ahead of him. The bankers had gone into court the previous June and had been granted an injunction against the Quinn family, demanding that they cease and desist in all attempts to put properties beyond the reach of the bankers and, therefore, the State. In February 2012 they went back to court to launch an action designed to put manners on the Quinns, once and for all.

The contempt of court proceedings against Sean Quinn, his son Sean Junior and Petey meant that if the Quinns failed to hand over the keys to the properties in Russia, Ukraine and India, they would be liable to whatever penalty the judge decided was appropriate. If the Quinns didn't comply, the judge would have only one option.

Prison.

During the hearing, the court heard how the Quinns had been asset-stripping on a massive scale. In the witness box, Sean Quinn admitted for the first time that he'd given the green light to the plan that he'd hoped would allow him to hold onto the properties, but said he'd brought an end to it when the injunction was issued against him the previous June. When it came to his turn, Petey admitted his role in the creation of a 'smokescreen' or, in other words, a multinational blizzard of companies designed to keep the €500m worth of properties under the control of the family.

In her lengthy judgment, Miss Justice Elizabeth Dunne was excoriating of the Quinns, finding them guilty of contempt of court. The only way they could 'purge their contempt' was by handing over the keys and all the information they held on the ownership of the properties. If they didn't, they were going to prison.

Their case wasn't helped when, on the Sunday after the verdict, the *Irish Daily Mail* published a damning video of Sean Junior and his cousin Petey filmed in a Kiev restaurant the previous January, when both were under the injunction to help the bankers recover the properties. According to the paper, 'The recordings feature Sean Quinn Jnr and his cousin Peter Quinn with Russian-speaking businessmen as they discuss payments to the Quinns ranging from US$100,000 (about €79,000) to US$5m (€3.95m). The damning videos also contain a strikingly nonchalant admission from Peter Quinn, a nephew of Sean Quinn Sr, who says he is prepared to mislead a court looking into the Quinns' affairs. "I'd have to lie to the court. That wouldn't overly concern me," he says, laughing.'

The film, and the timing of it coming into the public domain, couldn't have been worse for the Quinns. They had both been caught out in court and on camera. But had Petey's plan worked? He said he wasn't worried about lying in court – was that because of the financial upside of the deals they were making in far-off restaurants? Had the Quinns made that calculation and decided that losing their freedom was a small price to pay?

Rumours began to circulate on the border that, while the Quinns appeared to be losing, somewhere in a secret bank account they had stashed away the millions they had secured in Russia and Ukraine. Sean Quinn hadn't become a billionaire without showing cunning. He couldn't, surely, be putting himself and his family through all this misery for nothing?

***

In July 2012 the quarryman, his son and nephew, Petey, were back in court. Justice Dunne had ordered them to tell the banks everything they knew. The only question to be answered was had they complied with Justice Dunne's order to tell the banks everything they knew. But before the hearing could start, the drama began.

Petey failed to turn up. It became clear that he'd sworn an affidavit at his lawyer's office in the morning but instead of walking the short distance to court, he headed for the border and home. He left a message with the court that he was sick. His lawyers said they were as shocked as anybody that he'd failed to turn up.

As his uncle and cousin took their seats, they weren't impressed with Petey. He'd been loyal and committed to the cause up until now, but something had changed since the court case and the publication of the video. It was as if he'd decided that he'd done all he could to help the family and now it was time to put himself first. It was true that the relationship between his father, Peter and Sean Quinn had been put under strain due to the crisis that had engulfed them. Dara O'Reilly had walked away after Quinn accused him of being disloyal. Now it was a family member who was refusing to stand shoulder to shoulder.

Sean's daughter Ciara told an *Irish Independent* journalist that she didn't know where Petey was and she hadn't spoken to him. 'When you are ordered to do something which physically cannot be done, it leaves you in a very difficult and frightening place.'

Miss Justice Elizabeth Dunne ruled that by their actions in attempting to put the property beyond the State, there had been an 'outrageous' contempt of court, and therefore sentenced both Sean Junior and Petey, in his absence, to three months in prison. Sean Quinn would escape jail, for the moment. It was reported that Sean Senior held a white handkerchief to his face as his son was jailed.

According to court reports, the Quinns' lawyer described the court's decision as an 'almost medieval approach of holding the son to see what the chieftain father will do in terms of freeing the son's liberty'. Effectively, the lawyer was implying that Quinn Junior was a hostage. The father now had to decide what to do – free him by telling all, or risk joining him.

After the hearing, Quinn told *Mail on Sunday* reporter John Lee: 'The family have taken steps to fight back and I fully endorsed their actions. They are standing up to the bank that took everything from them.'

Quinn's response was not to call up the bank and back down, but to call his supporters out onto the streets. Ostensibly, the rally in Ballyconnell on the last Sunday in July 2012 was organised by the Concerned Irish Citizens, but it was really a gamble by Quinn that in the face of public uproar, the courts and the banks would back down.

An estimated 5,000 people lined the streets and then crowded around a flatbed trailer for speeches from Quinn's supporters. Rodney Edwards was one of the journalists who covered the march for *The Impartial Reporter*. He recalls how split opinions were at the time between those on the border and elsewhere on the island. 'I remember standing there tweeting the event live. It was very early on in the days of Twitter, but I can remember one tweet in particular that I got, in which it referred to those people who had gathered in the street that day as being "peasants" and that was tweeted that particular weekend by another member of the media and that really was, I suppose, the impression that some outside the border counties had of this area.'

On stage, speaker after speaker rose to address the crowd, some of whom were carrying placards denouncing the bankers and the press – 'Trial of Injustice by the Media' and 'No justice in Ireland. Quinn held to ransom' read two. According to reports, family friend Father Brian D'Arcy said that 'when Northern and Southern governments wouldn't give us a penny, when not a single one of them provided a job, it was Sean Quinn and his family who took up the battle'. GAA All-Ireland winners, Mickey Harte, Jarleth Burns and Joe Kernan were among those on the platform.

The plan was for Sean Quinn to stay away, but as he got word of the size of the crowd, he couldn't resist making an appearance. There was loud cheering and applause as he arrived on stage. Clearly emotional, he said that a propaganda war had been waged against him and that an 'untrue story' was being told. He also gave his public support to Petey, saying 'the Quinns always stick by each other'.

Whatever Quinn had hoped that the protest would achieve, in reality, the rally and the support only widened the gulf between the people of the border and the rest of the island. Fintan O'Toole, in *The Irish Times*, questioned the 'collusion of many respectable people' in what Quinn was doing. 'His shamelessness is made possible by those who tell him that he has nothing to be ashamed of, that, on the contrary, he is the victim in all of this,' he wrote.

But in Cavan, Leitrim and Fermanagh, as Rodney Edwards was finding, there was a growing sense of anger that no one was listening – never mind understanding – the people's hurt and frustration at how their chieftain and their community were being treated.

In October, a second rally was held in Ballyconnell the Sunday before Sean Junior was due to be released from Dublin's Mountjoy Prison. Peter Quinn and Sean's daughter Ciara both spoke this time, both fiery, both angry. Ciara told the thousands of people who turned up that 'have no doubt, this is a war. Our lives have been torn apart, as has our life's work.' Her sister Colette spoke to tell the crowds that the family wanted to bring prosperity to the area again. On stage, Sean and Patricia Quinn broke down as a poem was read in support of their son.

There was a strategy to what the family were doing. They were cementing the view that it was 'them and us', rural and urban, bad bankers versus the self-made billionaire who'd created thousands of jobs for his community.

Buoyed by the rallies, the phone calls, the letters, the GAA family support, Quinn decided it was time to get out on the front foot and tell their story. He believed that with the force of the people he could face down the bankers and the courts. Inside his bubble, it seemed that there was support from right across the island. There wasn't. A poll for one of the Sunday newspapers showed that 85 per cent didn't believe him when he said he hadn't tried to put the properties beyond reach of the State. Over 75 per cent said the financial regulator was right to oust Quinn and his family. But 56 per cent of those polled in Cavan/Monaghan felt the opposite, that Matthew Elderfield was wrong, and 65 per cent believed that Quinn would have repaid what he owed. The poll underscored the acute difference of attitudes to Sean Quinn and his family. He might have been winning the PR battle in his home constituencies but, outside of the border, he simply was not trusted any longer.

***

With his son having served his sentence, it was Sean Quinn's turn to face the inevitable in court, particularly after lawyers for the bank told Miss Justice Elizabeth Dunne that there had been no meaningful attempt by Quinn to restore any of the property assets.

For the hearing at the Dublin High Court on 1 November 2012, Quinn had turned to a highly respected Northern QC, Eugene Grant, to represent him. Grant told the judge that his client had a serious heart complaint and that she shouldn't send him to prison. He allowed that his client admitted that he alone gave the green light to Petey's asset-stripping plan but stated that Quinn believed he was lawfully protecting the assets. The highly experienced criminal barrister argued that Quinn had done all he could to purge his contempt. He pointed out that while he had sanctioned the scheme he had not been aware of the 'nuts and bolts'. Sean Quinn, after all, didn't do small print.

The judge said she would consider her verdict overnight and at 11 a.m. the next morning, Quinn, accompanied by his son, filed back into the same court to hear Miss Justice Dunne say that the quarryman had only himself to blame for the situation he'd gotten himself into. She sentenced him to nine weeks in prison.

The judge gave him time to consider an appeal, but Quinn used it to get drunk. He went to a bar in the Four Courts with his family and friends. 'It didn't panic me. Nothing would panic me,' he said. 'When Elizabeth Dunne said, look it, we are giving him nine weeks and he has a week or whatever time it was to consider what he wants to say or do.' I just stood up in the court and said, "I'm going this evening." She was shocked. She didn't want me going that evening for whatever reason. She said, "I'm not asking you to go this evening." "I'm going this evening." What was the point in going home this evening and going back the next day, the next week or ten days' time thinking about it? So I went to the bar along with a couple of friends of mine, locals. I had two pints of beer and two or three double brandies and headed straight for the white van into Mountjoy.'

Asked what it was like when the door of his prison cell closed behind him, the former billionaire remarked: 'I was drunk. I was right tight so I didn't pass too many remarks.'

Father Gerry Comiskey, Sean and Patricia's parish priest, was the first to visit him in prison that evening. 'I was in the courtroom and I was very pessimistic and I said that to Sean on the evening before he was sentenced. I said it looked bleak. Within a couple of hours of him being taken into Mountjoy, I went in to see him. Truthfully, it was devastating. To go and see this giant, a colossus really, in the community, being reduced to being a prisoner with a number and a uniform and to be so humiliated by the fact that he was taken in a prison van and escorted with all the sirens and sounds. It frightened him and astonished all of us, and may have astonished the nation as well,' said the priest, who added that Quinn, still tanked up from his session earlier, was defiant. 'I guess there were some words that I couldn't repeat. I suppose what I remember most was his spirit. He was crushed, down, and in prison. His phrase was, "I'll be back," and everything would be rectified. I do remember him repeating often, if I'm given seven years I will be able to repay all I owe and get the show back on the road again.'

Back up on the border, his former colleagues were angry, with one recalling: 'I always think back to the time on the jet about him talking up Anglo, and he was basing that judgment on the information that he had. And because of that he ended up in jail. Like, it was just crazy, crazy stuff. And when you think, when you look back and think of maybe some of the bankers and some of the crooked politicians, maybe they're more entitled to go to jail. But look, they had to get a scapegoat and I suppose Sean was the scapegoat at the time, you know.'

Alan Dukes, who was by that point chairman at IRBC, said that, for the bankers, there was no sense of victory. 'It wasn't a situation that we wanted to see come about. Our concern was to go to the courts, to establish the bank's right to get access to these assets. The last thing we wanted was any obstacle, or any new obstacles, to be put in the way of getting access to assets that would pay part of the money that was owed to the bank.'

While Quinn adjusted to life behind bars, his frustrated supporters were planning their response. Days after his imprisonment, workers staged a walk-out, and tractors and farm machinery were parked across the main roads in Ballyconnell and Derrylin.

The Molly Maguires were also back meeting on the mountain, planning. Their first response was to attack another electrical substation, this time at the wind farm Quinn had built on Slieve Rushen. But, knowing that the IBRC were intent on selling off Sean Quinn's business, they were going to have to step up their campaign. Paul O'Brien was still in charge in the company headquarters. If he wasn't moving, they were going to have to target any potential buyers of the business.

That meant that one of Quinn's old business adversaries was now going to find himself a target.

12

Is This What You Want?

As 2012 neared its end, life couldn't have been much worse for Quinn as he stewed in prison, stripped of everything he had built. Jail-time had failed to diminish his sense of injustice; if anything, it only strengthened it. The bankers had stolen his business and he was prepared to do whatever it took to get it back. His nine-week sentence would soon be up and he'd nothing else to do on the outside other than make life difficult for the bankers.

Paul O'Brien was the man who had usurped his office – he'd even gotten rid of Quinn's red chesterfield chair – but he knew that, despite sacking several workers for disloyalty, Quinn still had eyes and ears inside the company. O'Brien also knew that they couldn't run these businesses for ever. The bankers wanted to get their money back and the only way to do that was to break up the quarryman's empire, close the bad businesses and sell the good ones.

Quinn was temporarily released over Christmas 2012, to attend the christening of his granddaughter and to spend time with his family. It also allowed him to speak with his supporters, get updates on what Paul O'Brien was doing, and to consider his next move. The lawsuit against the bank that he'd launched the previous year was supposed to come to court mid-2013 and, at the time, the advice they were getting from their legal team was that they had a very strong hand. Their legal argument, and firm belief, was that the €2.4 billion in loans that Seán FitzPatrick and David Drumm had given the company, in the names of the children, were illegal, as the bank knew they were to help shore up its share price. Furthermore, the children had no legal advice and had no idea what they were signing. That was the big picture and Quinn still clung to the belief that, ultimately, the bank would negotiate. They'd see it made sense and he'd get the company back.

But there was a risk. And it was Paul O'Brien. If he could sell off the family silverware, as Quinn saw it, before they got to the negotiating table, there would be nothing left that was of any value. That Christmas, around the tree in the living room, Quinn contemplated what could be done to stop that from happening.

What worried the quarryman most was the announcement on 21 December by Paul O'Brien and his counterpart at Lagan Cement, Jude Lagan, Kevin Lagan's younger brother. The two companies were planning a joint venture and had signed a memorandum of understanding that could lead to them 'pooling their operations'. *Construction Index* magazine said the two companies hoped to complete a merger inside three months. 'The businesses that would become part of the joint venture are the combined cement and building products businesses based in Ballyconnell, Derrylin, Kinnegad, Belfast, Cork and Benelux. Lagan Cement Group would put in its cement, concrete, quarrying and roof tiles businesses. Quinn Building Products would put in its cement, roof tiles, quarrying, pre-stress and lightweight blocks. Quinn Therm, Quinn Litepac, Quinn Tarmac and Lagan Sand are not included in the proposal,' it reported.

A joint statement from the two companies said a merger would be good for both businesses and their customers. 'By combining two stable Irish businesses the proposed JV will create a sustainable independent cement manufacturer that can continue to support its customers on a competitive basis,' said O'Brien and Lagan. Separately, the CEO at the Quinn Group announced a €15m investment to upgrade the Ballyconnell cement plant. In other words, O'Brien was upgrading the cement plant ahead of closing a deal with Lagan.

Time was running out for Quinn to keep the family silverware together.

***

The quarryman was forty miles from the border when he knew for sure that he was back in Quinn Country. On the main street of Virginia, Co. Cavan, a JCB forklift had been used to raise a huge banner that simply stated, 'Welcome home Sean Quinn'. It was 6 January 2013, he was a free man and on the road home.

When he got there, he kicked off his shoes and spent a little time with Patricia before inviting BBC television cameras in for an interview. He was going to waste no time in getting his message out there, telling Julian Fowler, reporter for the evening news programme *Newsline*, that he'd enjoyed the 100 per cent support of his fellow prisoners, even if the experience had been somewhat taxing. 'I found it tough but when you come to sixty-six years of age I suppose you have been through many a thing over that period. I could fit into most environments and I fitted in,' he said. 'Of course, when you find a door slamming at nine o'clock at night and you close for the night, it's not nice, it's not something I'm used to and it's not something I felt I deserved. I wouldn't call it frightening but it would certainly make you think.'

Quinn knew there was still a chance that the court could return him and his son to prison if they found that he hadn't actually let go of any of the properties in the Ukraine, Russia or India. But, in reality, they'd abandoned all attempts to retain the properties by this point and had no intention of doing anything that was going to see him back behind bars. All focus now was on ensuring that the plants, the factories and the hotel that he looked out at from the window of his home would remain intact until he could force the bank back to the negotiating table. At the end of the interview he could have been talking directly to the bankers: 'The Quinns are not killed off. The Quinns are still there.'

Paul O'Brien responded within days, inviting *The Impartial Reporter*'s Rodney Edwards into his office for a twenty-five-minute interview. 'I don't do photographs. I don't do many interviews either,' he said before launching into a defence of the actions of the bankers and, in doing so, sending a clear message to Sean Quinn: he wasn't going to win. 'Even if they win the case, they don't get their companies back. It is only a claim for damages. The people who own our businesses are the institutional investors: banks, bonds, not IBRC,' he said. Warming to his theme, he continued: 'There is a lot of rubbish being talked,' he said. 'I know there are a lot of people in our 2,800 staff who would have a lot of sympathy for Seán Quinn. Do I have sympathy? Absolutely. On a business level, there was a decision taken because the debt couldn't be paid. If I don't pay for the mortgage on my house, someone else will take it off me. It is that simple. Everybody is entitled to an opinion. But if people are putting out misguided facts – worse than that, incorrect facts which create unease – that's mischievous and dangerous and not right.'

Recalling the interview later, Edwards said, 'Paul O'Brien wanted to erase all memory of the Quinns from that business.' It was well known that Paul O'Brien, who only met with Quinn twice during his time as CEO, thought that Quinn believed he was more important than he really was. He talked of an old phrase his father had used: 'You have two ears and one mouth and you should use them in proportion. Sean Quinn never did that. He has a complete inability to take advice.'

With Quinn now back home with little else to do but brood on where it had gone wrong and how to put it right, the scene was set for a climatic showdown. Since the Quinns had been jailed, the atmosphere on the border was raw and, now, more defiant that ever. The Dublin political classes and intelligentsia, who'd never done anything for the area, refused to listen. The mainstream media was ranged against them. They were the underdogs, the forgotten, the misunderstood. Quinn had clearly gambled and lost. That they understood. But why not let him pay off his debts, just like anyone else? Why put him out on the street? On the mountain above Derrylin, the Molly Maguires met, their next step already decided.

***

Peter Lagan ran a trucking business before he became a quarryman. When he retired in the late 1970s, he handed the business over to his two sons, Kevin and Peter, who between them built an international group of quarries and cement plants, as well as brick and asphalt businesses. They paved the runway at Hong Kong International Airport and built roads in the Caribbean. It was natural that Lagan, the only other cement manufacturer in the North, would be looking at the opportunity provided by the collapse of Sean Quinn's business. Kevin Lagan and Quinn had history, of course, going back to the 1980s and, later, when Quinn surreptitiously attempted to prevent Lagan from opening a cement plant in Co. Westmeath. Quinn was unhappy at the idea of Kevin Lagan owning his former businesses. Some of those involved with the Molly Maguires felt the same way.

For Lagan, bringing together Quinn's cement and concrete businesses and his own company was very appealing. He approached the administrators, looking to make this happen. Soon after, it looked like a deal would occur. The prospective deal would be structured as an amalgamation with agreement that Lagan would purchase the former Quinn companies at an agreed price, subject to a green light from the then Competition Commission in the UK. 'It was a huge deal for Lagan and for the industry on the island,' said a source who had knowledge of the negotiations. 'We were very close to an agreement,' he added. Sensing this, the same saboteurs who had been wreaking havoc on the border since April 2011 sped into action.

At the end of January 2013 a package arrived at Lagan's offices at Clarendon Road in Belfast's docks. When it was opened, a .243-calibre rifle bullet fell out of a cigar box onto his desk. A note made from newspaper cuttings was attached, which read: *Quinn. Is this what you want?*

Lagan had built a business through the worst of the Troubles in the North. He had lived through conflict. Still, it was the first time he'd received a death threat. The PSNI were called and removed the bullet and the note for forensic examination. In a company statement, Lagan said it wasn't going to put him off the joint venture. 'This is clearly an attempt to intimidate myself and the Lagan Group at a time when we are engaged in discussions with Quinn on combining our cement and building products businesses,' he said. 'The proposed joint venture is a positive move for everyone and will create a sustainable, independent cement manufacturer that can continue to support its customers and employees on a competitive basis. The people behind this crude, intimidatory tactic clearly aren't interested in protecting jobs, but we will not be swayed from our determination to complete our discussions successfully.'

It was a defiant tone. However, two weeks later, it was announced that the joint venture would not be going ahead. 'Discussions have now concluded and both companies have decided not to progress further with the proposed joint venture,' they said in a statement.

It was a major blow to Paul O'Brien and the bondholders, who couldn't hide their anger in the statement they issued to the media, which also accepted that it was the Molly Maguires' intervention that had led to the venture's collapse. 'We are well aware of the grave upset and annoyance this causes our colleagues and their families. Whatever cause is espoused by those who perpetrate and/or sponsor intimidation of this kind, it is absolutely clear that these people have no concern for the preservation of jobs. Further, they have no concern for the families of individuals who are dependent on the success of these businesses and they have absolutely no regard for the image of the locality and the community,' a Quinn Group spokesman told *The Impartial Reporter*.

It was particularly frustrating for O'Brien because he knew who was carrying out the attacks on behalf of the Quinn case; he knew those who were appearing to do their job by day and leading the sabotage at nights. And he knew that the police knew who they were – because he'd told them. It was an open secret on the border who was involved, yet there were no arrests, no charges, no convictions. As far as O'Brien was concerned, the police forces on both sides of the border had failed him. Others felt the same way: 'If the attacks were in Dublin on Apple or Facebook or Intel, they wouldn't be tolerated. But because we were up on the border, it seemed not to matter. We were constantly worried for our lives; we were on our own. The damage being caused to the business was astronomical but, again, it didn't matter in Dublin or Belfast,' said one of those involved in the business at the time.

For those seeking to keep the Quinn companies intact, however, it was cause for celebration. No one was ever arrested or questioned for the threat. Furthermore, in a shed on Molly Mountain, they now knew that a bullet in the post had caused more damage than burning down an electrical substation. The tactic had worked. Lagan had withdrawn.

Still, the physical attacks continued. A month later, there was an attempt to burn a fibre-optic cable connected to the Quinn Group's communications department and a fire bomb attack on machinery in Ballinamore, Co. Leitrim. The arson attacks reminded the bankers of the opposition they faced on the border. It kept them under a constant sense of fear of what was coming next in terrain they didn't know with a community that was violently hostile to them.

Police and gardaí continued to have no success in breaking up the attacks. Paul O'Brien met with Garda Commissioner Nóirín O'Sullivan and told her in no uncertain terms that Irish territory on the border was 'lawless'. She, of course, denied it, but the facts were stark: not a single charge had been brought, never mind a conviction secured.

In the North, their PSNI counterparts were doing no better, but they, at least, were making some attempts to apprehend the gang behind the attacks on the electrical grid. PSNI detectives based in Fermanagh, in Enniskillen and in Lisnaskea, came up with a cunning plan. When the previously destroyed Power NI (NIE) telegraph poles, almost fifty of them by this time, were being replaced, they were coated with a special dye. The hope was that when they were attacked again, the dye would transfer onto the gang's clothes, allowing police to identify and apprehend those responsible. When a new spate of attacks began again in February, it was just the opportunity they were looking for to spring a surprise raid of their own. The hope was that when they raided the Mollies' homes, they would find the incriminating clothes using ultraviolet light that would show up the dye and therefore link them directly to the attacks.

In a dawn raid involving dozens of police officers in February 2013, four properties on Molly Mountain and the surrounding area were searched, three men arrested and clothes seized for forensic examination.

Evidence was found of the dye, but a police officer who was involved in the operation accepts that those arrested had a solid defence. They had all been dipping sheep in the days and weeks before their arrest and obviously the animals had previously rubbed up against the telegraph poles and had transferred the dye onto their clothing. The chainsaws used were never recovered in the police operation, which was a major disappointment for the detectives involved.

One of those arrested in the raids was Sean McGovern, from Springtown, Kinawley, who denied any involvement in cutting down telegraph poles or with the Molly Maguire gang. He later told the *Fermanagh Herald* that between fifteen to twenty police officers arrived at his home at dawn. 'They put on white suits and forensic masks and they proceeded to search out houses and cars in the yard. They did forensic tests on two chainsaws, but didn't take them away. They didn't do the search manually, as they normally do, but they seemed to use an ultraviolet light to detect chemicals that was probably spread on the poles. I have never worked for Sean Quinn, but I do have sympathy for his plight. In my case, they didn't find anything, but I do think they should be targeting their searches at the people who have taken over from Sean Quinn for stealing his property.'

The police tactic hadn't resulted in charges, but it did put an end to the targeting of the poles. However, it didn't end the attacks.

Meanwhile the bankers took some solace in the fact that, despite the violence, the restructuring overseen by Paul O'Brien was starting to yield results. They had backed O'Brien and invested €15m to upgrade the Ballyconnell Cement Plant. In an announcement, reported widely, the company said that, 'The use of solid recovered fuel (SRF) as an alternative fuel is long established in the cement industry worldwide. SRF is a fuel produced from segregated waste and its use will bring Quinn Cement cost of production more into line with its Irish and European competitors.' It was a significant signal from O'Brien and the bondholders that they weren't going to allow the cement factory to get run down or be shut down; they were investing in its future viability.

The Quinn Group at this point had revenues of over €600m and had made a profit of almost €26m in the previous year. Given that the group was back on a firm footing, as they saw it, they felt that the time was right for a significant cosmetic change. They decided to break with the Quinn name, in order to put distance between the company and its former owner. In November 2013 they announced that the manufacturing division would be rebranded as the 'Aventas Group'. A company spokesman explained that it was a combination of the Latin for 'Ave' (hello) and 'advent' (arrival).

Explaining the change of name, Paul O'Brien said, 'While respecting the achievements and heritage of the past, we have chosen a name, Aventas Group, which puts a greater emphasis on looking to the future.' O'Brien had already rebranded Quinn Plastics as 'Polycasa', saying it was doing so after a significant restructure of the company, which included the shelving of the plant outside Leipzig that Quinn had spent more than €300m in building. The decision was taken when it was realised that it would cost another €200m to complete and no partner could be found. Polycasa still retained six manufacturing plants across Europe.

O'Brien also made clear that the other divisions would be rebranded.

While the names changed over the doors, the Quinns and their supporters took some satisfaction from the fact that the manufacturing companies remained largely intact.

Still, Quinn had more pressing concerns. Throughout 2013, his main focus had been on the court case, which had yet to get a start date. They were now receiving an avalanche of disclosure in their action against the former Anglo Irish Bank, and were taking heart from what they were finding and the fact that IBRC had attempted and failed to have the case thrown out of court.

Quinn was growing in confidence that an offer would eventually come. Even with all the legal action and the jail sentences, Alan Dukes and IBRC were still chasing around Eastern Europe and India, trying to get control of the property portfolio. All Quinn had to do was wait them out, and keep reminding his supporters that he was the victim. There was a real chance, he felt, that they might still come out of this back on top. 'Hopefully the court will tell the tale on this over the next six, twelve months, and that the true story will come out of what was done and, more importantly, why it was done, and who are they covering for and why were they covering for them,' he said to *The Impartial Reporter*. 'That's my ambition and that's why I'm keen the kids run the court case, because I think there's an obligation and a duty on us to clear our name, even though we're not innocent, even though we made mistakes, but I think there's a duty on us to let the truth be known,' he said, explaining his motivation.

Some of his supporters, however, remained focused on disrupting the company. Two weeks after the Aventas rebranding, these supporters made clear their response. Shortly before Christmas 2013 an oil lorry belonging to Cassidy Oils was stolen from its depot near the cement plant in Ballyconnell. It would have taken the driver no longer than two minutes to reach the headquarters of the newly named Aventas Group. There were bollards to prevent any vehicle entering after office hours, but the driver drove the oil lorry straight over them. He then manoeuvred the vehicle in the car park and reversed it at high speed straight through the main doors to the building before setting it on fire. The Aventas Group sign, which had replaced the famous 'Q' logo that had been there for thirty years, was blackened by the flames. When the fire brigade arrived they tackled the blaze, knowing that the lorry could explode at any second. Thankfully, it did not. 'This latest incident is part of a continuing campaign of sabotage, intimidation and vilification against this company and certain of its employees,' the company said in a statement that was widely reported across the island.

The new year began as the old one had finished. This time a coach was filled with tyres and set alight at the entrance to the therm plant. A sign on the side of the fifty-two-seater bus said: 'Paul O'Brien Disaster Tours. Leaving Soon.'

Prior to this, Quinn had been launching attacks of his own in the media. In another interview with *Impartial Reporter* journalist Rodney Edwards, he said that his former businesses 'have been destroyed' and claimed that taking over his companies had 'cost the Irish taxpayer two million every day yet they want to deflect the limelight by saying the Quinns stole our assets. They want to blacken the Quinn name, and they have done a fantastic job of it. They have destroyed the family's reputation.'

The bankers began to see a pattern emerge: Sean Quinn making highly contentious statements, which were followed by some sort of attack on the company. What they didn't know was whether it was co-ordinated or simply disparate groups acting in support of Quinn but independently of one another.

***

Cyril McGuinness was a career criminal with a past in paramilitarism. Born in Dublin in 1964, he'd made the border his home, living first in Rosslea until he became involved in a land dispute and was 'chased' out of the village. Next he ended up in a house in Teemore not far from the Quinn Group headquarters. He was well known to the RUC from when they were fighting IRA terrorism. One former officer spoke of the threat he posed in the 1980s: 'You worried every time you seen him. If he was in the area, you could be sure an attack was imminent. He was a real threat.' He'd been identified as the driver of the lorry carrying a massive bomb that ripped through London's Docklands in 1996. He came to be known locally as 'Dublin Jimmy'.

After the IRA ended its campaign, he'd aligned with dissident Republicans, while continuing to smuggle cars and heavy machinery. He was convicted of various criminal offences, including the illegal transportation of waste, but avoided prison. He did do jail time in Belgium after being found guilty of a multimillion-pound smuggling operation in which he'd stolen twenty trucks and cranes and shipped them back to Ireland where he used some of them to steal ATMs from banks across the island.

By 2013 he was back on the border, living with his partner. Quinn admits that he met Dublin Jimmy in the pub a couple of times, but that he didn't know him. Police suspect it was at some point during 2013 that the criminal offered his skills and expertise to the Quinn supporters. Six months after he'd returned to the border, McGuinness was reported as the chief suspect in the theft of the oil tanker from a fuel depot that was driven into the Aventas headquarters, causing significant damage to the front doors and foyer. The owner of the depot, Tommy Cassidy, told Sheehan that he'd been tipped-off that McGuinness had been 'eyeing up' his tanker. 'I didn't believe that they would start stealing from the local community to do damage,' said Cassidy. 'I said to the police straight off "I know who did this job." I know exactly who did it, and I gave them McGuinness's name – I had no hesitation in saying it was McGuinness,' Cassidy told the *Sunday Independent*. Despite this accusation, Cyril McGuinness was never arrested nor charged with any offence linked to the tanker theft.

Quinn's more hardline supporters were certainly aware of Dublin Jimmy and what he was capable of. At the start of a New Year, they likely felt that the co-ordinated, targeted and sustained attacks of 2013 were going to have a demonstrable impact on the business and its future. In the first weeks of 2014 the attacks continued, with two telecoms cabinets demolished and set ablaze. Soon after, a petrol-bomb attack cut off all broadband and phone services to dozens of homes along the border.

Events were undoubtedly escalating.

In February 2014, *Impartial Reporter* journalist Rodney Edwards was leaked an internal email from a senior manager at Aventas. Quinn Rooftiles, established in 1983, was to be sold to Kevin Lagan's Belfast-based company. In his story, the journalist quoted from the email: 'The sale enables us to achieve our two objectives of a satisfactory price and continuity of employment for our Rooftiles employees,' it said. Despite getting a bullet in the post, Kevin Lagan had come back, not for the cement plant, but for the roof-tiles business, which would be a much smaller deal for both sides.

The response was violent and costly. Over the course of two evenings in February, co-ordinated attacks were mounted on Lagan businesses in Comber and Lisburn in the North and 250 miles away in Cork. In Comber, two large dumper trucks and other machinery were set on fire and destroyed. Heavy plant machinery was also the target at Lagan Asphalt premises in Carrigtwohill in Co. Cork. In Lisburn, the attackers daubed graffiti, making clear the motivation for the attacks: 'Stay out of Co Fermangh [sic]' and 'hands off Quinn'.

The cost of the damage was estimated to be €1 million. For a time, Lagan's company was warned that it could not be insured against further violence. Regardless, for several weeks, it appeared that Lagan would continue with his purchase of the roof-tile business. That was until the morning of his wife's death.

Kathleen Philomena Lagan died on 27 March 2014. She was sixty-five years old and had suffered from cancer. The couple had five children, two of whom joined the family business. On the day of her death, Kevin Lagan received a letter. When he opened it, he realised it was another threat. This time, he was warned that if he went ahead with the roof-tile deal, he 'would not live to see the benefits'.

After burying his wife, Lagan pulled out, saying his company had sustained criminal attacks that were executed with the sole purpose of 'creating a toxic atmosphere and intimidation in order to illegally dissuade potential investment and investors into the area. We have repeatedly said that it was only a matter of time before such attacks switched their focus from property and plant to people,' a Lagan company spokesman told the *Belfast Telegraph*.

The attacks on Kevin Lagan and his business were particularly vicious. In the aftermath, Lagan met with PSNI Chief Constable George Hamilton to voice his frustrations that police were failing to bring those responsible before the court. Lagan was told that a south Armagh fuel smuggler had likely co-ordinated the attacks on his business. Another businessman from Fermanagh was also a suspect. Police may have been briefing that they knew who was responsible, but despite the threats to kill and the millions of euros of damage caused, they failed to bring anyone to court. The lack of charges only served to encourage those involved. They, like the IRA before them on the border, were able to strike at will and with impunity.

Cyril McGuinness was living openly on the border, and while linked to a series of attacks, he was never charged with a single offence. For some, this only raised suspicions that he was a protected species. That he was of some value to police. That he was an informer.

In an interview with the author in October 2021, Sean Quinn refused to outright condemn the threats and attacks on Kevin Lagan's business, still blaming the decision to send in over a hundred security guards to help seize his companies ten years previous for setting the tone. 'There was lots of things done, lots of things said which shouldn't have been done or shouldn't have been said. But at the end of the day, I suppose if you see the hundred people coming from Dublin down into your local, rural area, [which during] the early part of the last century didn't have anything, there was nothing there, and all of a sudden they come in to where there was seven or eight thousand jobs employed, and they come in with heavy security and taking over a business, which was one of the most successful in the country, it did lead to a lot of anger. It did lead to a lot of people disappointed. And I was one of those people. I was very, very angry. And I made no secret of that. The heavy-handed approach, by an Irish government selected by the people, to go in with a heavy hand into a rural area, who had done nothing but good in that area, to take it over and destroy it, I mean, it was criminal. And of course it was going to raise tensions, and of course things were going to happen and did happen. Was I part of it? Absolutely not. Was I angry, was it done because of my anger? Was it done because I was telling the truth about what the position was? Maybe. But was I involved in planning it or involved? Absolutely not.'

***

For Paul O'Brien it was not only the failure to close the Lagan roof-tiles deal but the manner in which it had fallen apart that caused most concern. 'The underlying strategy seems to be one of damaging value, striking fear into our employees and to discourage any genuine prospective acquirers of our businesses,' he said in a statement published by *The Impartial Reporter*.

It was the first time that the owners of Quinn's businesses came close to admitting that the attacks were having an impact on their ability to sell any of the companies. Two weeks prior to the Lagan announcement, a transport firm which had a deal in place with Aventas to transfer 200 of its fleet drivers to Ceva Logistics, a global company specialising in supply chain services, also pulled out. The decision came after a transit van was driven through the gates of Ceva's commercial unit in Little Island, Cork, and set alight.

With the Lagan and Ceva Logistics deals falling apart, speculation mounted as to the viability of Aventas's strategy. Concern was clearly growing, with *The Irish Times* reporting that a number of the international investment groups – i.e. the bondholders who now owned the business with IBRC – had made representations to the Dublin government and to the Executive at Stormont in Belfast. 'US concerns, such as the $3.2 billion hedge fund and private equity group Strategic Value Partners, global investment group GSO Blackstone, the Prudential financial services group, and a US teachers' pension fund are among those on whose behalf concern has been expressed to Minister for Justice Alan Shatter and his counterpart in Belfast, David Ford. Some of the investor groups have offices in Ireland and have other significant investments in the Irish economy,' it reported.

In any similar situation, the financiers would have expected a management buyout (MBO) to be an option if an external buyer couldn't be found, or a mix of both with the MBO coming with investors on board to buy out the business. However, given his history, the Irish bankers were never going to do a deal with Sean Quinn – regardless of what Quinn himself believed – and the attacks were only hardening their position. By this point they firmly believed that, if not directly involved in the attacks, Sean Quinn's anti-banker rhetoric was a significant factor in motivating those who were carrying out the attacks.

Quinn was out of consideration; but that didn't mean they would turn down an offer from within Quinn Country.

Bernard Farrell's LinkedIn page details his three years as the managing director of the Construction Industry Supplies Division of Quinn Building Projects. He'd joined after the takeover and, according to his page, 'oversaw the re-engineering and re-structuring of the Construction Industry Supplies Division, managing 500 staff across multiple ROI/NI/UK manufacturing locations with revenues in excess of €100m. Grew revenue by +30% and developed a five-year plan to treble market share of key product in export market.' But it was a casual remark at a meeting in a hotel in Leitrim's county town, Carrick-on-Shannon, that led to arguably his most significant role in the company's history.

Back in 2013 he was attending a local business forum when someone at his table said the 'elephant in the room' was the future of the Quinn Group. It sparked a conversation about the company and led to a general agreement of those in the room that the business should be brought back under local control.

John McCartin just happened to be at the meeting. A Fine Gael Councillor in Co. Leitrim, he was very well aware of the situation at the business. He'd been invited to attend some of the meetings organised by one of the Quinn-supporting protest groups, Concerned Irish Citizens (CIC), and had met with one of its leaders, Patricia Gilheaney. McCartin had also previously met with Quinn. 'I wanted to see inside that big house,' he said.

His own party had been in power since before the takeover in 2011 and he'd spoken to the Taoiseach, Enda Kenny, about developments at the border business. Quinn wanted to know about Enda Kenny's position and what McCartin could do for him. 'I told him the Dáil couldn't give him back Derrylin,' said McCartin. 'Two weeks later he rang me and asked how I had got on. I didn't even know I was supposed to be doing anything for him. He chastised me for not doing any work.'

Quinn had identified McCartin as 'the man who is going to sort this out'. The councillor was not at all confident that he could meet the quarryman's expectations; although there was still enough self-confidence following that business forum to give it a go. 'My ego told me to keep going,' he admitted.

Meanwhile, Quinn's close friend Tony Doonan claims he made the first approach to Liam McCaffrey on behalf of the quarrymen, to see if the former management would be prepared to become involved in a bid to bring the company back under local control. McCartin would achieve nothing if Liam McCaffrey, Kevin Lunney and Dara O'Reilly were not prepared to get on board. Even if Quinn was behind it, he needed the old team back together.

Tony Doonan and Padraig O'Donohoe were highly active at the time, lobbying and campaigning for Quinn. 'We met Alan Dukes twice, we met Paul O'Brien and we actually had met the then Taoiseach, Enda Kenny, in Drumshanbo.' Their aim, Doonan says, speaking for CIC, was to 'keep the business running, and keep the money turning and keep the employment levels, which was our first and foremost objective'. He added that 'Kevin [Lunney] did come and support us and was at some of the meetings that we held in Sean Quinn's house, and did put in a good bit of work, you know, as part of our group. And in the beginning of 2014, and this was us three years at these sort of tactics, Paul O'Brien was [still] there but at least all the businesses were there, so the employment was there. So we had achieved that [goal]. But the next step was to put in a local management team or put in some management structure.'

By this time Liam McCaffrey had moved on, travelling from his home in Enniskillen to establish a new business, Nuspan, based in Suffolk, England, specialising in precast insulated floors. Doonan still decided to approach him. 'I rang Liam McCaffrey and I asked to meet him, it must have been a Friday or a Saturday. And he said what was it about, and I told him. And he said he was very busy [with] his own business. And I said I needed to meet him, that we weren't able to continue to keep the business, it was going to be sold, but we had to have an alternative, we had to have a management buyout. And I met him in the Westville Hotel [in Enniskillen]. And I explained to him what had to be done, and he went through the different figures. [It] was going to be in the region of €125 million to buy the cement and construction and supplies and packaging, and then the glass was going to be another €400–500 million. I think the figure that Liam was talking about was, I think, was about seven and a half times EBITDA which, I think, amounted to €525 million,' said Doonan. Their figures, they would soon find out, were way off what O'Brien was expecting for the business.

Doonan, and the prospective bid, had clearly piqued McCaffrey's interest. 'Liam said he would arrange to meet all the directors, the past directors of Quinn Group, and they all met the following night. And every single one of them agreed, you know, that they would throw their shoulder to the wheel and they would get on board,' explained Doonan.

Following this development, McCartin went to see Paul O'Brien regarding the idea of a local buyout. 'Paul O'Brien was a big strong-looking rugby man,' said one of those involved. 'He kept McCartin waiting for twenty minutes in the Quinn boardroom and he got so annoyed he sat himself down in the head seat. When O'Brien came in, he was eating a salad. McCartin had the feeling it was just something for O'Brien to get out of the way on his lunch break.'

O'Brien ultimately told McCartin that if he was serious about a local buyout he should go away and put it together and come back with a proposal.

McCartin went to see Sean Quinn after the meeting and filled him in. Quinn beamed. 'He couldn't sell the assets. I was delighted.'

It was game on. They had Quinn's backing and the management team in place. But there was a very significant piece of the jigsaw still to be found: the finance.

***

Approaches were made to Bosco O'Hagan, a highly respected business-man from Ardboe, Co. Tyrone who, in the late 1980s, set up Specialist Joinery, manufacturing high-end bespoke joinery. Bosco knew Peter Quinn through the GAA and his company had helped fit out the Slieve Russell Hotel and the Quinn's lakeside mansion. O'Hagan, who had helped Quinn raise well over £1m from sympathetic donors to help pay Quinn's huge legal fees to fight the takeover, later told a secretly recorded meeting that the first approach had come from Liam McCaffrey, although he'd also spoken directly to Quinn himself. 'I got a phone call from Liam McCaffrey and he said, Bosco I was talking to Sean – we've been talking to Sean back and forth and thinking of putting a grouping of people together to try to buy out O'Brien and those people and whatever, see can we put a bid together to get the place back, would you come on board? So I said who else, and he said Ernie Fisher, John McCartin and yourself would be the three business people in the North of Ireland that we're talking about in this area and Liam McCaffrey, Kevin Lunney and the people who ran the place. And if we, moving forward, our three names and our three faces are the face of credibility in that group – the bank's checked us, the government's checked us, everybody has checked us so therefore we're honest and truthful and business people – there was nothing about us that they could say these boys are crooked or anything. So we were the face of credibility to allow Liam and them to make a bid for the property, CIS and Glass and all at that time,' explained O'Hagan.

Ernie Fisher was the other Northern self-made businessman who agreed to be involved. Fisher Engineering, and particularly the late Bertie Fisher (Ernie's brother, who died in a helicopter crash in 2001) had a very strong relationship with Quinn, having supplied the steel for many of the plants on the Ballyconnell Road, although Sean had little or no relationship with Ernie.

Quinn viewed O'Hagan and Fisher's roles as 'trustees' who would ensure that any deal struck between QBRC and his family would be honoured. But that wasn't necessarily the way O'Hagan and Fisher understood it.

With Fisher and O'Hagan on board, as well as the former managers, and McCartin prepared to be the face of the bid, the Quinn Business Retention Company (QBRC) was officially registered on 31 January 2014 with its address given as O'Hagan's offices in Magherafelt, Co. Derry. Its shareholders were John McCartin, Bosco O'Hagan and Ernie Fisher, who had 10,000 shares each. Two weeks later, in February, Kevin Lunney, Dara O'Reilly and Liam McCaffrey came on board officially as directors. The shareholding hasn't changed since the company first registered.

It wasn't long before the new company was making headlines. In a story published by *The Irish Times*, journalist Tom Lyons reported that 'eight former senior executives in the Quinn Group are backing a bid by three northwest businessmen to buy back the manufacturing arm of the business, now called the Aventas Group. The eight include former group chief executive Liam McCaffrey, former group development director Kevin Lunney, former group finance director Dara O'Reilly, and former radiator division chief executive Denis Doogan.' Doogan, a firm Quinn loyalist, had stayed on with the company after the takeover, but had ultimately resigned to Paul O'Brien without negotiating a severance package for himself.

Liam McCaffrey set out his stall to Lyons, who wrote that 'the consortium was in talks with banks and private equity funds to support a bid for the entire business of Aventas, which has five manufacturing divisions from glass to cement. "KKR [a US $40 billion private equity fund] was prepared to offer us finance in 2011 to fund a management buy-in," Mr McCaffrey said. "Finance is a lot easier to raise now than it was then."'

The former CEO condemned the recent attacks on Kevin Lagan's companies, saying they were not helping the cause of the consortium, and told the paper that they wanted to be treated fairly and equally. But arguably the key sentence in the story was: 'We will be bidding for all of the assets, we think they are much more valuable kept all together.' QBRC were setting out to buy the cement business, along with plastics and the glass.

The bondholders' valuation of the three different parts of the former Quinn Group was in excess of €800m. In a meeting with Paul O'Brien, QBRC opened discussions with a valuation at half that, €400m. They were a long way apart. It would later become a significant issue, but at the time, it was clear that at least some of those involved in QBRC still had their eyes on the prize of retaining all the Quinn businesses along the border. Asked by Tom Lyons if Sean Quinn or his family were going to be involved, Liam McCaffrey responded: 'I don't know. I can't rule anything in or out.'

At this time QBRC were akin to the Magnificent Seven, preparing, planning and getting ready for battle. But when pushed by O'Brien, they were still missing the one thing that would ensure their bid was taken seriously: the finance. They could show no credible evidence to prove they could raise €400m, never mind the €800m O'Brien and the bondholders were still seeking for all the businesses. Until they could do so, O'Brien couldn't take them seriously. The problem for QBRC was that until they did, O'Brien would continue to do all he could to sell off the businesses and recoup the money owed. 'I went to Dublin [with Liam] to meet – I'll just use his Christian name, Derek – to look at getting finance in place,' said Doonan. Nothing concrete came from that, at least not at first.

John McCartin's focus was on ensuring that the former Quinn Group was still intact by the time they could get the finance together. He was working hand in hand with Patricia Gilheaney's group, Concerned Irish Citizens, who had helped establish a Facebook page that was constantly lambasting Paul O'Brien in person and the bankers in general. As reported in *The Sunday Times*, in an email on 27 February 2014, after QBRC had been formed and McCartin met with O'Brien, he updated Gilheany: 'we need to get out the message that our bid is credible and there are many interested funders', but he also complained how 'O'Brien is trying to block our efforts by refusing to show us the financials. He's probably doing this to keep us away long enough for him to make a grab [for] some of the more profitable parts of the business.'

Soon, however, McCartin grew more optimistic. In a group email on 8 March, he told the leaders of the Concerned Irish Citizen group. 'We're making progress lately and I think we have OB [O'Brien] under pressure. I think there's a great "good cop, bad cop" thing going on between QBRC and CIC. We're playing it cool and level, but the pressure you're putting on is very important. It shows what the alternative to dealing with us will be like.'

In a 'mission statement' document prepared and sent to the Concerned Irish Citizens group around the same time as the email exchanges, QBRC set out to explain to the community what it was all about. 'The combined businesses of the former Quinn Group have created a critical mass of high-quality employment within the otherwise economically and socially deprived areas of Fermanagh/Cavan. The retention of this economic base is critical to the well-being of the area from an economic, social and political perspective,' the document read, adding: 'It believes that the economies of scale arising from the combined structure of the former Quinn Group are significant and necessary to be competitive. With this objective the company now states its intention to acquire any businesses of the former Quinn Group that are presented for sale.'

It is notable that nowhere in the mission statement does it say that QBRC's plan was to return the business to the Quinn family.

The covering letter also made clear its concerns at what could be happening in the background. 'Aventas management appear to be pressing ahead with the sale of a number of individual businesses including the rooftile division and the outsourcing of the transport division. We have requested that these actions, and any further sales, be put on hold for a short period until QBRC has finalised its bid for the overall former Quinn Group.'

Within days of the document being prepared, Kevin Lagan, on the day of his wife's death, received a death threat in the post. There was little doubt that those who prepared and sent Lagan the letter knew exactly what QBRC were planning.

Other companies within the group continued to be shopped around, however. Quinn Packaging was another highly successful company based on the main Derrylin to Ballyconnell road, supplying every major UK and Irish supermarket with food-packaging products. Aventas had found that despite what Sean Quinn believed, there was little financial upside from the integration of the group businesses. 'There was no real integration; all the businesses could stand on their own two feet. We couldn't find the savings or benefits of the great integration of the group that we'd been told about,' one source said. So packaging was up for sale. But as with Ceva and Lagan, Quinn supporters quickly found out.

'[We] obviously got word – probably internally, naturally, in Quinn's

– that Paul O'Brien was selling the packaging business, and that there were three runners, three businesses in the running for this,' said Tony Doonan. 'So [one of the management team] rang me up to say that that [Quinn Packaging] was important, that it was crucial that it would stay within the group, as it was quite a sizable part of the business. I wouldn't have known any of the potential suitors from Adam. So he informed me of who they were, and then said that we would have to write to them. Call a spade a spade, it's a blackmail letter, whatever shape or form you want to [call it], words – and I wouldn't be renowned for my diplomacy, so there's no point in me starting now – that's what it was, to persuade them not to pursue their interest in that. And that's exactly what [he] wanted done. I came back then, [and he] basically outlined, you know, what we should say.'

The letter from one of the campaign groups sent to RPC Containers, based in Blackburn, which was the lead bidder for the packaging company, stated: 'We believe your company is currently tendering for the purchase of Quinn Packaging. Since 2011, when the company was reprocessed [sic] and the local management team was displaced and replaced by the current management team (none of which are local), our area has experienced redundancies for the first time in 40 years, depletion of assets and displacement of local employment which has led to violence and unrest. All the local community are supporting the current QBRC bid. The QBRC group consists of all the previous local successful management team who built the group in the first instance and are going to keep the group in its entirety. As your bid ultimately means the break-up of The Quinn Group we cannot see this as the best solution for our area and therefore ask you to reconsider your bid,' warned the protestors in the letter.

Meanwhile, John McCartin was spending a huge amount of time around the kitchen table at the Quinn family home, discussing nothing else but the QBRC bid. For many of those involved in bringing QBRC together, there was no doubt whatsoever that it was operating on behalf of Sean Quinn, and that too was Quinn's own unqualified belief. But there was nothing in writing, no legal document to support that understanding. Quinn was still in bankruptcy, after all, and wasn't going to be trusted by lenders, and he and his family were still fighting the bankers through the courts. Quinn understood this and fully appreciated that it made sense that it was the former managers, backed by two of the most respected businessmen in the North, and a well-connected Fine Gael councillor in the Republic, who were putting the deal together.

Setting the Quinn relationship with QBRC aside, two key questions now arose: how much could they raise, and how much of the business would that buy? McCaffrey had continued meeting with the Dublin financier, 'Derek', to test out the appetite for Irish funding. According to the leading campaigner, Tony Doonan, at this stage it was recognised that QBRC wouldn't be able to get all the businesses back in one go. 'I was saying to Liam, you know, can we not buy the whole lot, lock, stock and barrel? And Liam said that initially, you know, they'd have to buy everything excluding the glass, you know, and that would be in the ball park of 125 million. And Derek had set about, you know, to look for funds for that.'

While McCaffrey focused on the finance, McCartin was the smooth talker with the political contacts. In a key development, Michael Noonan, the finance minister who had agreed the original liquidation, wrote to a border politician voicing his support for McCartin's involvement in QBRC. At one stage in the process McCartin spoke to Alan Dukes, who had advice for him: 'You'll never get a deal good enough for Sean Quinn.' Still, it was clear that McCartin was plugged in at the highest levels of government and they, in turn, were showing support for QBRC.

However, they weren't the only ones he and the rest of the QBRC team had to convince. While Paul O'Brien was CEO at Aventas, the group of twenty US bondholders behind the Barclays syndicate would have to see the value in any proposed deal. Perhaps understandably, O'Brien was sceptical of QBRC and, in particular, its ability to raise the finance. However, when they requested time to put together their bid, he signalled that he was prepared to give them it.

Separate to his discussions with 'Derek' in Dublin, Liam McCaffrey sounded out the potential of financial support with Endless LLP, a UK private equity house co-founded by Northern Ireland businessman Garry Wilson. Doonan recalled how, 'Liam [told me about] Endless and that he had been over to meet them, and ... there was €125 million secured [from] them.' Doonan recognised that this wasn't going to be anywhere near enough to take back all the companies. 'I said to him, you know, Liam, what about the glass? You know, because it was the jewel in the crown. And he said, look, we can't bite off more than we can chew. We bite off this and get this and make a success of this; [anyway] the glass is going nowhere, it'll always be there, you know. So I said, right, that sounds sensible and logical,' admitted Doonan.

It was decided: QBRC would not be bidding for the glass business. They would have to come back for it at a later date.

Following negotiations through the spring and early summer, an agreement was reached whereby Endless would back a partial buy-out if the figures stacked up. Everything looked like it had clicked into place when, on 8 July 2014, QBRC released a statement saying it had secured a deal with Aventas valued at €100 million for the cement and manufacturing companies. Despite their previous stated intentions, there was no mention of the glass or plastics plants. The deal valued the cement business at almost €85m with another €3m of costs and with the agreement of a €10 million bank overdraft to help the new company get on its feet. Due diligence would begin with completion due by the end of the summer. 'It was very cheap at that,' said Quinn. 'It was worth a hell of a lot more,' he added.

John McCartin was quoted by TheJournal.ie as saying: 'It's basically a consortium I put together after I got tired of people asking for a political solution to the Quinn problem, so I decided to put together a business solution.' In a statement reported by the *Belfast Telegraph*, Liam McCaffrey pointed to the benefits of returning the companies to local ownership: 'We are delighted to have reached an agreement with Aventas for the acquisition of the Construction Industry Supplies (CIS) and packaging businesses and are excited with the prospect of returning to these businesses that we have previously worked in and managed,' he said. 'We will work with Aventas to facilitate stability in the local community that will enable Aventas to achieve its corporate objectives.'

QBRC were admitting publicly what they had already faced up to privately: they couldn't raise the €800m valuation Aventas had placed on the entirety of the former Quinn Group, and were, instead, settling for the CIS part of the business.

The bondholders, while relieved at QBRC's commitment to help them achieve their objectives, were concerned that while QBRC – and in particular Sean Quinn – appeared to have settled for what they could afford, they had not given up hope of bringing the glass plant under their control. As a result, they worried that the business could again be targeted to frighten off any potential buyers and force the bondholders' hand to sell to QBRC.

***

Paul O'Brien said he was pleased to reach agreement with QBRC; privately, however, he could barely hide his contempt for the deal. He struggled to form any relationship with Liam McCaffrey and had little respect for John McCartin, who he couldn't work out. 'He was a politician one day, a musician the next and a businessman the day after. O'Brien couldn't get his head around him and his role in the whole QBRC set up,' said a source.

However, with everything seemingly set, there was another twist. With Endless backing the deal, three of the bondholders quickly conferred, wondering if they were missing a trick. Brigade, Contrarian and Silver Point stepped forward to open up discussions about potentially becoming involved with QBRC, the bondholders having come late to the conclusion that they could make more money by staying involved in the border business.

The bondholders sent representatives to negotiate a deal. Mike Gatto had graduated from Cornell University with a BA in economics before helping build Silver Point from a hedge fund with $120 million of assets in 2002 to over $8.5 billion. Matt Harnett was Head of European Research and Trading for Brigade, who'd studied European business at Dublin City University before becoming an analyst and trader covering 'high yield and distressed situations'. Gatto and Harnett became the lead negotiators for the bondholders. Alan Dukes had met both and warned McCartin that they'd take no nonsense.

It all came down to a meeting at London's Mayfair Hotel. Liam McCaffrey and John McCartin met with the bondholders' representatives. Liam already knew the principals involved as during his time as CEO he'd regularly take the private jet across the Atlantic to brief them on the business and to give comfort that they would be repaid their €1.2 billion. But this was a very different time with a very different dynamic. QBRC had the Endless deal on the table but a deal with the bondholders would be much more attractive and would mean they would pay less for the borrowings. 'Liam was unflappable, he was very cool,' said a colleague. Gatto warned that if 'they fucked around, if there was any more community violence, you will get no economic benefit from the company'. Having delivered this warning, the bondholders ultimately offered a better deal than Endless.

They shook hands in agreement and headed for home. McCartin went straight to update Sean Quinn on the new situation, which was that Endless had been pushed out, ultimately walking away with compensation fees. In its place, some of the sellers, i.e. three of the twenty bondholders who were owed the original debt, had stepped in to back the buyer, QBRC.

While Brigade, Silver Point and Contrarian were going to support QBRC to buy out the cement and packaging business (CIS), they would still, along with the other seventeen bondholders, own the other Quinn businesses – glass, plastics, radiators and a wind farm – and, of course, wanted to sell them off as quickly as possible.

Quinn now had to come to terms with the fact that it would be the 'Yankees', as he called them, calling the shots.

A six-page document given to the author, which is described as 'an indicative proposal' for the QBRC–bondholders deal, gives some indication as to the understanding reached by the two parties in the summer of 2014. 'Brigade, Silver Point and Contrarian ("investor group") will back QBRC's purchase of CIS and Packing from Quinn ("OldCo") for €85m,' reads the first line. But on page two of the proposal, from the 'investor group' or bondholders, it sets out 'Newco MIP examples' (MIP standing for 'Mixed Integer Programming'), which is a way of setting out potential business outcomes, taking various variables into account. The first heading, over a series of mathematical equations designed to set out how QBRC stood to benefit, stated: 'Example 1: "If Glass is sold at month 12 for €425 of net proceeds and no Community Interference has occurred."' The second example, which would see QBRC benefit a huge amount less than the first, was if glass was sold but 'community interference has occurred'. A final example was if glass was not sold for three years and no 'community interference has occurred'. The document also put in place an incentive for the sale of the plastics plant – QBRC receiving 5 per cent of net proceeds over €75m, even if there was community interference. Plastics was sold for €120m, giving QBRC a potential return of over €2.2m. The bondholders were dealing with QBRC, but on terms that would incentivise the border businessmen to allow the much more valuable Quinn plants to be sold off. But the deal also, on the face of it, linked QBRC directly with the violence.

The violence was being addressed head on. QBRC was being left in no doubt about the bondholders' concern regarding the risk of the continuing attacks on the former Quinn business. On page two, the incentive was spelled out. If glass was sold and there was no community interference 'defined as actual sabotage, threats of sabotage or buyer intimidation', QBRC would receive 1 per cent of the net proceeds from the sale. With a valuation of €400–€425m, that would give the QBRC team a return of $4m. Plus they'd earn an extra 4 per cent equity in the CIS company. The bondholders were offering QBRC an initial equity stake in the CIS business and if profit levels were met over the following five years, their shareholding would increase to 26 per cent, which would give QBRC a share in the company valued at over €46m.

The document also set out the salaries for the executives. Liam McCaffrey, as chief executive, could earn up to €487,500 per annum if he hit his targets. Kevin and Dara could take home €345,000. Tony Lunney would earn €277,500. All of them were on much higher salaries that Quinn had ever paid.

There was also a provision in the proposal for higher salaries for the executives in the event that both plastics and glass were not sold and were retained as part of an all-encompassing deal with QBRC.

News broke of the new formation of the deal in early September, with a spokesman for QBRC quoted as saying they had the 'moral support' of Sean Quinn. The detail behind the deal structure also became known. There were heavy restrictions placed on the 22 per cent but, most importantly, the QBRC shares could not be transferred to a third party, including Sean Quinn or any member of his family. However, Quinn believed that, if all went well, it would be possible in time for the minority shareholders to buy out the bondholders by refinancing the debt. After all, it was a strategy used by administrators on a regular basis. The original owner came back into the business with a small shareholding, usually 10 to 15 per cent, but with the 'carrot' of being able to get back full control if they brought the company back into profit and then raised the finance to buy out the administrators, in this instance, the American bondholders. It was possible that Sean Quinn, if he played his cards right, could have his company back within five years.

Still, he was struggling with the realities of the deal. He had nothing in writing to give him comfort. He'd no guarantees this was going to work out the way he hoped. There were ways in which this could have been done, of course, such as through a share option agreement that could have been signed and placed in the safe of a solicitor. But there wasn't a share option agreement because some of those involved were not prepared to give Sean Quinn any written guarantees on any aspect of the deal. How it was all going to pan out, as far as they were concerned, was firmly down to Quinn's behaviour.

The main players had different thoughts on what would come next. While most of those involved may have been prepared to only sell the Quinns their shares at the market rate, for example, some others might have been prepared to hand them over to the Quinn family for little or no return. The fact that Quinn was involved at all was a reflection of their intentions and goodwill towards him, but that was it. For ownership to come back to the Quinns he would have to show loyalty to his colleagues and the company, and learn to live with having the majority owners – i.e. the bondholders based in Connecticut – calling the shots. It wasn't going to be easy for a man who'd had everything his own way for the previous forty years.

As the deal progressed through contracting, QBRC argued for Quinn to have some sort of role in the business. 'It was always going to be better to have Sean inside the tent than outside,' said a former colleague. In the end, the bondholders agreed to the proposal that Sean Quinn would be brought back into the company as a 'consultant' and would be paid €500,000 a year. Sean Junior would also be offered a consultancy role.

Even with this offer, though, would Quinn go for the deal?

13

Mission Accomplished

By November 2014 it was crunch time for all sides. It was now or never for the deal with the bondholders. Since the summer, though, much had changed.

Paul O'Brien had to work on the basis that the deal with the bondholders could fall apart at any moment. Therefore, he had to have other options for the business. In parallel to the QBRC negotiations, he had opened up talks on the glass plant with one of Europe's leading glass manufacturers. Vidrala was founded in Álava, in the Basque region of Northern Spain, by the Delclaux family in 1965. By the time Vidrala became interested in the former Quinn Glass, the grandson of the founder, Carlos Delclaux Zulueta, was the company president, owning a 30 per cent shareholding. They had significant market share across Europe and, by buying Quinn Glass, would immediately have 30 per cent of the UK and Irish market.

Since 2011 the Quinn Glass plant in Derrylin had been the key target of the saboteurs. Yet, inside the plant itself, the majority of the workforce, which was more religiously mixed than the other parts of the business, were against the attacks and made their positions very clear: they wanted their jobs more than they wanted Sean Quinn back. The Cheshire base had been beyond the reach of the attackers. The bondholders crunched the variables through the autumn, knowing that any new attack could put the Spaniards off the deal. But it got to the point that they had to declare their hand to QBRC.

John McCartin went to Quinn to explain that glass was going to be sold and would no longer be part of the QBRC deal. Quinn, displeased to say the least with the prospect, looked to stall, asking for time to put together his own bid.

Zulueta himself flew into Dublin and travelled up to the border to meet with Quinn, who'd asked for the opportunity to talk with the man. Out of nowhere, the quarryman proposed that he take a 25 per cent share of the business. His reasoning was that he, and only he, could ensure the critical continued supply of sand to the business, even though he no longer owned any of the quarry from which the sand was being drawn. Zulueta wasn't interested in having Sean Quinn as a minority shareholder. He was putting a €400m bid on the table and had no need for partners. Anyway, Quinn wasn't offering a single cent for his 25 per cent. When it was clear that the meeting was going one way, Quinn became frustrated and angry, darkly warning the Spaniard: 'You know what happens when you corner a rat.'

Zulueta left for Dublin where, later the same day, he dined with Paul O'Brien at a top restaurant off St Stephen's Green. With the Quinn meeting having gone badly, McCartin – as Quinn's emissary only and not working on behalf of his QBRC colleagues – asked if he could join them. Zulueta and O'Brien expected him to come with a commitment that Quinn would do nothing to prevent the deal from happening despite his behaviour at the earlier meeting and that the deal would not be opposed on the border. Instead, it became apparent that McCartin had travelled to Dublin in a last ditch attempt to stall the deal.

As O'Brien walked Zulueta back to his hotel, he promised him, despite the obvious opposition of Quinn and McCartin, that the deal would go through. 'O'Brien was impressed by Zulueta. He wasn't going to be put off at all by the trouble. His family had been targeted by ETA [the Basque separatist group] in the past so they had some experience of violence. The Spaniards had balls of steel,' said a source.

Liam McCaffrey and his colleagues had already accepted that glass and plastics could not be part of their deal. But now, for Quinn, the penny finally dropped. Glass, and indeed plastics, were all but gone. He could withdraw his backing for the QBRC deal for the cement and manufacturing businesses or stay in and hope that it played out in his favour. He was rattled. As far as he was concerned, this wasn't what he had envisaged.

Before finalising the deal, the QBRC shareholders met at the Westville Hotel in Enniskillen. John McCartin drove Quinn up from the border. Not long into the meeting, Quinn announced that he wasn't sold on the deal and began to aggressively argue against it. Everyone else in the room was stunned. It was the best possible outcome; how could he not see that? It was Dara O'Reilly, who'd previously shown no concern about standing up to Quinn, who told him bluntly: 'This deal is happening with your support or not.'

John McCartin told *The Irish News* later that 'we said back to Seán, "Jesus, we're in for a song and in control of management. We are on the pig's back here."' However, Quinn remained far from convinced. 'I do remember him being very belligerent,' McCartin added.

Quinn got up from his seat, grabbed the keys to John McCartin's car, and left. In his absence, everyone in the room agreed that they were signing the contract. 'We knew there was going to be trouble but let's get it done and maybe the atmosphere will change,' said one of those present. By the time Quinn came back, according to McCartin, 'he had changed his mind and decided he would go with it'.

Legally, QBRC could not compromise themselves by signing up to an agreement with the bondholders, a deal that explicitly stated they weren't acting as proxies for Sean Quinn, while at the same time acting on behalf of Quinn. There is no doubt that Sean Quinn believed QBRC was for the benefit of himself and his family, but he had nothing in writing and had to buy into the deal on the basis of the commitments he believed he was getting from those involved. Liam McCaffrey's attitude was that if Quinn wanted to buy his shares from him, he could do it at the market rate, just like anyone else, if he ever decided to sell. 'Sean Quinn understood that,' claimed one of those involved. 'He knew the deal wasn't right but was of the belief that he would get in and sort it out,' he added.

On 23 December, the deal was formally concluded. The cement factories, quarries, tarmac, roof-tile and insulation businesses, along with the packaging division, were now back under local control. The 700 employees in the manufacturing and packaging companies were no longer working for the bankers.

With the deal closed, Dara O'Reilly, Liam McCaffrey and Kevin Lunney gathered in the boardroom with Ernie Fisher and Bosco O'Hagan. It had been agreed that Sean Quinn shouldn't turn up on the first morning, so as not to spook the bondholders, who were now investors. QBRC and Aventas would be replaced by a new company, Quinn Industrial Holdings Ltd (QIH).

There were jubilant scenes at the company headquarters, reported *The Impartial Reporter*'s Rodney Edwards, who was the first journalist on the scene. 'Employees took a sledgehammer to the Aventas Group sign, removing it to uncover the previous sign – the letter "Q". One of the Aventas signs was later set on fire as some employees jumped up and down on it,' he wrote. An *Irish Examiner* report described the scenes as being 'reminiscent of the fall of Baghdad during the US invasion of Iraq'.

Inside, Liam McCaffrey, back again for a second time as chief executive, told Edwards it was the beginning of a new chapter. 'This company had a unique culture that was built in fairness around the profile and ethos of Seán Quinn and that uniqueness sustains and develops it. Over the years there has been a lot of trust in this company and a lot of people willing to work with each other. For Seán and the local community there is a sense of pride in collectively proving a point. I think it's a return of a significant part of it. Today is the start – it's not a finish. We are taking over a business that we have to drive forward.'

As the executives celebrated in the boardroom at the back of the headquarters, they began to hear loud cheers from the entrance hall. Sean Quinn couldn't stay away. As he walked up the steps, employees shouted: 'Welcome home, Sean!'

The investors were nervous about Sean Quinn. The plan was to keep the media away, but the quarryman hadn't signed up to that deal either. Quinn emerged with a tray full of Budweiser beer and whiskey, providing the waiting photographers with the money shot of the day. It was Christmas; Quinn was back in his old office.

In a rare public comment, Ernie Fisher told Rodney Edwards how pleased he was to be part of the deal. 'I think it's very important for all the businesses in Fermanagh, Leitrim and Cavan to have this business back managed by local people. People in these counties are great workers but they work better with local management. It is a very viable business. I think it's important to see Seán Quinn back involved in giving the business his support,' he said.

John McCartin, now a non-executive director in the new company, was also keen to talk up Quinn's role. 'I am looking forward to seeing Seán Quinn around here and bringing back energy, enthusiasm and expertise. There is something very poetic about it; the place was taken in hostile fashion and we've come back to run this business with the right message and intentions. My message to Seán Quinn is: we are very proud to be here maintaining your legacy,' he told Edwards.

There was a clear strategy – give Quinn all the credit for the forty years' work he had put into building the business, but at the same time, remain vague as to how things would work out moving forward. What they did know is that they had control of the board, not Quinn. They had the support of the investors and if things went sour with Quinn, the business was going to continue, with or without him. Dara O'Reilly was the most outspoken of the executives, having long run out of any reserves of respect for Quinn. Liam was clear-eyed about the future. Quinn was closest to Kevin Lunney and, despite everything, the two still had a very tight bond. All three executives knew it could never be what it was before, but as they broke up for Christmas they hoped the New Year would bring a new, collaborative, collegiate attitude from the quarryman.

Meanwhile, for those who had led a relentless campaign in support of Quinn, it was a moment to celebrate. As far as Tony Doonan was concerned, it was the work of the campaigners that had brought about QBRC. 'Our group, between signs and protests and anything we could do that could deter Paul O'Brien from breaking up the businesses and selling them off to interested parties, and Lagan was one of those,' he said. 'And we wanted to maintain and keep what Sean Quinn built. Because no one else was going to build those factories in our area, you know – south Fermanagh, west Cavan – there was nobody, nobody going to do that. So this was a one-off opportunity that we had. And actually Christmas 2014 ... We thought at that stage, you know, mission accomplished, we can take a breather, thankfully, you know, through all our protests and actions, someone was listening to us,' said Doonan.

Sean Quinn flashed big smiles to everyone that day, but deep down he was smarting. The glass factory was gone, plastics would go too. He'd come through the loss of his businesses, bankruptcy, jail time. Now the world thought this was his comeback, his second coming, but Quinn was full of resentment. He believed he'd been played.

***

The New Year brought a slew of announcements from Paul O'Brien. Quinn Radiators was sold to an investment company led by Tony Mullins, the former CEO of Barlo, the company Quinn had bought from Dermot Desmond after his week at the Cheltenham Races in 2004. The Slieve Rushen wind farm's eighteen turbines were also sold to a London company for €127 million. The plastics company, Polycasa, was sold for €120 million to a Swiss company, Schweiter Technologies.

Over a three-month period O'Brien had successfully disposed of all the major Quinn businesses for €700 million. In return, according to accounts filed later, he was paid more than €2.5 million in dividends. Aventas chairman Mike McTighe was paid €1.27 million and its chief financial officer and chief accounting officer took home just over €1 million. Aventas, before it was broken up, had returned a profit of close to €115 million in its final year.

The QBRC deal was worth around 10 per cent of the value of the total Quinn business estate on the Border. But for the bondholders it triggered the unhindered sale of the most valuable assets. One of those involved in the QBRC deal made the frank admission: 'We only got the [QIH] business back because of the violence.'

From 2011 there had been almost a hundred separate attacks. The pattern that emerged in 2014 suggests that those behind the violence were aware of the growing possibility of the companies coming back into local hands. From January through to April 2014 there had been at least eight separate attacks alone, including the death threat sent to Kevin Lagan. In March a car with the roof cut off was loaded with tyres, petrol and gas canisters and crashed into the front foyer of Quinn Packaging before being set alight. More than thirty employees were in the building at the time and some €600,000 of damage was caused. In early April the Molly Maguires destroyed two excavators and damaged a third in an attack on Doon Mountain. A week later a bomb warning was phoned into the glass factory, causing it to be shut down. The final attack prior to the QBRC takeover coincided with the interest Vidrala was showing in the glass company. From then until Sean Quinn walked through the doors of the company headquarters, there wasn't a single attack. Those behind the violence were very clearly aware of when, where and what to target. When their work was done, they could go back to the day jobs.

Given the ferocity of the violence, it was clear that relationships based in crime had been established. Given the geographical spread of the attacks, from Cork to Comber, a wide network of men and women willing to risk jail in support of Sean Quinn had come together – as many as a hundred people may have been involved. They had shown sophistication and co-ordination in the attacks and had evaded police detection.

In the maelstrom of violence in the first four months of 2014, even Quinn had become a target. On Good Friday, according to a report in the *Sunday Independent*, he 'had to hurriedly leave a reception after gardaí uncovered a threat to kill him ... Mr Quinn was socialising in his native Derrylin, in Fermanagh, at the start of the Easter bank holiday weekend when gardaí learnt that a death threat had been issued against him. They immediately made contact with Mr Quinn, urging him to return to his family home across the border in Ballyconnell, Co. Cavan. Once he got there, he was briefed by detectives who informed him that Garda headquarters had received intelligence about a "credible" threat on his life from an unknown source,' the paper's Ronald Quinlan and Maeve Sheehan reported the following July.

Despite being targeted himself, it was later alleged that Quinn was financing the attacks, something which Quinn has always categorically and vehemently denied. The Molly Maguires and many of the others who were involved were not doing it for monetary gain. They saw their actions as being in the interest of the community.

However, Dublin Jimmy was mercenary. He had no dog in the fight for control of the Quinn business. Money was his motivation. Rumours about who was paying him to orchestrate the attacks were rife. But police were never able to even disrupt his campaign, never mind bring him to justice.

One former RUC officer who knew him claimed: 'McGuinness had no fear. He had a confidence about him. I didn't recognise it at the time, but now I know it came from him knowing he was a protected species. No matter who was paying him, his real bosses were MI5 – they were protecting him.' The former policeman had been stationed in Rosslea in the early 1990s. At the time, Cyril McGuinness was living in a caravan positioned across the border. When the caravan was approached by the RUC, he would move his possessions into the Republic, and vice versa should the gardaí visit. At one point, the officer sought to have a camera fitted outside McGuinness's home in order to monitor his movements and the vehicles he was using. But senior officers refused. When he asked why, he claims to have been told, 'Cyril is working for the boys, MI5.'

In 1996 the IRA ended its ceasefire with a huge bomb attack on the London docklands, killing two men and causing damage estimated at £150m. In the aftermath, Scotland Yard issued a photofit picture of the man who was suspected of having driven the bomb to its target. It was clearly Cyril McGuinness. Police later claimed that he'd escaped to the Irish Republic. However, the RUC officer was suspicious of the police claims, as he knew that McGuinness was still on the border. All of this only reinforced his suspicion that McGuinness was indeed working for British intelligence. After all, at the time, the British and Irish governments were working hand in hand on the peace process. Any application to have McGuinness extradited would have surely been done with pleasure by a Dublin government keen to underscore its even-handed approach to the North. Instead, he remained 'at large'.

All of these factors were in mind when the new Quinn Industrial Holdings team gathered around the boardroom table in the early weeks of 2015. What was described as Sean Quinn's 'destructive impulse that could not be controlled' was clear to everyone in the room. 'They realised Quinn didn't understand the basis of him coming back during the very first meeting,' said someone who was in the room. 'He should have settled down and had a bit of wit. It wasn't done for him, it was for the community, but he thought it was all about him.'

Liam was keeping his distance from Quinn, Dara too was staying out of his way. Quinn was back in his office, but he was struggling with the dawning realisation that he was no longer in control. Everything looked the same – the offices, the people, the decoration – but it was different, very different. The business no longer revolved around him. No one reported to him. He couldn't even buy lunch for clients in the Slieve Russell without the bill being authorised by Liam McCaffrey.

Soon, relationships began to be strained. 'I brought people in here that were ex-employees who worked for me before but they had left or were sacked during Paul O'Brien's time, and I brought them into the house here and agreed new terms and what we were going to be doing,' Quinn explained. He believed he had the authority to make decisions such as rehiring former employees, but the CEO, Liam McCaffrey, had no idea what was happening at the mansion, nor had his agreement been sought. The former employees ultimately got their jobs back but this overstepping was an early sign that Sean Quinn was confused by what exactly QBRC was all about. 'Day by day, week by week, you could see that there was something wrong,' said Quinn.

A recording of a meeting attended by John McCartin and Bosco O'Hagan was leaked to the Quinn family. The Magherafelt businessman can be heard explaining how he got involved in QBRC in the first place: 'It was agreed to buy the place and always, always, always, we were only buying it for Sean Quinn, we weren't buying it for ourselves, we were buying it for Quinn and the Quinn family, putting them back into what we thought was their rightful place. That is still the same to this day. This never changed with anybody,' said O'Hagan.

McCartin struck the same note. 'We didn't get involved to get 22 per cent or 27 per cent or any per cent of this business for ourselves, we got involved in this to straighten out the mess that was here and look after the Quinns. That's what we wanted to do,' he was recorded as saying. He went on to explain his understanding of the bondholders' plans for exit. 'They have no interest in here, they are going to flip the business, they are going to flip it as quick as they can and establish exactly how much they can make on it and I think the job we should be looking at now is making sure that we stay trusted by financial institutions and that we make sure that we manage their expectations and make sure that we don't let them think that they can get too much out of here but they think they can just get themselves paid for and get out the door. That is what we need them to think and while they are going to give us a reference and say, "Those are bankable, lads, let them at it." That is what we need. That is what our plan was. That is what we find out there. That is what I want to do and when we get it the Quinns can have it.'

It was unambiguous. QBRC, according to O'Hagan and McCartin in January 2015, was there for one reason only: to get the company back for the Quinn family. At the time, the relationship between O'Hagan, Fisher, McCartin and Quinn was still amicable.

But Quinn was getting more and more frustrated about the businesses that had been sold: he couldn't let go of them – the radiators, the plastics as well as the glass. But rather than blame himself, he began blaming his QBRC colleagues. He was especially angry when he discovered that Paul O'Brien had put in place a ten-year agreement to provide the Spanish owners of the glass factory 'special prices' for their raw material, i.e. the sand from the former Quinn quarry.

The business may have already been broken up and sold off, but Sean Quinn was still fighting through the courts for compensation for the €2.8 billion in loans he claimed had been given to his family illegally by Anglo Irish Bank. After his 'second coming' in December 2014, it was thought the mood music might have changed, allowing for mediation in the case the family had launched. Again, John McCartin became the key player, shuttling back and forth to Dublin to meet with politicians and IBRC representatives to scope out the parameters of a potential settlement. The political wind had changed, which could have allowed for the government to be seen to do a deal with the businessman. Some of the property developers were beginning to get back on their feet so why not Quinn?

But McCartin discovered that, while he was making all the running, when it came to the key meetings, Quinn was keeping him out of the room – and behaving in an unprofessional manner within the room. The journalist Ian Kehoe reported in *The Currency* how Quinn had behaved during one set of talks. 'Previous attempts at settlement talks had failed. During one meeting at a five-star Dublin hotel, Quinn removed his shoes and walked around the room in his socks. For reasons completely unrelated to his attire, the talks lasted a matter of minutes. There was no bridge between the two sides. The family was offered €20 million in various assets to end the battle. They refused,' he reported.

Sean Quinn admits that he was offered the Slieve Russell and two pubs in Dublin in a deal in return for ending his legal action against IBRC. The one proviso: he had to accept there and then. But he stalled for a week – so that he could consult his family, he claims – and when he went back to accept, the offer was off the table, as he'd been warned. Quinn's reservations had cost him the deal. 'If he had accepted it,' said a source close to the negotiations, 'he knew it would be viewed as justification for everything that [the bankers had done to him] and he couldn't accept that.' The source viewed it as a key moment. 'He could have taken the deal and built back. The vast majority of those who have gone through what Sean Quinn suffered want a deal so that they can move on. He could have rebuilt in months and been a hero.'

Quinn had once again misread the room and missed a chance to return his family to the status of multimillionaires. He seemed unable to swallow his pride. 'Quinn never once came to a meeting with specialist advisors,' said another source. 'In the meetings he would say "if Sean Quinn was here" and he had to be reminded "but you are Sean Quinn and you are here!" It seemed to be a device he used to avoid taking responsibility for what had gone wrong. It also became clear that it was all about winning. It wasn't about the assets or the money anymore at that point. He had to get the victory that he'd created in his mind. He believed there was always a better deal and could never get to the point where he could tell himself, I've won.'

Furthermore, his colleagues became concerned that Quinn was adopting a strategy designed to devalue the QIH companies, in order to make it easier for him to buy them back at a later point. It was a kamikaze business plan. 'Why are you working towards profits here? It's only putting it out of our [the Quinns'] reach,' Quinn is reported to have said at one meeting. 'They didn't know what to do,' said a colleague at the time, talking about the executive team.

Another colleague claimed that Quinn wanted to inflate payments to certain suppliers with whom he had personal debts, 'mates he owed or owed favours to that he wanted to sort out through the business', which caused serious friction with Dara O'Reilly, the chief financial officer. 'Dara had a sense he would be asked to do things he was uncomfortable with,' a colleague said, adding. 'Did they leave him at it? No, they couldn't. He wanted to drive the value out of the business and they felt an obligation to the local community to not let this happen.'

His frustration growing, in May 2015 Quinn demanded that he meet directly with the American investors. It was decided that Matt Harnett was the right person to take the meeting. Quinn recalls how 'They came over in August and I talked to them. I said, this business can't succeed, lads. It's not managed. I said, these men are not capable of running this business. This business needs forty-five million capital investment. And the fella, Matt Harnett, said, oh, we don't believe that, we believe these are great men, these men are going to do a great job, and these men have convinced us that they will be able to make a go of this. I said, well, sure it'll take a few years to tell, but I'm telling you, these men are not capable of running this business, and I said the proof of the pudding is in the plant, and machinery has not been maintained, and it's not been invested in, and the raw materials are not being invested in. And some of the management decisions that are going on just don't make any sense. So, I said I can't see how this business can succeed. I know this business. I built this business. What you are talking about doesn't make any sense. And I told that to the Yankees, but nobody would hear me.'

Quinn had laid out his concerns to the investors directly. Harnett had no sympathy for the quarryman but recognised the position management were in. If they ended Quinn's contract, could that spark renewed violence? They were in a no-win situation.

Quinn felt that others had already turned Harnett and the other investors against him. 'They were after telling so many lies about me, and that I wanted to destroy the business and I wanted to run the business into the ground and buy it for nothing, and that I was mentally ill,' recalled Quinn. 'And they told that to my son as well, that I was mentally ill, and they had to look after the business for me because I wasn't a well man, I had been through a rough time and it may take me a few years to settle down. And they were trying to look after the business. So I was hearing all this back,' he said.

The executive team looked to the family, hoping that they could help Quinn to see sense, make him realise that this wasn't going to end well. On that matter alone, Quinn agreed with them.

***

The one-year anniversary of Sean Quinn's 'second coming' should have been a moment for celebration, but instead it was a month of increasing tension that would see a very significant change in direction in terms of the attacks.

All through 2015 Quinn had been raising hell in meetings about QIH agreeing to give right of way to the French company that had bought his former wind farms at Snugborough and Slieve Rushen. While he disputed the access in Quinn headquarters, others were taking much more direct action on the mountain – namely, the Molly Maguires. Boulders and spikes were placed on roads to block access, contractors were being harassed – bullets were sent to one and, in another incident, a security guard was chased by a man wielding a gun.

Quinn's argument was that the right of way shouldn't have been agreed over the heads of the farmers who owned the land. He'd made previous agreements with the farmers and therefore these rights should not have been included in any deal. 'All of those farmers, I dealt with them for the last twenty, thirty, forty years and I bought land off them for shale, stone, wind farms, limestone, made roads and everything. I must have dealt with sixty, seventy farmers in the local area. And I always showed total respect to them. And all of a sudden these boys came along and they allowed [a] French company to walk all over them through the wind farm.'

There was no doubt that during the back end of 2015, Quinn had no relationship or confidence in the executives who had been closest to him, including now Kevin Lunney, who had almost been like a second son to him, the man who had led the insurance company and built the family's property portfolio, who'd been a staunch defender and supporter of Quinn through thick and thin. It was clear that the quarryman's most zealous supporters were watching on.

Two weeks before Christmas, Kevin Lunney became a target for the first time in a gruesome incident at their home. His wife, Bronagh, had taken their children to Enniskillen to see Santa Claus. When they arrived back home, the children ran from the car to the house, only to discover a pig's head on their doorstep with a threat attached. On the same night, a can of petrol and matches were left at the door of a substation serving a small five-turbine wind farm owned by Kevin Lunney and his two brothers. Graffiti was scrawled along a wall: 'Tony, Kevin – it's your choice'.

The incidents marked the end of Kevin Lunney's almost twenty-year relationship with the man he once saw as a business genius, and more, a friend.

Lunney wasn't the only former disciple against whom Quinn had now fully turned. The day before the company was to break for Christmas, Sean Quinn called Dara and Liam into his office. His decision was clear and final. 'Liam and Dara, you are going to have to go. I want you to resign.' Quinn, back in the company as a consultant, but without any authority, had decided that the best course of action to deal with the now toxic atmosphere was to sack the two executives. McCaffrey and O'Reilly knew that treating Sean Quinn with disrespect wasn't going to help but they made it clear to him that although he was sitting in an executive chair, back in his old office, he no longer called the shots. He could refuse to recognise that fact, but it was still a fact. As they broke for the holidays, the executives knew they had reached breaking point with Sean Quinn.

The new year certainly didn't bring any respite. The first week back in the office, Quinn demanded a showdown meeting with the executives. His son Sean Junior, daughters Aoife, Brenda and Colette would attend, at their father's invitation, along with his son-in-law, Stephen Kelly. He was going to bring two businessmen, Freddie Walsh and Martin Maguire, to act as observers. Christmas at the Quinns had allowed the family to discuss the ongoing disputes, both at the company and in the courts. They wanted to see a settlement on both fronts.

The 8 January meeting in the boardroom at the company headquarters, they hoped, would clear the air and allow for a frank discussion. *Sunday Times* reporter John Mooney later published minutes of the meeting. Quinn took the chair at the top of the table, and according to Mooney, 'opened by asking McCartin to outline who owned and controlled QIH. McCartin explained that QBRC owned 11% of the equity and the management team a further 11%, which he suggested could increase by another 2.5% if they met performance targets. The remaining 78% stake was owned by the bondholders: Brigade Capital, Contrarian Capital and Silver Point Capital.'

After that explainer, 'the conversation turned to the issue of who was in charge and the raison d'être of QBRC. Aoife Quinn said she believed her father had been isolated in QIH and was no longer making decisions. "My father can be difficult but he is not an unreasonable man, and it appears there's a deliberate intention by the management to isolate and exclude him," she said.'

Foremost on Quinn's mind was not his treatment, however, but when ownership of the company would be returned to his family. He had expected to regain control of the company within two or three years of QIH's establishment in 2014, with QBRC's help.

'How could this be possible?' asked Fisher.

'That is QBRC's mandate,' Quinn pointed out.

According to the notes of the meeting, Quinn repeated his demand that Liam McCaffrey and Dara O'Reilly leave the company, accusing them of treating him in a 'dreadful manner' and not showing him respect. (The notes do not make any mention of Quinn's attitude towards Kevin Lunney.) Aoife Quinn said she never thought she would be 'sitting here fighting with the management team', reported the paper. 'McCaffrey replied that he had never thought he would be asked by the police to check his personal security – a reference to the ongoing attacks on the company.'

It was clear to all in the room that the relationship between Quinn and the QIH team had broken down. The question now was how best it could be managed. The time had come to rip off the plaster.

***

Quinn followed up the meeting by writing to the QIH board, reiterating the demands he'd made at the boardroom meeting. An internal memo dated March 2016 recorded that the American investors were 'growing increasingly uncomfortable with the escalating acts of violence and intimidation'. The investors demanded that Quinn withdraw his demands for an equity stake in the business, a seat on the board and his separate allegations of impropriety against the management. (Quinn had accused Liam McCaffrey of fraud, sparking an independent investigation, which cleared the executive.)

Up on the mountain, there were fresh attacks. A package containing bullets, a funeral wreath and a handwritten note were left, warning the French company operating the wind farms to 'stay away from Slieve Rushen or face the bullet'. The three executives were singled out in April when a threat was sent to the company headquarters warning McCaffrey, Lunney and O'Reilly to 'remove the UDA and UVF off our mountain or face the gun' – a reference to a security team that the owners of the wind farm had brought in from Belfast to protect their business. Locals had detected that they were Protestants – the note writer therefore made the leap to suggest they were members of a loyalist paramilitary organisation.

A series of letters were exchanged between the investors and Quinn, which led to the inevitable in May: Sean Quinn resigned from his consultancy position. His son also left the company for the second time. In a statement to Rodney Edwards at *The Impartial Reporter*, Quinn attempted to position the move as being in the best interests of himself and the company. 'I confirm that an agreement has now been reached with QBRC which creates a pathway for the Quinn family to potentially realise its ambitions over time. Arising from this positive development, I have agreed to stand aside from my contract with Quinn Industrial Holdings to facilitate that process.'

Tony Doonan and the others involved with the Quinn support groups had been very aware of the deteriorating situation. He claims that the management, in the spring of 2015, had committed to setting up a 'steering group' to manage the family's relationship with QIH or, depending on interpretation, to manage the handing over of shares to the family. Doonan goes further and claims that the Quinn family were told that unless Sean Quinn resigned, there would be no steering group established. The steering group was seen as the pathway for Quinn to regain control. 'They would meet regularly and [agreed] that something would be put in place, a structure, and over time, you know, something tangible would transfer to the Quinn family,' said Doonan.

After Quinn's departure, Tony Doonan led a delegation of the campaigners to meet with Liam McCaffrey, Kevin Lunney and Dara O'Reilly to explain his exit from the company. 'The explanation was that you couldn't work with Sean and that, you know, [he was] too disruptive, [they] couldn't work with him and they couldn't get on with him and [Quinn's behaviour brought about] the hostile environment, hostile attitude, which was never, never, never in any Quinn business or Quinn Group or Quinn office or Quinn anywhere. We accepted that and we said, right, okay, okay, we understand that Sean would want to do things his way and that he wanted to get back into control and he couldn't do that and we understand, naturally, he couldn't do that,' he said.

However, following discussions with Sean Quinn, the protest groups wrote to QIH, warning that they were not sticking to the agreed mandate with the local community. The Quinn family were not being looked after as had been agreed. QIH responded by telling the Quinns that unless Tony Doonan and the others backed down there would be no steering group. In response, the Quinns told Doonan and the campaigners to cease all social media posts and remove the signs that had been placed along the main Derrylin to Ballyconnell road.

While this played out in the background, the management sent a carefully worded statement to staff, which was leaked to several newspapers, explaining why Quinn had left. 'Following the acquisition of the businesses by QIH we entered into a consultancy agreement as a framework to facilitate Sean Quinn's involvement in the businesses. We believed that this would enable us to benefit from the wealth of experience that Sean had built up since he founded the businesses and was a role intended both as a mark of respect for Sean and to assist in creating a unified sense of purpose in support of a local management team and local businesses that sustain local employment and prosperity. As time has progressed it has become evident that Sean's expectations for his role and the ownership structure of QIHL are at odds with the strategic direction of the businesses. Accordingly, it has been mutually agreed between the parties that QIHL's consultancy arrangement with Sean Quinn and Sean Quinn Junior will be discontinued.'

Sean Quinn blamed the executives he'd hired in the first place. Dara O'Reilly and Liam McCaffrey had both stood up to him; their relationship had all but fallen apart not long after he'd gone back in. The shock for Sean Quinn was Kevin Lunney and his brother, Tony, backing the investors. Two men he believed in and believed he had their total support in return. 'I mean, I'd be very angry with the Lunneys. I know they were good friends of mine and I promoted both of them to very senior positions, and I had great respect for them. But, I mean, you just can't go back there. What they've done to me is wrong,' Quinn said later.

The protestors melted away, hoping that QIH and Quinn would come to an amicable agreement. 'The boys bought eighteen months of no social media, no signs, so they had a free reign,' said Doonan, explaining that, 'We didn't want to be the ones standing in the way of the Quinn family. How stupid would that be of us, to be actually standing in the way of the Quinns getting something out of this business?'

With no job to go out to in the mornings once again, Quinn himself withdrew behind the high walls of the lakeside mansion and brooded. Before, it was the banks, the Dublin politicians, who'd turned against him. Now, it was the three executives he fixated on. They were the cause of everything, from agreeing to the security on the property that caused him to lose the insurance company in the first place, to doing a deal behind his back with the American investors. They'd allowed the glass, radiator and plastics factories to be sold off. They'd allowed 'outsiders' access to the wind farms across his neighbours' land. It was all their doing now. Yes, he had made mistakes, but he'd been loyal to them and that loyalty hadn't been repaid. Quinn felt they had betrayed him.

Looking out of his living-room window, he could see the businesses he'd built rising up to the skyline: the cement factories, the glass plant, the Slieve Russell Hotel. Over 200 acres of businesses. His lifetime's work.

It was all gone now.

14

Border People

The rise and fall of Sean Quinn over the last fifty years has, in many ways, become the story of the Cavan–Fermanagh border. In the Dublin media, Sean Quinn is a caricature. At first there had been the story told over and over again, across thirty years of reporting, of the man who borrowed £100 to start his own business, who played cards for fifty pence with his friends on a Tuesday night and eschewed everything that became synonymous with success or the Celtic Tiger. However, whether during times of success or at the point of his ultimate downfall, he was depicted as something of a freak of nature who came out of a lawless place. For the news industry in Dublin, there was Ireland, the North and a third jurisdiction, known simply as 'the border'. Sean Quinn was defined by that border.

***

It was in late 2018, two and a half years after he left the company, that I first met Sean Quinn at his home on the border. Rodney Edwards introduced us.

The house was impressive, although the pool no longer had any water, a window pane in the main living room was shattered and wallpaper had come away from the wall. Over coffee and biscuits, we discussed the family's situation with regard to the company and the still-to-happen legal case. Despite all that had occurred, Quinn continued to believe that the family could get a favourable result from its case against IRBC. Throughout our conversation, he constantly flicked the top of a pen bearing the famous Q logo. When we discussed a date to meet again he opened a Quinn diary. All that he had left of the empire: a pen and a diary.

He told me it was time the Quinns told the truth about what had happened and that now was the right time. Listing off figures of hundreds of millions, he set out how the State had robbed him of his company in the first place and how his executives had stabbed him in the back. When asked, he dismissed the recent violence and those involved as a sideshow. The real story, he said, was in the corrupt practices of regulators, bankers and politicians who had colluded to steal his empire and blame him for the economic meltdown in 2008. He hadn't the connections in Dublin to fight back in the way other Irish businessmen with access to power had done. He was a border quarryman with no formal education who had become a billionaire. The family, he said, were fully behind him and were looking forward to their day in court.

A few weeks later he sat down for his first interview and over the coming months we met several times, going over the past, the case, the wrongdoing, the treachery. He seemed no closer to truly owning any of it than he was on the day he left in May 2016. While he was of course prepared to put his hands up, admit to some mistakes and accept that he had to take some punishment, he remained adamant: he was ultimately more sinned against than sinner. He was the real victim.

As we parted after the initial meeting, Quinn said the legal case would be the final chapter in the relationship between the family, CFDs, banks and the Quinn Group. He was clearly still fully immersed in the events of the previous ten years; time had not healed any of his wounds. He was frustrated at the pace of the case, which was initially supposed to go to court in mid-2013. He wanted action, any action, more quickly than the courts or the process would deliver. He was desperate to restore respect to the family name.

Others continued to strive to restore the Quinns to what they saw as their rightful legacy. Along the Ballyconnell Road out of Derrylin, there was a constant and visible reminder of the conflict. It wasn't British Army bases, Land Rovers or helicopters. Posters were once again hung on electricity poles along the main road. Pictures of Kevin Lunney and his brother, Tony, with the words 'Grabber', 'Wanted' and 'Traitor'. A large white poster with black and red writing claimed: 'Liam McCaffrey's Salary – £487,500 plus expenses. Tony and Kevin Lunney's Salary – £345,000 plus expenses. Sean Quinn zero pounds.'

Doonan produced email correspondence between himself, the Quinn family, Kevin Lunney and Liam McCaffrey. After Sean Quinn left the business, McCaffrey wrote to Doonan to advise that 'QBRC is engaged constructively with the Quinn Family. This engagement is continuing and the Family have nominated a committee to deal with QBRC and other parties regarding the various initiatives.' Quinn supporters believed QBRC were still intent on coming to a deal with Sean Quinn. But two years later, in the summer of 2017, Sean Quinn's daughter wrote to Kevin Lunney to express her growing frustrations. She accused QBRC of breaking commitments, despite the family and supporters promoting a 'message of harmony in the local community' while encouraging the removal of the anti-QBRC signs and Facebook pages. The email from Colette Quinn makes clear the family were expecting shares in the business and an 'ultimate goal of securing future ownership of the company'. She said there had been a 'plethora' of meetings since 2014 which, in the family's view, were designed to 'create the impression that QBRC were genuine in their efforts to assist the family'.

While the family were at loggerheads with QIH, Quinn's supporters claimed the company was sacking employees who had 'liked' pro-Quinn material on Facebook. There was also anger at the growing number of legal actions the company executives were launching against locals, alleging harassment and defamation. In the summer of 2017, there was a poisonous atmosphere on the border. Whatever the truth, one thing was clear: there would be no detente between QIH and Quinn.

As a result, it was no surprise when the attacks returned. Dara O'Reilly's car was burnt out in an attack at his home in Butlersbridge on the southern side of the border. Ten days later, at the end of October 2018, Tony Lunney's car was also destroyed when a petrol bomb was thrown into it outside his home in Ballyconnell. The substation at the wind farm on Molly Mountain was again targeted.

In February 2019 Dara O'Reilly and Kevin Lunney went for lunch in the service station café across the road from the headquarters. CCTV captured what happened next. They failed to notice the young man who came in behind them and took a seat to Kevin's left. When the waitress asked what he'd like to have he ordered a tea. She came back with the teapot and filled up his white cup. The young man then got up and walked around the back of the café to Dara and Kevin's table where he engaged with them both, Kevin recognising the young, muscular man as Bernard McGovern, an All-Ireland boxing champion. The same young man would later claim that he'd been approached to keep lookout when the electrical substation was attacked on Molly Mountain in 2011. Bernard McGovern's father, Sean, had been arrested in relation to the cutting down of the telegraph poles on Molly Mountain.

It's clear from the video that neither of the executives wanted to talk, but then neither did McGovern. He picked his moment, threw the mug of tea into Dara's face and launched an attack on Kevin, raining punch after punch down on him. As Kevin fell off his chair, the attack continued until others in the café pulled him off. Blood was streaming from Kevin's face. He'd sustained a broken nose and other facial injuries in the attack, which lasted less than thirty seconds.

Until that Friday afternoon in the cafe, the attacks had been on property. Now it had escalated to physical violence. McGovern's family and the Lunneys are neighbours on Molly Mountain. Their fathers and grandfathers had farmed the land, side by side, helping each other in times of need, as those in close rural communities do.

McGovern's father, Sean, had worked in the road service but left after thirty-two years to join QIH after Quinn's return. He supported Sean Quinn, though he didn't know him personally. But he'd fallen out with the management after Sean Quinn had left the company, and had been sacked. The prosecution in the subsequent Bernard McGovern case claimed that his father's departure from the company was the motivation behind the vicious assault he'd launched on Kevin Lunney. Outside the court, the McGovern family said the attack had nothing to do with Sean's sacking but was related to how Bernard had been treated by those involved in the attacks on Molly Mountain.

Bernard McGovern, who lived with his parents on the Northern side of the border, was extradited from the North and spent several months on remand in Castlerea Prison, Co. Roscommon, having been refused bail on five separate occasions. Being incarcerated for such a lengthy period on what are, in the eyes of the judicial system, relatively minor charges, was unprecedented. His family said in a statement published on bernardmcgovern.co.uk, a website they established to campaign for his release, that McGovern was being wrongly linked to other crimes. 'It must be remembered that the allegation that Bernard is facing is one of assault against two individuals, however, both the media and the states in both jurisdictions have attempted to link Bernard by proxy to other more significant incidents which Bernard has had nothing to do with.' However, Bernard McGovern would also claim that as a thirteen-year-old he'd been asked to participate in an attack on an electrical substation on Molly Mountain.

Following the assault on Kevin Lunney, QIH stepped in to launch a series of civil actions. Just weeks after the incident, junior counsel for Lunney, Peter Girvan, told the High Court in Belfast that the QIH executive was bringing an injunction against Bernard McGovern to prevent him from coming within 100 metres of Kevin Lunney or his family. In court papers, it was later alleged that Bernard McGovern 'stalked the family despite the injunction'. Later, QIH itself, along with Kevin and Tony Lunney and a number of their colleagues, were listed as the plaintiffs in a civil action against Sean McGovern, Teresa McGovern and two of their sons, Patrick and Kevin, which banned the family from protesting outside QIH headquarters against their son Bernard's incarceration.

The QIH executives would return to the courts time and time again to seek protection from allegations and protests but, on the border, many saw Bernard McGovern as being held as a hostage by the Irish State, hoping that it would, at the very least, send a strong message to others who had violence on their minds. In reality, for those still supporting Quinn, it only increased their sense of injustice and anger.

**

By the time of our meetings, Sean Quinn had resigned himself to never being back in his office again. He walked the golf course at the Slieve Russell each morning and, sometimes, he drove the Range Rover that belonged to QIH around the quarry, a journey that only seemed to further convince him that machinery wasn't being looked after, and the business, without him, was being mismanaged. But there was nothing he could do about it now. He'd written to the 'Yankees' a few more times to voice his concerns and to offer to do a deal, but there was no longer a response.

In the spring of 2019 the family's case against the bankers was finally listed in the Four Courts in Dublin. It had taken eight years to come to trial, during which time Anglo Irish Bank's former chairman, Seán FitzPatrick, had been found not guilty of concealing the personal loans he'd drawn down from his own bank, while his former CEO, David Drumm, had been convicted and was spending two years and eight months in prison for conspiracy to defraud the public and false accounting.

First into the witness box was going to be the baby of the family, Brenda, who had been at university when her father was drawing down the Anglo loans to meet his CFD margin calls. Brenda had to go to the main office in the university to sign the back page for loans she claimed to know nothing about. The argument made by the Quinns' legal representatives was that the five children had no independent legal advice when they were asked to sign personal guarantees and share pledges. As a result, they could not legally be held liable for them.

However, prior to her testimony, lawyers for IBRC and the Quinns got into a huddle. An agreement was reached. Under the settlement, the five children consented to a judgment for €440 million, or €88 million each, being made against them. However, it would be 'stayed', or not enforced, if they helped the bankers secure ownership of the outstanding properties, particularly a tower block in India that had evaded them. None of the children would be bankrupted under the settlement, although they faced legal bills running into millions of euros.

Their father's gamble had always been that the bank would eventually make them an offer to go away. Indeed, there had been a number of attempts – including that offer of €20 million in assets – but Quinn had always held out for a better hand, and now he had ultimately lost.

Speaking in the aftermath, he was reconciled with the defeat. 'Ach, disappointment with the way that we handled the case, disappointed at the way that we were set up, disappointed probably that we moved the assets back six, seven years ago at all, disappointed with the whole thing, I suppose. We felt very strongly that the assets that Anglo were taking from us in India, Russia and Ukraine, they didn't own and didn't finance them, so we felt we had every right to move them. Of course we know that was a major mistake and we shouldn't have, and the court found that we had no right to move them, even though we felt that we owned them and that Anglo were going to steal them, the court didn't see it that way. The court seen it as Anglo were innocent until proven guilty, and the Quinns were guilty until proven innocent. And that's the way it turned out. I suppose, what we found out anyway very simply is it's not easy beating the government. When you have all legs of the State against you, and all the big legal firms and all the big accountancy firms, and when you are on your own, small operator, it was foolish for us to take them on.'

Liam McCaffrey and Kevin Lunney were also going through a legal action of their own. In May 2015 the Central Bank had set up an inquiry to examine allegations that McCaffrey and Lunney had 'been involved in eight subsidiaries of the company providing guarantees against loans to the wider Quinn Group, without the knowledge of the insurer's board or investment committee'. The two executives had gone to the High Court in a failed attempt to have the inquiry halted. The inquiry, which cost several million euro, heard evidence over seven days in May and June 2019. One of those to give evidence was Sean Quinn himself, who told the inquiry that he'd only learnt that guarantees had been given against the loans in March 2010 and that he'd relied on his executives to read important documents.

In his evidence, Liam McCaffrey said it was a 'gross exaggeration' to say that 'nobody was reading anything'. *The Irish Times* reported that McCaffrey had received emails in September 2005, ahead of the initial refinancing transaction the following month, that clearly identified that the QIL subsidiaries were to guarantee group loans. 'This is a very deliberate decision, there is no mistake here – a clear decision is being made to include the QIL subsidiaries,' said Eoin McCullagh SC, of the legal team assisting the inquiry.

RTÉ reported Kevin Lunney telling the inquiry, that 'he was aware of the Quinn Group's refinancing operation in 2005 but had practically no role in it. He said he had an understanding that, as QIL was part of the wider Quinn Group, it would have to be part of the transaction but carved out. He claimed that the papers showed how A&L Goodbody had advised that QIL would be kept insulated from the process. He said he was shocked and surprised when it later emerged that it had not been.

He added that he did not have any recall of how four key documents were signed by him. But his work often included confirmatory signing of documents in normal course of business,' reported the State broadcaster.

The Central Bank ultimately announced that it had reached a settlement with the two executives, but refused to give any further details due, it was suspected, to the violence on the border.

Meanwhile, moving on from all the courtroom drama, the Quinn family took some comfort from a new business they had established in 2017– Quinnbet, which offered betting on sports fixtures and an online casino. An old friend of Quinn's, Val Flynn, who had worked with him on the financing of the first cement factory, had joined the board of the company, which already employed eight people at its office in Ballyconnell. 'The new betting company is doing very well and it's given a great interest to the family and they are all working in that. It took the mind away a little bit and it reduced disappointment, of having to settle the case or having to walk away from the case, the fact that we had something else to go back to,' said Quinn.

Perhaps it offered the opportunity of a fresh start.

If the Quinns' minds were possibly on the future, there were still those on the border who were intent on revenge for the past. Since the attack on Dara O'Reilly and Kevin Lunney, there had been one further incident, when a man was captured on camera in an attempted arson or burglary at Eco Tyres – a Ballyconnell business owned by Tony Lunney. The Lunneys, especially since the assault on Kevin, knew that they had to keep up their guard, but they didn't want to be in a security bubble either. They wanted to live as normal a life as possible.

Over the course of the summer of 2019, things suddenly appeared to ease off for them; there was little sign of activity. The posters were still up, of course, but they'd grown used to that, as well as the online abuse. Perhaps they even allowed themselves to think that the worst was over.

This easing off may have had something to do with rumblings from within Quinn Industrial Holdings. For over twelve months there had been persistent rumours that the bondholders were seeking to exit from their shareholding in QIH. It had always been accepted that the bondholders were not going to be long-term investors, that they went into the deal with an exit plan in mind, which would be aligned with the interests of the QBRC shareholders, i.e. that they all sell and walk away with a huge profit, or QBRC buy out the bondholders. *Sunday Times* reporter John Mooney reported that Quinn and his supporters 'were convinced the manufacturing company was about to be sold privately through the Irish division of Investec bank. It is understood QIH did examine the possibility of attracting new investment into the business but did not proceed with this for logistical reasons. The plan had been discussed among the board and with senior managers.' Mooney also reported that Sean Quinn had sought a meeting with the American bondholders about the potential sale but his request was declined. Anonymous letters had also been sent to the board of QIH, criticising the way in which the company was being managed. Simon Carswell, writing in *The Irish Times*, said the company had explored a sale through Investec, but shelved their plans due to the uncertainty around Brexit.

These reports seemed to demonstrate that Quinn and his supporters were still being leaked information from the heart of the company. Liam McCaffrey and his colleagues knew that they could keep very little secret from the local community and, by extension, the former owner.

Tony Doonan said Quinn had taken him into his confidence regarding the possible sale on the very evening of the Lunney kidnapping. 'On that Tuesday night – we play cards every Tuesday night – Sean Quinn told me that the business is for sale. I was sworn to secrecy.'

***

When Kevin Lunney pulled out of the headquarters of Quinn Industrial Holdings around 6.30 p.m. on Tuesday, 17 September, driving his Toyota Land Cruiser, he had no idea that he was being followed. He turned left out of the office and drove along the Ballyconnell Road to Derrylin, where he turned left again and from there 'it's a straight run home'.

But he was driving into an ambush.

Minutes later, his masked kidnappers rammed his car, pulled him forcefully from his vehicle and bundled him into the boot of their getaway car.

He later told the trial of the four men accused of attacking him, how, 'As soon as the boot closed, pretty much immediately I could hear the vehicle taking off at speed out of my lane. I remember thinking I should recall the way the vehicle would go. I remember it turned left. I was starting to try to reach for the opening mechanism for the boot. I was able to pull the carpet from the latch area and to feel for the metal string that opens the car from the inside. I pulled that hard and it broke. So then I felt for the actual little lever mechanism and I was able to open that and it opened. The car was going at speed. There was quite loud shouting from inside the car and I could words of "he's opened the f'n boot!"

'I was aware I was close to the border. The road seemed somewhat familiar to me. I noticed a tractor going in the opposite direction. Then another vehicle, a small vehicle in the opposite direction, I waved at it but clearly they didn't see me. I was trying to identify [where I was] but I wasn't able to. I thought about jumping out but it was going so fast, I thought that I put my left foot slightly along the road to gauge how difficult it would be to jump.

'Then the car was slowing down at that stage. I was thinking about jumping still. By the time the car had slowed to a point where I could reasonably think about jumping out, one of the individuals had come through [the back seat]. I was half [out], one foot on the road and about to jump, and they grabbed my right foot so I couldn't get out. The car was slowing and then it came to a stop. The individual was still holding onto my right foot. My shoe had come off my right foot. My next recollection, the individuals had surrounded me [shouting] ... "we are not going to kill you, we just wanted to talk to you. If you don't get it, we are going to kill you." The individual [who] had the Stanley knife hit me on the right hand side of the face with a wooden object. I was dazed and I don't think I resisted much after that and they put me [fully back] in the boot. The individual who had come through the seats in the back was then lying inside on top of the folded-down seats and they were holding my hands through the opening between the boot and the back seat. They were holding my hands so I couldn't use my hands.'

With Lunney subdued in the boot, the car crossed the border. The car journey continued for forty-five minutes before Lunney was pulled from the boot and taken to a horse box. Lunney told the court: 'The individual who was the person who was driving the Audi, the heavier of the individuals, was standing beside [me] with the Stanley knife and was pressing it to my neck. Just inside the door he said something like "you know why you are here?" I said no. "You are here because of Quinn Industrial Holdings. You are going to resign. You have destroyed the company." He named two other directors and said they are going to resign as well. It was clear that I was going to resign or they were going to do something else to me. It wasn't a question. It was you are going to resign. It was also said, you are going to stop these charges and injunctions north and south. [The attackers appeared to be referring to court action against those who had published materials online, to injunctions against a number of people on the border from approaching Lunney or his family, and to the charges against Bernard McGovern.] I was saying, look, don't kill me, I will do whatever you want.'

The attackers told Lunney that they had been watching him for six weeks and they knew about his daughter – and 'her GAA top'. Kevin had been at an event the previous weekend with his daughter.

Then a vicious attack ensued. They used the Stanley knife to scrape under his fingernails, in order to remove any DNA, and then one of them, having gone to a local store first to purchase it, poured bleach over him. He told the court that at one point the attackers said 'QIH' into his ear as they 'quickly scored QIH down my stomach with a Stanley knife'. In an attack that lasted forty-five minutes, he was also slashed across the face – wounds that would require twenty-six stitches – and had his leg broken. Kevin Lunney said he thought he was going to be killed. Afterwards, he was put back in the car and dumped at the side of a road before being discovered by a passer-by who called the police.

During the trial for the kidnapping, a doctor who had examined Lunney soon after the attack gave evidence. Court reporter Eoin Reynolds wrote: 'Dr Muhammad Ashraf Butt of Cavan General Hospital told the court that he examined Mr Lunney on October 25, 2019, more than one month after his abduction. The doctor noted a 7cm long scar from Mr Lunney's right ear to his cheek and a 10cm scar from his right ear to his jaw-bone where he had been slashed with a Stanley knife. Mr Lunney used a beard to hide the scarring but it was still partially visible, the doctor said. He also had scars on his right upper arm, left wrist, an 8cm long vertical scar on his lower chest and upper abdomen and a 13cm scar on the left side of his abdomen. Scarring remained on his left lower leg where surgeons had inserted a nail from his knee to his ankle to repair a fracture to his tibia or shin bone. In the middle of the shin area the doctor noted a "bony swelling".'

Kevin Lunney had given a major interview to the BBC's Jim Fitzpatrick in November 2019, during which he'd told of how his chest was scored with the company initials. Eoin Reynolds said that no medical evidence was given in court of QIH having been scored onto his chest. Opening the trial, prosecution counsel Seán Guerin SC said that 'his chest was scored with the knife and as this was being done the man said the letters QIH as though he was carving them into his chest'.

**

The attack on Lunney caused an outpouring of sympathy for the father of six. How could an industrial dispute end up with a man being subjected to such a vile and brutal ordeal?

John McCartin told the press that a 'paymaster' was behind those who carried out the attack. Even the church became involved, with the priest in the Quinns' parish, Father Oliver O'Reilly, delivering a scathing homily on the Sunday following the attack, blaming 'a Mafia-style group with its own godfather' and condemning the 'paymaster or paymasters' for the Lunney attack. The priest, who had published his homily before the Mass and invited the press to attend, later told the gardaí in an interview that he'd 'no hard evidence about anything'. John McCartin called on the police on both sides to 'get to the root of the problem. If we don't get that paymaster brought to heel, we can look forward to more of the same,' he told Virgin Media News in Dublin. There was little doubt in anyone's mind, particularly amongst the Quinn family, to whom the priest and John McCartin were referring.

Sean Quinn condemned the assault on his former friend and advisor as 'despicable and totally barbaric' but said there was 'not a scintilla of evidence' to support Father O'Reilly's claims. Indeed, Quinn visited the priest to put him right. He said he was very nice to him but that he was 'wrong, wrong, wrong, wrong'. Father O'Reilly told *The Irish Times* he'd listened to Quinn for ten or twelve minutes. 'He just reprimanded me. He was angry. I just listened quietly.' *Irish Times* reporter Simon Carswell later wrote that Quinn had accused the priest of 'scuppering his attempt to buy QIH through Investec when he angrily confronted the cleric at his home'. Whatever the reality behind this prospective Investec deal, it is true that, following the attack on Lunney, the bondholders pulled back from any immediate plans to exit.

For Quinn loyalists, such as Tony Doonan, there was little sympathy for Kevin Lunney. 'Now, what happened to Kevin was wrong, you know; I can't condone what happened to Kevin. The reason I have no sympathy for him is, he put himself in the position to allow a situation in a community to fester. And if you can't see what you are doing, or just are so high and mighty and "I'm above this," well, then, that's naive and that's stupid,' said Doonan, who also claimed that the QIH management had created many enemies along the border.

One evening, several weeks after the Lunney attack, Sean and Patricia Quinn sat at their kitchen table overlooking a dark and choppy Aghavoher Lough. Patricia, who'd made tea and had laid out a platter of biscuits, said it had been a hard time for the family. 'Every morning you get up it's no different. You have just this heavy load every morning, enormous pressure, yeah. And it translates onto the children and everybody in the house. Because everyone is in bad form.'

Her husband, sitting at the head of the table, said it was 'beyond belief' that he was being blamed for the attack. 'Now they try to make us criminals. It's soul-destroying. It makes no sense. I'd say these boys are gangsters at a level that's way beyond anything that's ever been seen before.'

Patricia channelled her anger at two men she had hosted at her home many times. 'I would be very disappointed with the priest, a man that used to come in here to céilí. He named us, even though he said he didn't, he did name us. And I'd be fierce disappointed with him. I'll never forgive him. Never. Never. And he céilíed in here in this house and he had tea and he had wine and he had everything he wanted, and that's what he did. Back-stabber. That's what he is, a pure back-stabber. And I'd be very disappointed with John McCartin, a man that lived in this house for I don't know how long. He had his breakfast, dinner and tea here.'

Since the attack, she no longer went into Ballyconnell or Derrylin, but chose instead to go to Cavan or Enniskillen for her shopping.

As far as Sean and Patricia Quinn were concerned, they were the real victims. Kevin Lunney's wounds would heal, but they would never get back what they'd lost, what had been stolen from them.

The quarryman had an ability to hide what he was really thinking. A good trait for the card table. But in the weeks and months after the attack on Lunney, Quinn knew that he'd lost the support of his beloved community, the people he'd lived among all his life, those who'd benefitted most from his entrepreneurialism. Many had turned their backs on him. And it clearly hurt.

He admitted that the mood had changed in Derrylin and Bally-connell. 'I suppose they have got used to the criticism and got used to bad publicity. I suppose we were one of the most popular and highly respected families in the country for maybe twenty or thirty years, and now all of a sudden it's just gone downhill. Every move we made, in fairness, wasn't a good move. I could have done things better,' he admitted.

***

Pressure came onto police, North and South, to take action.

At 7 a.m. on 8 November 2019, officers from Derbyshire Constabulary, supported by colleagues from the PSNI, burst through the door of a house at Rockfield Road in the town of Buxton, twenty miles south-east of Manchester. Inside, they arrested Cyril McGuinness. They handcuffed him and began to search his home, where he had been living for most of the previous year. McGuinness sat on a sofa, smoking cigarettes and drinking tea – with difficulty, one imagines, given the handcuffs – while the officers went about their work. His seeming indifference did not last, however. Around 9.30 a.m. he suddenly collapsed and was pronounced dead at 10 a.m. A coroner's court was later told that Dublin Jimmy had a serious heart condition and had died from a cardiac event.

Back on the border, there were mixed emotions. Very few knew that McGuinness had a 'safe house' in England. It was presumed that when he disappeared for long spells, he was somewhere in the Republic. Some of those who knew him best were aware of the heart complaint – he'd told them six months previously that he'd had cardiac treatment at a private Dublin clinic. Following his death, it was widely reported that McGuinness was the ringleader in the Lunney attack, having been paid by the 'paymaster'. In fact, the raid on McGuinness was part of a much wider police operation on both sides of the border in which twenty houses were raided.

Four months later Sean McGovern and his wife Teresa were arrested along with their son Bernard, who was, at that point, on police bail charged with the assault on Kevin Lunney the previous February. In an interview with *The Irish News* after their release, Sean McGovern denied having 'any act or part' in the Lunney kidnapping but had 'no trouble saying we have supported Quinn from the start, from the first day he was thrown out of his business. It was an injustice in my eyes, a major injustice.' The McGoverns said their home had been searched several times and members of their family regularly stopped and searched by police. Teresa McGovern, who is a nurse, told the paper the experience of being arrested has left her feeling 'anxious' but that 'I have nothing to be ashamed of or embarrassed about. I am annoyed and it's very stressful.' The PSNI said they sent a file on the McGoverns to the Public Prosecution Service. Despite extensive PSNI investigations, no one in the North was ever charged in relation to the Lunney attack.

In the Republic, four men were arrested. Luke O'Reilly, from Kilcogy, Co. Cavan, along with Darren Redmond and Alan O'Brien from East Wall in Dublin, and a fourth man, Alan Harte – who was referred to as YZ during the subsequent trial as he could not be identified at that time for legal reasons– were all charged with false imprisonment and causing serious harm to Kevin Lunney. They went on trial in Dublin's Central Criminal Court in June 2021. Because of the nature of the crimes they were tried in front of three senior judges rather than a jury. In court, the prosecution said it would not be ascribing a motivation for the attack on the QIH executive but would simply prove that the four men charged were those who were involved. Evidence was given of how two of the men in the dock had been in direct telephone contact with Cyril McGuinness in the days before and on the evening of the attack.

Luke O'Reilly was found not guilty but the other three, Harte, O'Brien and Redmond, were all convicted and given lengthy prison terms. Harte, who was described as the ringleader, was given thirty years; O'Brien was sentenced to twenty-five years and Redmond to fifteen years. All three lodged appeals in January 2022.

In a victim impact statement, Kevin Lunney said he was 'saddened at a human level that they have ruined their own lives as a result of their actions' and he sympathised with the families of the three men who had been convicted of the vicious assault on him. He said he trusted that those involved realise there will 'never be a place in our community for violence or any other form of intimidation'. Outside the court, the gardaí said they were continuing to pursue others involved in the attack and had a series of investigations ongoing linked to the former Quinn business.

**

The trouble on the border began with the hijacked dumper truck being driven into the company headquarters in the days after the 2011 takeover by the bankers. Over the eight years that led to the attack on Kevin Lunney, there had been two distinct periods of violence, pre and post the QBRC comeback in December 2014. The first period of up to a hundred attacks was all about keeping the company intact for Quinn's 'second coming'. The latter – over thirty incidents, including the vicious assault on Kevin Lunney – was largely due to the fallout of his second departure.

The cost of the first series of attacks is estimated at €10m. The second series was predominantly about threats: graffiti, pig's heads, posters and constant online abuse of the executives at QIH. These were the attacks on the homes and businesses of Tony Lunney and Dara O'Reilly and culminated in the assault on Kevin Lunney. The estimated damage caused was less than €200,000. For the Irish taxpayer, the saboteurs who led the campaign of attacks between 2011 and 2014 ensured that they never saw a single cent of the 2.4 billion that Sean Quinn borrowed from

Anglo Irish Bank. No one has ever been brought before a court for any of the dozens of incidents during this period. Police on both sides of the border say they're still investigating.

While the gardaí refused to produce statistics for the attacks on the southern side of the border, the PSNI issued a statement in January 2022, detailing reports they had received during the two distinct periods of trouble. 'During the period April 2011 and December 2014 police have investigated more than 40 reports of criminal offences in the area, including reports of incidents such as arson, criminal damage, theft and assault,' the statement said. 'In addition police have also received over 100 further reports of incidents including suspicious vehicles, signs erected and a number of protests in the area. During the period May 2016 and November 2021 police have investigated nearly 50 reports of criminal offences in the area, including reports of incidents such as kidnapping, harassment, threats to kill, criminal damage and assault. In addition police have also received over 150 further reports of incidents including suspicious vehicles, signs erected and a number of protests in the area.'

A year after the Lunney attack, the famous 'Q' logo disappeared once again from the Mountain Road. QIH had decided it was time to rebrand and get rid of the Quinn name from the business. It was now to be called 'Mannok', which, they explained, 'like the company itself, is deeply rooted in the region of Cavan and Fermanagh. It reflects the culmination of a 5-year re-positioning journey from regional commodity supplier to a trusted building and packaging solutions provider capable of competing and winning alongside leading global brands, and doing so in an increasingly environmentally sustainable manner,' a QIH statement said.

Quinn told *The Irish Times* that he was shocked. 'That company was twenty-five years old when any of those boys got involved. What right they seem to have to rebrand it, but that is entirely up to them. They weren't even around,' he said. Still, it later became clear that the Quinn children in fact wanted the world to forget about their name in another terrain: the Internet.

In the autumn of 2021 the *Sunday Independent* broke the story that the search engine Google had removed dozens of articles relating to the quarryman and his five children. Quinn's son-in-law Niall McPartland, who is married to Ciara Quinn, told *The Irish Times* that he had applied to Google under the European Union's 'right to be forgotten' regime. McPartland told the paper he made the requests for a number of reasons, stating some were 'inaccurate, outdated and relating to proceedings which have long since been resolved'. He referred to an article about his wedding fourteen years ago that went into detail about the cost and expense of the celebration. 'That material is not relevant to who I am. I don't think people should form their opinions of me based on what comes up on a search engine,' he added.

As for the Quinns' 'exotic' international property portfolio, the Irish government has given IBRC's special liquidator, Kieran Wallace, until 2024 to recoup what he can. Wallace has assiduously led a team that has unravelled the complex network of ownership of buildings across Eastern Europe and Asia put in place by Quinn's son and nephew. It is estimated that the Irish taxpayer will see a return of €500m after costs when the portfolio is eventually sold. The property bought by Quinn for his children includes the Slieve Russell and Buswells hotel in Ireland and others in England and the Czech Republic. They all have to be sold by the government-imposed deadline. Sean Quinn is rumoured to still have his eye on the Slieve Russell, which remains one of the projects he is most proud of. Whether he, or his family, will be able to purchase it with profits from Quinnbet remains to be seen. According to the former chairman of IBRC, Alan Dukes, Sean Quinn still has 'large amounts of money and there's reason to believe that a good chunk of it was brought to Switzerland where it's probably in an inaccessible account, and that there's a substantial amount of money in India as well'.

For those living away from the border, the violent response to Sean Quinn's downfall only confirmed the area's reputation as being a third jurisdiction on the island; a lawless place. 'Border people have it in their blood,' said Alan Dukes. 'Because they are living in communities that have, you know, a long history of violence of different kinds, and they'd more easily turn to it than anybody else would, you know. And I'm not saying they're different animals from the rest of us, but whether they have Provo links or B Special links or whatever, you know, it's something that's nearer to the way they think than it would be to somebody in south Tipperary or anywhere like that,' said the former Fine Gael leader, damning a large section of the population of his own country.

Looking back at meeting him in 1986, the author Colm Tóibín thought Quinn enjoyed being the inscrutable businessman. 'He had a sort of gruffness about him to start with, a sort of plainness. I think he found, certainly I had a feeling that those places like Dublin, Dublin business journalists or Dublin courts, or *The Irish Times*, would not have been part of the world in which he wanted respect. He wanted respect locally. It's very sad the story of Sean Quinn, because it shows hubris, it shows somebody rising and falling, and their pride or something wrong in them made wrong decisions. I think it is too far-fetched to say he sort of represents something in the society, because he seemed to operate alone; not to be like anybody else, not to represent anybody else, that all around him were people locked into this really dreadful political and economic situation. And he rose above that,' said the first journalist to ever interview Sean Quinn.

In October 2021 the quarryman gave his final interview for an RTÉ documentary. His focus on the events of the previous fifteen years had again changed. This time he ruminated on allowing former chief executive David Mackey to leave the company in 1999 and the bad decision he'd made not to replace him with someone much more experienced. Instead, he'd promoted Liam McCaffrey. That was where it had all gone wrong, he mused. He also now solely blamed his executives for setting up the CFD company in Madeira. 'They financed the shares by taking hundreds of millions from Quinn Insurance without the approval of the board or the Central Bank. They used a mechanism called CFDs which, at the time I'd never heard of.'

None of it was his fault.

He was now seventy-five years old and clearly his age was a burden; his time was running out. He wanted his story told, his version, his truth. He refused to see that even he shouldn't trust his memory of the events that had shaped his life.

'Any big regrets?' I asked.

'Well, a lot,' he admitted. 'I could have done things differently, but as regards growing the business and the manufacturing, growing it in the property and starting what I believe was one of the most successful businesses ever in the history of the State, the insurance company, I think they were all good. And no big regrets there.'

The quarryman finally broke down when addressing his legacy. 'All I can say is, that in my seventy-five years I never knowingly ... I never knowingly took anything that didn't belong to me,' he said into the camera, tears running down his cheeks.

Epilogue

The violence may have gone, but the seething mistrust and anger on the border caused by the events of the past fifteen years remains. Many people, with some justification, fundamentally believe Sean Quinn was taken out by the Dublin establishment, who had neither affiliation nor affection for the border billionaire, or the generations of families whose lives he had singlehandedly enriched over four decades in business. The loyalty that led to a sign appearing on the side of a border house at the height of his troubles – 'Sean Quinn was never in my home but I wouldn't be in my home if it wasn't for Sean Quinn' – is still there. Many hundreds of workers first employed by Sean Quinn now work for Mannok and the American bondholders – some have been joined by their children – or for the Spaniards who still own the glass plant. Quinn might be long gone and his businesses out of his ownership, but his vision has helped the people of the border to benefit from good, secure jobs that neither Dublin nor Belfast had ever created in the area.

Walk into any pub or GAA clubhouse in the region and you'll hear a very different version of the events that led to the attack on Kevin Lunney. Very few believe the Dublin media version of the story, even if they have total sympathy with Lunney and his family. No one doubts he endured a vicious, unwarranted attack. The what, when and where are not challenged. It's the why that still arouses debate, much of it coming from a continued suspicion of policing both North and South.

A case taken by the Mannok management and reported in *The Impartial Reporter* newspaper early in 2022 was seen by Sean Quinn supporters as evidence of the company's complete lack of understanding or engagement with the local community. An eighty-three-year-old farmer, Patrick 'Pa' Treacy, was found to have broken a prohibition order banning his cattle from land owned by Mannok, who had brought contempt proceedings alleging Treacy's cattle had strayed onto their land on six occasions. In his defence, the octogenarian farmer had told the court the trespassing was 'isolated, inadvertent and accidental'. He was found guilty and fined £500. A judge, who was told that Mannok's 'substantial' costs in bringing the case were over £27,000, ordered that both parties seek to agree how the bill should be split.

Away from the border, the dominant narrative is that Sean Quinn is the paymaster and he paid Cyril McGuinness, 'Dublin Jimmy', to carry out the 2019 attack on Kevin Lunney. On the face of it, the decision by the gardaí to raid Sean Quinn's home on the morning of 20 April 2022 confirmed that the authorities were still on the case. They'd been granted a warrant to search the 15,000 square foot house. It was Quinn himself, wearing no shoes as usual, who let them in through the front door, where they spent two and a half hours going through each room, while the quarryman and his wife, Patricia, sat at their kitchen table. Later, in a statement, a garda spokesperson said they'd acted as part of 'an ongoing criminal investigation into alleged criminal activity in Cavan and the wider border region'. They made no mention of the attack on Kevin Lunney. Quinn's solicitor, Chris McGettigan, said he'd been told the searches were the result of complaints of alleged intimidation from the management at Mannok. In an interview with the BBC, the quarryman himself said he'd been told the raid was about 'coercion, deception and harassment, stuff like that. It's a fishing expedition.' Quinn's diary and phone were among the items seized.

For some onlookers, the raid was linked to a case launched against QBRC in the Belfast High Court by the 'Cavan, Fermanagh Community Group', claiming that the former Quinn team now leading the company had made commitments to hand the former quarryman's business back to the people of the border. Solicitor for the group, Chris McGettigan, had, in the weeks before, sent letters to the owners of QBRC seeking responses to a series of questions in relation to the commitments alleged to have been made prior to the former Quinn executives and supporters becoming involved with the US bondholders.

Around the same time, the Dublin based *Village* magazine, 'Ireland's political and cultural magazine', published the first of two articles examining events on the border. The headline was stark: 'Quinn was our champion when the State did nothing', and the story below didn't miss and hit the wall. For the first time, the author, Michael Smith, revealed in public that the three bondholders and QBRC had drawn up an agreement which allowed for what he described as a 'covert donation' to QBRC from the sales of the glass and plastics plants. According to Smith, 'nobody knows where the money went'. The article said that it was the Cavan, Fermanagh and Leitrim (CFL) group that had encouraged the QBRC deal, but according to Smith, 'CFL should have been following what was going on more closely,' going on to state: 'What happened [i.e., the deal with the bondholders] couldn't have worked without QBRC's involvement which depended on CFL's support, so it had to be timed during the window when the incendiary local community was well disposed to the new [old] management.'

Three months later, in July 2022, the magazine followed up its story with another article under the headline 'Media ignore Lunneys' background in campaign of sabotage'. Michael Smith again set out in some detail the events that had led to the QBRC–bondholders deal. He published a letter from the PSNI to Sean McGovern, father of the young boxer, Bernard McGovern, who had been convicted of assaulting Kevin Lunney and throwing a scalding cup of tea over Dara O'Reilly. Dated 21 February 2022, the letter from the PSNI's Criminal Investigation Branch advised Mr McGovern that they were following up on claims he'd made in the witness box while being prosecuted for alleged intimidation of the former Quinn executives: 'Police have been made aware of comments made during a recent court appearance in

Enniskillen Magistrates Court on 31st January, 2022. Police have been informed that you have said that your son was the victim of Gareth Lunney, Tony Lunney and Kevin Lunney and that he was used to do work that was illegal on Doon Mountain when he was a teenager. Detectives from the Criminal Investigation Branch at Enniskillen Police Station would be willing to meet you to discuss what you have said in court and for you to provide a written statement outlining any information that you may have in your possession so that the matter can be thoroughly investigated.'

The PSNI, and the gardaí, refuse to provide any details of their separate investigations. In response to Chris McGettigan's letter, Mannok moved to have the High Court case against them thrown out before it could get on its feet. The case is ongoing.

For Mannok, it was business as usual, albeit under extraordinary circumstances. Ten years after the violence first began, its executives were advised that there were still serious threats against their lives. Announcing year-end results in May 2022, Liam McCaffrey said the business had undergone a 'quiet but determined transformation' over recent years. *The Irish News* reported that higher energy and raw material costs had weighed heavily on the company after its revenues rose in 2021 but earnings diminished. Sales were up 16 per cent from €233.2 million to €269.9 million (£231m), but earnings at €25.8m were lower than the previous year's figure of €31.1m. The Belfast daily newspaper reported McCaffrey as saying the company would need to raise 'more than €200m green investment to transform production and distribution processes' in order to make the company carbon neutral by 2050.

A month later, in June, the *Irish Independent* reported that 'armed Garda officers have been deployed to protect Tony Lunney, John McCartin, and Dara O'Reilly, who have been deemed as being most at threat due to the latest threat'. The paper's crime correspondent, Paul Williams, reported that police on both sides of the border had warned the men that the threat against them remained high.

Every day of the working week, Mannok's distinctive green, blue and white liveried lorries leave their border base, loaded with deliveries of cement manufactured in the plant built by Sean Quinn. On Slieve Rushen, the blades of the wind turbines still turn. Below, the Slieve Russell Hotel may still be in administration, but it remains busy with weddings and events. The golf course still attracts patrons from around the country. Driving the Ballyconnell to Derrylin road, the area is an industrial oasis as far as the eye can see.

Underneath the visage, the people of the border remain wary, particularly those now employed in the old Quinn businesses. The certainty they once had is gone, replaced by constant speculation and rumour: that Mannok is in debt and in danger of being sold.

The one constant is Sean Quinn, whose presence is still felt along every road, in every home and at every kitchen table. He may be determined, but he's also acutely aware of his own mortality. His life has brought him unbounded success and wealth, making him a local hero and a renowned national and international entrepreneur. All of which make his downfall and demise all the harder to take for him, his family and the families of those who helped build his businesses in the first place. His story will live long on the border.

Trevor Birney,
September 2022,
Belfast

Bibliography

Books

Byrne, E.A., *Political Corruption in Ireland 1922–2010: A Crooked Harp* (Manchester: Manchester University Press, 2012)

Carey, B. and Lyons, T., *The FitzPatrick Tapes: The Rise and Fall of One Man, One Bank, and One Country* (Dublin: Penguin Ireland, 2011)

Carswell, S., *Anglo Republic: Inside the Bank that Broke Ireland* (London: Penguin, 2011)

Daly, G. and Kehoe, I., *Citizen Quinn* (London: Penguin, 2013)

McWilliams, D., *The Pope's Children: Ireland's New Elite* (London: Macmillan, 2013)

Quinn, P., *Peter Quinn: The Outsider* (Dublin: Pigeonhouse Books, 2013)

Shiller, R., *Irrational Exuberance* (New York: Doubleday, 2009)

Tóibín, C., *Bad Blood: A Walk Along the Irish Border* (London: Picador, 2010)

Urwin, M., *Fermanagh: From Plantation to Peace Process* (Dublin: Wordwell Books, 2021)

Newspapers/Magazines

Belfast News Letter
Belfast Telegraph
Bloomberg Businessweek
Construction Index
Export & Freight
Fermanagh Herald
Irish Construction

Irish Daily Mail
Irish Examiner
Irish Independent
Mail on Sunday
Plantman International
Sunday Independent
Sunday Tribune
The Anglo-Celt
The Currency
The Impartial Reporter
The Irish News
The Irish Times
The Phoenix
The Sunday Business Post
The Sunday Press

Websites
Anglo-Irish Report – www.yumpa.com
BBC – www.bbc.co.uk
CMC Markets – cmcmarkets.com
Dáil Records – www.oireachtas.ie
Fermanagh Civil Rights Association Report, 1972 – https://cain.ulster.
    ac.uk
Grace's Guide to British Industrial History – gracesguide.co.uk
TheJournal.ie

TV
BBC
RTÉ
Virgin Media News

Acknowledgements

I was born in Enniskillen in the year Sean Quinn's father died: 1967. By the time I began secondary school he was already on his way to being a millionaire. He was probably the only one in Fermanagh at that time.

Despite having a father who was a part-time Reservist in the RUC, we grew up largely untouched by the Troubles. My father has good friends in Quinn Country, working in the 'electric board' with the local historian Brian McManus. My mother worked as a school dinner lady in St Joseph's Secondary College where Bryan Gallagher was the principal for a time, a man for whom she had huge admiration.

I played for Enniskillen Rangers from when I was at the Model Primary School and was lucky to meet friends for life who just happened not to have the same religion as me. Denzil McDaniel was heavily involved in the club and later became editor of *The Impartial Reporter* newspaper, where I first worked. Myself and my two brothers were born into Unionism but were not defined by it. That was the Fermanagh I grew up in. I loved it then, I'm proud of it now. Fermanagh and its neighbours, north and south, rest easily. They live, work and play together, but its people see themselves living in a place apart. As Mervyn Dane, another former editor at *The Impartial Reporter* was known to say, 'Fermanagh is normal; it's the rest of the world that's mad.'

I first became aware of this man known as 'Quinn' in the 1980s. He was a mythical figure, never really seen in Enniskillen, where no one seemed to know him personally. But we all knew one thing about him: he was rich and successful.

Writing a book about him was first floated by two colleagues, Brian and Brendan, during the lockdown of 2020. Because of the pandemic, and for legal reasons, we had been stalled in the production of the series for RTÉ and it was thought that I could use my time wisely by writing a book. It was not something I immediately embraced but with a significant period of working from home ahead of us all in 2021, I contacted Conor Graham at Merrion Press.

Thanks to Conor, Patrick, Maeve and Wendy at Merrion, and to Noel O'Regan, my editor, who have all been a great source of support and guidance and who have also shown great patience throughout the writing process. Thanks also to Djinn von Noorden for her careful proofread of the text.

A big thank you to my friend and colleague Andrew Tully, a young man with an old head on his shoulders, who I'm forever indebted to, along with Michael Fanning, Sabina Cherek, Michael Paisley, Carol Murphy and Eimhear O'Neill at Below The Radar and Fine Point Films, and to Andy Tohill and Greg Darby, who have all put up with so much for so long on this project.

Thanks also to those who talked to me off the record for giving me so much of their time, knowledge and experience.

A very special thanks to Denzil McDaniel who has not only helped in the research and in reading drafts, but has been a constant source of good advice and support throughout my life. And also to the incomparable Rodney Edwards, without whom I would never have been able to tell this story in the first place. Thanks to Susan McKay, who also read an early draft of the book and whose input was invaluable.

Thanks to Fearghal, Marcus and Brendan who have patiently listened to me wrestling with some issue or other over pints of Guinness in the Parador. Niall Murphy and Barry McCaffrey are friends who have proven most reliable, whatever we've faced together. Thanks to them for their advice and support.

To my mother, Jean, who at eighty-three years of age still remains a source of inspiration, particularly for her energy, love and ability to socialise seven days a week. And to my brothers, Nigel and Ian, for their continued support.

Those who've made the greatest sacrifices to allow me to pursue my work are my wife, Sheila, and our daughters, Ella, Mia and Freya. Lockdown was a challenge, but writing a book in the middle of it just added an extra source of stress for them all. For months I disappeared into the 'gin room', as it is known, where no alcohol of any kind is kept. I could rely on them to point out any procrastination, an important role that they took on with great passion.

Trevor Birney,
September 2022,
Belfast

Index

9/11 terrorist attacks, the, 134–5

Adams, Gerry, 78, 81
Ahern, Bertie, 124, 133, 154, 165, 178, 191
AIB, 160–1
Airtricity, 147
A&L Goodbody, 188, 286
Allen, Philip, 114
Amazon, 127
Ambassador Hotel, The, Kildare, 92
American Home Mortgage Investment Corporation, 168
Anglo-Celt, The (newspaper), 65, 76, 82, 83, 93, 154
Anglo Irish Bank, 86–7, 138, 152, 159, 160–3, 169–70, 171–3, 174–6, 179–80, 182–3, 192, 210, 218 (*see also* IBRC (Irish Bank Resolution Corporation))
Anglo Republic (book), 86
Ansbacher Cayman Ltd., 51
'Anti-landlord agitators,' 211
APC (Associated Portland Cement Ltd), 49, 53
APL (Anti-Partition League), the, 9
Ardagh Group (Irish Glass), 103, 136, 138–9
Arora, Surinder, 150
Arthur Andersen, 111
Aspdin, Joseph, 48–9
Athlone Extrusions, 142
Aventas Group, 236, 242–3, 248, 250, 254
Aynsley, Mike, 183, 184, 197, 210–11, 218–19

B Specials (Ulster Special Constabulary), the, 25
Bad Blood – A Walk Along the Irish Border (book), 69–70
Bailey bridge at Belturbet, the, 30–1
Ballinabrackey Residents' Action Group, 118
Ballyconnell cement plant, 116–17, 236 (*see also* cement-making business, the)
Bank of Ireland, 160–1
bankruptcy, 217–19
Barclays Bank, 196
Barlo, 142–3, 144, 145, 175, 264
Barlow, Aiden, 142
Bazzely V Consultadoria Economica E Participacoes Sociedade Unipessoal LDA, 156–7, 173, 299
Bear Sterns, 168
Beatson Clarks glassworks, 10
Belfast News Letter (newspaper), 139
Belfast Telegraph (newspaper), 102–3, 241, 254
Best Mate (horse), 141, 143
Bezos, Jeff, 127
BGC (British Glass Confederation), the, 103–4
Bill, P.T., 56
Bin Laden, Osama, 133
Blair, Tony, 124
Bloomberg Businessweek (magazine), 209
Blue Book, the, 109
Blue Circle, 53, 54, 55, 62, 65

bondholders and debt, the, 154, 187, 196, 197, 199, 209–10, 233, 236, 243, 248–9, 252, 254–9, 261, 268, 274, 288
Book of Kells, the, 87
Bord Fáilte, 61
Bord Pleanála, An, 117, 123
Border Campaign, the, 34, 35
border crossings, 29–30
Boyson, Rhodes, 55, 56
Brady, M.J., 117
Breslin, John, 165
Breton Precast, 119–20
Brigade, Contrarian Capital Silver Point (investor group), 254–6, 274, 275
British Army, the, 30, 31, 73–4, 78, 134
Bullock, Thomas and Emily, 25, 30
Bupa Ireland, 165
burning of electrical substation, 212
Burns, Jarleth, 223
Buswells Hotel, 175, 200, 298
Butt, Dr Muhammad Ashraf, 291
Byrne, Elaine A., 51

Canniffe, Mary, 107
Carey, Brian, 148–9, 171
Carey, Dermot, 145
Caring, Richard, 149–50
Carswell, Simon, 86, 128, 132, 133, 288, 292
Cassidy, James, 17
Cassidy, Tommy, 239
Cat & Cage pub, Drumcondra, the, 46
Cavan County Council, 116
Cement Limited, 49–50
cement-making business, the, 48–9, 52–8, 59–60, 62–3, 64–7, 116–23
cement patents, 48–9
Central Bank, the, 286, 287
Ceva Logistics, 242
CFDs (contracts for difference), 157–9, 162, 169–70, 171–3, 174, 175, 285, 299

Channing, John, 93
Charlton, Jack, 64
Cheltenham Festival, the, 141, 142
CIB (Concerned Irish Business), 193–4, 196, 204
CIC (Concerned Irish Citizens), 244, 245, 249
CIS (Construction Industry Supplies) businesses, 254, 256–7
Citizen Quinn (book), 150, 159, 175
Civil War, the, 10–11
Clarke, Arthur, 11
Clifford, Michael, 52
CMC Markets, 158
Collins, Michael, 121
Comiskey, Fr Gerry, 226
Competition Commission, the, 119, 232
concrete block plant, 100–1
Construction Index (magazine), 229
Cook, Bill, 104, 105
Cooney, Finbar, 88
Corley, Noel, 108
Cornered Irish Citizens, 223
corporate financial infrastructure, 148–9, 154–5
corporation tax, 104
Coughlin, Mary, 154
Coulson, Paul, 'The Cooler,' 103, 137, 138
court hearings, 220–2, 225, 284–5, 295–6
Cowen, Brian, 178, 191
CRH (Cement Road Holdings), 50, 51–4, 55, 56, 58, 62–3, 64, 65, 118, 119–20, 123
Croke Park, 81
Crowley, Des, 120
Currency, The (magazine), 269–70
Curry, Adrian, 138
Curry, Pat, 21, 22
Curry, Terry, 44

Daly, Gavin, 150, 159, 160, 162, 175
Danaher, Peter, 93

D'Arcy, Fr Brian, 223
Dassault Falcon 2000EX jet, 143
Davis, Steve, 83
De Vere Belfry golf club, Birmingham, 150–1
debts and borrowings, 154, 178, 179, 181–2, 184, 187, 192, 193, 196, 209–10, 231, 257 (*see also* bondholders and debt, the)
Department of Enterprise, Trade and Investment, 129, 133
Derrylin, Co. Fermanagh, 8, 10
Desmond, Dermot, 141–3, 145, 167, 264
Direct Line, 141
discrimination against Catholics, 9–10, 34
Dolan, Con, 44
Donegan, Joe, 84
Donegan, Samuel, 25
Doogan, Denis, 248
Doonan, Tony, 193–4, 204, 205, 244–6, 251, 252, 253, 264, 276, 277, 278, 281, 288, 292–3
'dotcom boom,' the, 127–9
Dresdner merchant bank, 133
Drumm, David, 161–2, 163, 171, 172, 175–6, 180, 229, 284
Dukes, Alan, 182–3, 184–5, 186, 193, 195, 196–8, 210–11, 227, 237, 245, 252, 255, 298–9
Dunne, Justice Elizabeth, 220, 221, 222, 225

Earthwatch, 117
Eco Tyres, 287
economic collapse of 2008, the, 174, 178, 179–86
economic optimism, 95–6, 112
Edwards, Rodney, 208, 223, 224, 231, 238, 240, 262, 263, 276, 279
effluent pollution charges, 37
efforts to bring Quinn Group back under local control, 244–64

EIA (Environmental Impact Assessment), 138
Elderfield, Matthew, 182, 187, 189, 190, 224
electricity market, the, 167
EMB, 195
Endless LLP, 253, 254, 255
Enniskillen Remembrance Day Parade atrocity, the, 57
environmental objections, 117–18, 138
Environmental Protection Agency, the, 117
Ernst & Young, 129, 156
euro, the, 136
Export & Freight (magazine), 32, 43, 44

Fabro, Hector, 83
Fair Employment Act, the, 77, 78
Fair Employment Tribunal, the, 77
fairy fort, Aughrim, 93–4
family background and early years, 11–20
family home, Ballyconnell, the, 147
family-owned property assets, 210, 220, 225, 227, 230, 285, 298
Farrell, Bernard, 243–4
Feehan, Sean, 84
Fermanagh: From Plantation to Peace Process (book), 9
Fermanagh Civil Rights Association, 10
Fermanagh GAA, 16–19
Fermanagh Herald, The (newspaper), 35, 37, 62, 105, 235
financial affairs, 35–6, 53, 57–8, 67–8, 85–6, 128, 136, 146, 154, 166, 181–2, 209
Financial Times, The (newspaper), 113
Fisher, Bertie, 247
Fisher, Ernie, 247, 262, 263, 269, 274
Fisher Engineering, 247
FitzGerald, Garret, 63
Fitzgerald, Kyran, 64
Fitzpatrick, Jim, 291

FitzPatrick, Seán, 86–7, 160, 161–2, 163, 171, 173, 175, 179, 228–9, 284

FitzPatrick Tapes: The Rise and Fall of One Man, One Bank, and One Country, The (book), 171

Fitzpatrick, Martin, 62–3

Fives-Cail-Babcock, 52–3

Fletcher, Pte thomas, 25

Flynn, Val, 58, 287

Foley, Ray, 108

Forbairt, 101, 102, 104

Forbes (magazine), 167

Ford, David, 243

Forrest, John, 93

Foster, Sammy, 101

Fowler, Julian, 230

Fyffe, John, 37

GAA, the, 79–80

Gallagher, Bryan, 11, 18, 21, 23, 93

Gallagher, Pat 'the Cope', 154

Gartmore, 142–3

Gatto, Mike, 255

Gilheaney, Patricia, 244, 249

Gilleece, John, 73

Gilleece, Michael, 44

Gilleece, Packie, 93

Girvan, Peter, 283

glass bottle business, the, 102–6, 115, 124, 136–9

golf club investments, 88, 149–51

Good Friday Agreement, the, 115, 124, 219

Google, 298

Goonery, Marie, 121–2

Gorman, Tommie, 180

Gortmullan roof tile plant, 42–4

Governey, Michael, 83, 87

government spending, 63

Grace's Guide to British Industrial History, 49

Graham, Cecil, 41

Graham, Ronnie, 41

Grant, Eugene, 225

gravel business, the, 23, 24, 26–33

gravel deposits, 21–2

GSO Blackstone, 243

guarantees on loans, 109, 178, 187–90, 286–7

Guerin, Sean, 291

Guinness and Mahon, 51, 52

Gunne, P.V., 76

Hamilton, George, 241

Hanly, Bertie, 48

Harnett, Matt, 255, 271–2

Harney, Mary, 129

Harp Bar, The, Dublin, 92

Harte, Alan, 295, 296

Harte, Mickey, 223

Haughey, Charles J., 38–9, 50–2, 75, 124, 142

Haughey, Eddie, 106

headquarters building, 38

Healy, Cahir, 9

Hill, Ronnie, 57

Hillgrove Hotel, Monaghan, 90

hotel developments, 61, 68–9, 76–7, 82–5, 87–91, 147, 298

housing discrimination, 9–10, 34

Hume, John, 55, 78, 81

hunger strikes, the, 40, 41

Hynes, Alan, 155

IBRC (Irish Bank Resolution Corporation), 197, 199, 218–19, 220, 227, 228–9, 237, 243, 269–70, 280, 284–5, 298 (*see also* Anglo Irish Bank)

IDA (Industrial Development Authority), the, 70

IDB (Industrial Development Board), the, 55–7, 101, 102, 104–5, 116

Illsley, Eric, 104–5

Impartial Reporter, The (newspaper), 42, 43, 82, 85, 100, 101, 208, 212, 223, 231, 233, 237, 238, 240, 242, 262, 276
imprisonment, 226, 227–8
Independent Concrete Manufacturers Association, the, 65
inheritance issues, 46–7, 69, 92, 97–8, 173
insurance business (*see* Quinn Direct Insurance)
insurance regulator, the, 129
intimidation and threats, 232–3, 240, 241, 250, 265, 273, 275, 281–4, 287, 288–92
Investec bank, 288, 292
investment and expansion, 38, 42–5, 46
IPG (International Property Group), 154–6
IRA, (Irish Republican Army), the, 10–11, 25–6, 30, 34, 41, 57, 59, 78, 95, 239, 267
Irish Cement Ltd, 50, 53, 57, 62
Irish Construction (magazine), 66, 67
Irish Daily Mail (newspaper), 221
Irish Examiner (newspaper), 52, 166, 262
Irish football team, the, 64, 75–6, 95
Irish Glass Bottle Company, the, 102, 103
Irish Independent (newspaper), 46, 117, 126, 140, 142, 147, 160, 166–7, 191, 222
Irish News, The (newspaper), 261
Irish Press, The (newspaper), 65
Irish Times, The (newspaper), 38, 49, 106, 107, 108, 118, 119, 120, 122, 123, 126, 131, 137, 141, 146, 147, 151, 176–7, 188, 189, 215, 223–4, 243, 247–8, 286, 288, 292, 297–8
Irrational Exuberance (book), 128
Irvinestown St Molaise GAA club, 17–18

job discrimination, 77–8

Keelan, Brian, 157
Kehoe, Ian, 150, 159, 160, 162, 175, 269–70
Kelly, Fiona, 217

Kelly, Seán, 154
Kelly, Stephen, 274
Kennedy, Robert F., 23
Kenny, Enda, 244
Kernan, Joe, 223
kidnapping and assault of Kevin Lunney, the, 288–92, 295–6
Killaskillen Co. Westmeath, cement factory proposal, 118, 120–3
Killeen, Conor, 140, 142, 153
Kilmore Hotel, Cavan, 76, 90, 110
Kilrane, Elma, 173, 174
King, Neil, 138
Kutuzoff Tower, Russia, 210

Lafarge, 133
Lagan, Jude, 229
Lagan, Kathleen Philomena, 240–1, 250
Lagan, Kevin, 54, 63, 118–19, 120–1, 122–4, 232–3, 240–1, 250, 265
Lagan, Peter, 232
Lagan Cement Ltd, 118–19, 229
Lagan Holdings, 54, 240
land ownership, 14–15
lawsuit against IBRC on loan legalities, 228–9, 237, 269–70, 280, 284–5
Lee, John, 44, 72, 100, 222
Lehman Brothers, 178
Lemass, Maureen, 51
Lemass, Seán, 50, 51
Lenihan, Brian, 180, 182
letsrecycle.com (magazine), 138
Liberty Mutual, 195, 198
limestone quarrying, 36, 37
London docklands attack, the, 267
Loughran, Gerry, 115, 116
loyalist attack in Belturbet, 30–1
Lunney, Kevin, 1–6, 111–12, 127, 129, 130–1, 141, 148, 154–6, 157, 188, 189, 196, 198, 199, 201, 204, 206, 209, 216, 217, 244,

247, 257, 262, 263–4, 273, 276, 277–8, 281, 282, 283–4, 286, 288–93, 295, 296

Lunney, Tony, 72, 100, 111, 144, 209, 216, 257, 277–8, 281, 282, 284, 287

Lynch, Jack, 23, 50, 74

Lyons, Tom, 171, 247–8

Mackey, David, 72, 76, 81, 84, 93, 100, 102–3, 107, 108, 126–7, 195–6, 299

MacSharry, Ray, 63

Maguire, Brian, 60

Maguire, Fr John, 17

Maguire, Jerome, 44

Maguire, John, 65

Maguire, Martin, 274

Maguire, Raymond, 88

Malholtra, Yash, 76

'Maple Ten,' the, 176

married life, 40

Martin, Pearse, 61

Matbro, 126

MBO (management buyout), 243

McAleese, Mary, 154

McCaffrey, Bernard, 22, 24

McCaffrey, Liam, 91–2, 127, 129, 148, 151, 153, 157, 171, 176, 184, 187, 188, 196, 198, 201, 216, 217, 244, 245–6, 247, 248, 252, 253, 254, 255, 257, 260–1, 262, 267–8, 273–4, 275, 276, 277, 281, 286, 288, 299

McCaffrey, Una, 137

McCartin, John, 244, 246, 247, 249, 251, 253–4, 255, 260, 261, 263, 268–9, 274, 292, 293

McCracken, Robert, 138

McCreevy, Charlie, 104

McCullagh, Eoin, 286

McDaniel, Denzil, 82

McEnaney, Tom, 106, 166–7

McGovern, Bernard, 282, 283–4, 295

McGovern, Paddy, 73

McGovern, Sean, 235, 282, 283, 295

McGovern, Teresa, 295

McGovern's pub, Drumcondra road, 47, 69

McGuckian, John B., 101, 104

McGuinness, Cyril 'Dublin Jimmy', 238–40, 241, 266–7, 294

McIlweeney, Pat, 24

McKillop, Murdoch, 196

McPartland, Niall, 298

McTighe, Mike, 265

McWilliams, David, 75, 180

Meath County Council, 121

media bias, 80–1

megalithic tomb, Aughrim, 93–4

MI5, 266, 267

Mitten, Robert, 22

MMA monomer, 144

MMA plant, Leuna, Germany, 144–5, 177, 236

Molly Maguires, the, 211–15, 227, 232, 233–5, 265, 272

Molyneaux, James, 55

Montgomery, Robert, 105

Mooney, John, 274, 288

Morgan, Colin, 187

Moriarty Tribunal, the, 142

Morrison, Shane, 156

Morrissey, Tony, 46

Mullarkey, Paddy, 129–30, 153

Mullins, Tony, 142, 143, 264

Murphy, Jack, 34–5

Murphy, Jim, 34, 35

Murray, Hugh, 44

Murray, Louis, 68

Murray, Michael, 154

Nally, David, 89

Nasdaq index, the, 127

NCB Stockbrokers, 140, 142, 147, 149

Neary, Patrick, 178, 180, 187
New Century Financial, 168
Newsline (TV programme), 230
NIE (Northern Ireland Electricity), 213, 235
Noonan, Michael, 202–3, 252
Norbrook Laboratories, 106
Northern Fisheries Board, the, 117
Northern Ireland Civil Rights Association, the, 34
Northern Rock bank, 174

O'Brien, Alan, 295
O'Brien, Noel, 54
O'Brien, Paul, 200, 204, 206, 208, 209–10, 211, 213, 214–15, 216, 227, 229, 231, 233–4, 235, 236–7, 242, 245, 246, 248, 249, 252–3, 254, 259, 260, 264–5, 269
O'Donohoe, Padraig, 205–6, 245
Office of Fair Trading, the, 120
O'Hagan, Bosco, 245, 246, 262, 268, 269
O'Hanlon, John, 130
O'Hanlon, Rory, 154
O'Leary, Olivia, 57
O'Neill, Pat, 207
O'Neill, Terence, 23
O'Reilly, Dara, 153, 157, 173–4, 196, 198, 199, 201, 206, 216–17, 222, 244, 247, 248, 257, 262, 263, 271, 273–4, 275, 276, 277, 282, 287
O'Reilly, Fr Oliver, 292, 293
O'Reilly, Geraldine, 30
O'Reilly, Luke, 295–6
O'Reilly, Rositta, 44
O'Sullivan, Nóirín, 234
O'Toole, Fintan, 39, 40, 41–2, 52, 66–7, 95–6, 112, 131, 224
Outsider, The (book), 11
overseas properties, 207, 210, 220, 230, 237, 285, 298

Parkes Hotel, Stillorgan, 68–9
partition, 15, 29–30
peace process, the, 114, 115
Pearson, Ian, 138
Phoenix, Eamon, 55, 56
Phoenix, The (magazine), 68, 86, 88, 90
Plantman International (magazine), 32
plastics businesses, 144–5, 177, 236, 264
PLM Redfearn, 105, 137
PNR (Programme for National Recovery), the, 63–4
police raids for forensic evidence, 235–6
Political Corruption in Ireland 1922–2010 – A Crooked Harp? (book), 51
poll on support for Sean Quinn, 224–5
Pope's Children, The (book), 75
Portland Cement, 49
Powell, Cpl David, 25
Powerscreen International, 125–6
Prague Hilton, the, 147, 152
Prague Spring, the, 23
Premier Direct, 110
price fixing, 119–20
Prime Time (TV programme), 180–1
property market collapse, the, 168–9
protests, 205–6, 223–4, 227, 231–2, 277
Prudential financial services, 243
PSNI, the, 233, 234–5, 241, 294, 295, 297 (*see also* RUC (Royal Ulster Constabulary), the)
public house investments, 46, 47, 69, 81–2, 92, 132
PWC (Price Waterhouse Coopers), 156, 178, 188–9

QBRC (Quinn Business Retention Company), 247–50, 251–4, 255–8, 259–61, 264, 268–9, 274–5, 276, 288
QIH (Quinn Industrial Holdings) Ltd, 262,

267–9, 270–1, 275, 276–8, 281–2, 283–4, 287–8, 292, 297

QIL, 188, 286

Quigley, Jim, 187, 189

Quinlan, Ronald, 266

Quinn, Aoife, 149, 152, 173, 274, 275

Quinn, Bernadette (Bernie), 12, 13–14, 20, 22–3, 24, 60, 66, 85, 90, 99–100

Quinn, Brenda, 97, 149, 152, 173, 274, 285

Quinn, Ciara, 92, 149, 152, 173, 222, 224, 298

Quinn, Colette, 92, 149, 152, 173, 224, 274, 281

Quinn, Hugh, 11, 12, 14–15, 16, 19, 20–1

Quinn, Mary (née Clarke), 11, 32, 90, 154

Quinn, Miriam, 12, 19, 22–3, 24

Quinn, Noreen, 60–1

Quinn, Patricia (wife), 32, 38, 97, 98, 149, 153, 224, 230, 293

Quinn, Peter, 11, 13, 14, 15, 17, 18, 20, 61, 79–81, 195, 224, 246

Quinn, Peter Darragh (Petey), 152–3, 206–7, 210, 220, 221–2

Quinn, Sean, 2, 3, 7–8, 17–18, 279–81, 293–4; business philosophy, 12–13, 26–7, 35, 36, 45–6, 69, 74, 98–100, 102, 106–8, 110–11, 131–3, 139, 140, 145, 151, 153–4, 159, 163, 164, 166–7, 170–1, 179, 271–2, 299–300; perceptions of, 40, 41–2, 66–7, 69–71, 74, 91, 112–13, 124–5, 131, 144, 146, 149, 159, 164, 165–6, 177, 180–1, 182–3, 184–5, 193, 198, 201, 202, 203–4, 205, 223–4, 231, 267, 269–71, 276–7, 279–80, 298–9

Quinn, Sean Junior (son), 92, 149, 152, 173, 177, 206–7, 220, 221, 222, 224, 258, 274, 277

Quinn Building Products/Lagan Cement joint venture proposal, 229–30, 232–3

Quinn Cement, 175, 182, 236

Quinn Direct Insurance, 107–12, 113, 125, 126, 127, 128–30, 131, 135, 136, 139–41, 146, 149, 152–3, 156, 170, 178–9, 182, 187–95

Quinn Financial Services, 140

Quinn Glass, 208, 212–13, 259

Quinn Group, the, 97, 119–20, 136, 146–7, 151, 166, 170, 198–200, 202, 236

Quinn Healthcare, 166

Quinn Investments, 149

Quinn Life, 130–1

Quinn-Lite, 100

Quinn Packaging, 250–1, 265

Quinn Plastics (Polycasa), 236, 264

Quinn Radiators, 145–6, 264

Quinn Rooftiles, 240

Quinn Tarmac, 213

Quinn Therm, 140

Quinnbet, 287, 298

Quinn's (McGovern's) pub, Drumcondra, 69

Railway Bar, Poyntzpass murders, the, 114, 115

Rathmines Inn, The, 81–2

ready-mixed concrete and blocks, 32, 33, 35

Readymix, 49–50

rebranding, 236–7

Redfearn, 137

Redmond, Darren, 295–6

Reilly, Gerry, 42, 43, 72, 100

Restrictive Practices Court (UK), the, 119

Restrictive Trade Practices Acts (UK), the, 119

Reynolds, Eoin, 291

'right to be forgotten' regime, the, 298

rights of way on farmers' land, 272–3

Ringsend Bottle Company, 103

River Mersey glass factory, Cheshire, 136–7, 138

Roadstone company, 49–50

Robinson, Mary, 75

Roche, Tom, 49–50

Rose, Howard, 88–9

Ross, Shane, 163–4

Royal Hibernian Hotel, the, 83

RPC Containers, 251

RUC (Royal Ulster Constabulary), the, 24, 78, 80, 239, 266 (*see also* PSNI, the)

Russian investments, 155

Ryanair, 159, 160

Ryder Cup, the, 151

sabotage of Quinn and Lagan factories, 212–16, 233–4, 237–41, 243, 259, 265–6, 282, 296–7

Sands, Bobby, 40–1

Saunderson, Lt Col George, 34, 35

Schweiter Technologies, 264

Seabrook, Robert, 147

Sean Quinn (Quarries) Limited, 47

sectarian tensions, 8–9, 14–15, 70

severance packages, 206–7

Shatter, Alan, 243

Sheehan, Maeve, 266

Sheridan, Harry, 64

Sherry, Adrianna, 76

Shiller, Robert, 128

Slieve Rushen wind farm, 96–7, 227, 264, 275

Slieve Russell Golf Course, the, 88, 284

Slieve Russell Hotel, the, 76, 82–5, 87–91, 92, 97, 134, 148, 166, 198, 270, 298

Smith, Brendan, 154

Smith New Court, 157

SRF (solid recovered fuel), 236

Stanley, Patrick, 30

stocks and shares, 113, 127–8, 142–5, 156–60, 162, 169, 171–2, 176–7, 181

Strategic Value Partners, 243

Stubbs Gazette, 218

subprime mortgage market, the, 168

Sunday Business Post, The (newspaper), 84, 116, 120, 128, 132, 150

Sunday Independent (newspaper), 62, 163–4, 165–6, 239, 266, 298

Sunday Press, The (newspaper), 61, 83, 88, 97–8

Sunday Times, The (newspaper), 162, 249, 274, 288

Sunday Times Rich List, the, 112, 167

Sunday Tribune (newspaper), 64, 67, 89, 106, 148, 162–3

takeover of the Quinn Group, 197–205

Taylor, Dennis, 83

Teemore Shamrocks GAA club, 16–19, 24, 27, 72–3, 79, 153, 205, 216

Terex Corporation, 126

Thatcher, Margaret, 71

TheJournal.ie, 253–4

Today, Tonight (TV programme), 57, 69

Tóibín, Colm, 69–71, 74, 91, 112–13, 125, 299

Touchline, 110

tourism investment, 77

Trainor, Damien, 114

Traynor, Des, 50, 51–2

Treacy, Noel, 154

Troubles, the, 24–6, 29–31, 33–5, 40–1, 57, 78, 95, 114, 215

UBS Warburg, 157

UDR (Ulster Defence Regiment), the, 25, 26, 41

UFF (Ulster Freedom Fighters), the, 35

Ukrainian investments, 155

Ulster Plant (*see* Powerscreen International)

United Health Group, 160

Urwin, Margaret, 9

Veitch, Pte Francis, 25
Vestas company, the, 96
VHI, 165
Vidrala, 259, 265
Vortex Hydra system, the, 43

Wallace, Kieran, 197, 298
Walsh, Freddie, 274

Wentworth golf club, England, 149–50
West, Harry, 41
Williamstown quarry, 32–3
wind farms, 96–7, 227, 272, 275
Wood, Jon, 157
Woodhouse, Richard, 183, 197, 210–11

Zulueta, Carlos Delclaux, 259, 260